THE UNBREAKABLE VASE

By

CALVIN WADE, GORDON JOHNSON & ALAN OLIVER.

The Final Book Of The 'Another Saturday & Sweet FA' Trilogy

This book is dedicated to the memory of Steve Garcia (1972-2016). Steve was a wonderful, charismatic, enthusiastic, gent of a man, who is hugely missed by everyone who had the privilege of knowing him.

Chapter One – Prior To Kick Off

So this is it, the final leg of the journey. After attending every round of the F.A Cup in 2013-14 and every round of the F.A Trophy in 2014-15, this season we are completing our F.A adventures with the F.A Vase. Alan Oliver, the groundhopper also known as 'The Casual Hopper', who I first met at the Extra Preliminary Round of the F.A Cup at West Didsbury & Chorlton, is predicting that it will be emotional. I am sure he will be right. We have been to every game together since that first meeting at West Didsbury (Alan is actually one up on me as I missed the F.A Trophy game between New Mills and Mossley) and although the adventure will end after the F.A Vase Final in May, I am sure the friendship will remain.

Based on the goings on in our lives since North Ferriby United lifted the F.A Trophy back in March, there will be plenty of stories to tell, not all of them pleasant. I could fill a book with everything that has happened since March, but shall make sure I cram it all into Chapter One. My events, other than one unsavoury Sunday lunchtime incident, are largely positive, but sadly Alan's last few months have been horrendous.

The week after the F.A Trophy Final, Alan's Dad, Stan, died. Stan had been unwell with Alzheimer's for some time, but Alan only really became aware of how severe it was when his Mum, Hilda, died in late 2013, during our F.A Cup journey. After Hilda's death, once Alan knew that Stan was not in a fit enough mental state to live alone, he moved into a care home and as his health deteriorated, he became a shadow of the man he used to be. One of the things that had upset Alan about his Dad's illness was that he could never speak to him about our F.A adventures. Prior to being ill, Stan had been a big football fan, a Manchester City fanatic who had spent several seasons watching them home and away with Alan, so if he had been mentally well, he would have enjoyed Alan's tales of visiting various grounds around the country.

Losing his Mum and Dad within the space of eighteen months has been a tough blow but later in the summer, fate conspired against Alan and his family once more. Jo, Alan's wife, discovered a lump in her breast which has subsequently been diagnosed as Stage Three breast cancer. As I write (in early September 2015), Jo is in the first of six, twenty one day cycles of chemotherapy, having already had a lumpectomy. I have only met Jo myself on a few occasions, so won't pretend to know her really well, but from everything Alan has told me, I know she is a strong, brave and resilient character, who is determined to fight and defeat this evil disease with every ounce of her being. Back in 2013, Alan began fundraising for Manchester's specialist cancer hospital, 'The Christie', in memory of his mother-in-law, Pat, but since then cancer has taken his mother and now his wife, Jo, is battling against it. I only hope this book goes on to relate positive news about Jo's battle.

I appreciate the sad news about Alan and his family is not the ideal nor the cheeriest way to start a book, but this whole footballing journey has been done by Alan to raise money to support the fight against cancer, so it would be remiss of me not to mention how it has cast its shadow over Alan's family once again. When Alan was telling me about Jo's cancer on the phone, he choked up a little when he said that his daughter, Jordan, had tearfully asked him,

"Why does everyone in our family have to get ill?"

Alan has raised over £15,000 for 'The Christie' now, but my contribution has not been as healthy as I would have liked. It is still early days but so far the two football books have added about £600 to the pot. Each time there is a download or a book sale I contribute 50p to Alan's 'Christie' pot unless it is a promotional 99p ebook sale when I contribute 25p a download. In total, there have been around 1,600 paid sales of the two books which is pleasing but I'm hoping the best sales may still be to come.

Early in 'Another Saturday & Sweet FA', I remember writing that I was an unhealthy sixteen stone and was aiming to be a far healthier thirteen stone thirteen pounds by Cup Final day. Two years down the line, how much do you think I weigh now? You guessed it sixteen stone (although I suspect some of you guessed more than sixteen stone)! I may not have managed under fourteen stone by the 2014 FA Cup Final but I now intend to get to my desired weight by the 2016 F.A Vase Final. If I don't make it this time around, I can't postpone it until future football books as there are unlikely to be any more after this.

With my sporting days behind me (other than as a spectator) my primary focus is now on the sporting development of my two sons, Brad and Joel. Over the last few months, Brad, our eldest son, has had an eventful time and I am hoping his sporting journey will form an interesting story that runs parallel to our FA Vase one.

Brad is fifteen now and since a very young age has been both a very talented footballer and a talented cricketer. A couple of years ago, his talent for cricket seemed to be surpassing his talent for football. He joined Chorley cricket club's junior teams when he was seven and it was soon noticeable that they had a rich crop of players at around his age. When he was nine, Brad played in the under 10s and under 11s teams that went on to win the local Palace Shield competitions which are open to teams largely in the Blackpool and Preston areas.

When Brad was twelve, Chorley under 13s were successful once more, winning the local Palace Shield final at Blackpool Cricket Club against Vernon Carus by eight wickets with Brad being awarded the 'Man of the Match'. Brad scored forty-six in a ninety run second wicket partnership with his friend (and footballing and cricketing team mate), Max Harper, as well as taking the prize wicket of Vernon Carus' star batsman with a caught and bowled.

At that stage, Brad was playing for Chorley District under 13s and was put forward for trials for Lancashire County Cricket Club and began playing for Chorley adults' third team. He was scoring runs and taking wickets and on the odd occasion he was even put into the second team. Brad didn't score many runs for the second team, as his defensive technique was not good enough against good adult bowlers, but he did manage to pick up a few wickets.

Fast forward two years and everything has changed. Just before the cricket season was due to start, Brad announced he didn't want to play cricket this year because 'cricket is boring' and devoting a Saturday afternoon and early evening to playing cricket was 'a waste of the weekend'. Whether this judgement was made purely on a sporting basis, I have my doubts. Brad had started dating his first serious girlfriend and perhaps time spent with her seemed more attractive than time spent on the cover boundary. After all, 'corkies' don't kiss! I was reluctant to allow him to pack in cricket altogether so I began negotiations that Kofi Annan would have been proud of and managed to come out of the talks salvaging his participation in junior cricket but sacrificing the adult matches. Brad agreed he would play for Chorley under 15s side and Chorley District u15s but would no longer be available for the Chorley Adults second or third team on a Saturday afternoon. One Sunday afternoon in June,

I was left momentarily wondering whether my persuasive skills could have cost Brad his life.

On 15th June, Chorley District under 15s were playing against Liverpool District at Eccleston Cricket Club. Liverpool had won the toss and had elected to bat and Brad and his Chorley Cricket Club friend, Joe Barker, had opened the bowling. Both lads were bowling well and generating a fair amount of pace on a lively wicket. Joe clean bowled one opener and then Brad had the other caught in the slips by Joe. Liverpool were two wickets down for not very many. Things were looking positive and other parents were telling me that it was a real shame that Brad wasn't playing adult cricket as he was bowling faster than he had ever bowled before.

Just after midday, Brad bowled a ball which was prodded into the covers and the batsmen set off for a quick single. Matthew Ragsdale, a big, strong fourteen year old lad sprinted in, collected the ball and from ten yards away, threw it with all his might at the bowlers end wicket. There was one major problem, between Matthew and the wickets stood Brad.

The whole incident seemed to play out in slow motion. I saw Matthew rushing in, I saw him pick the ball up and motion to throw and I saw where Brad was standing. In my mind, I was saying,

"Don't throw it, don't throw it!"

Then, once he had thrown it, I uttered one word and it was a four letter profanity beginning with 'S'. Brad didn't have more than a second to react and unfortunately his instinctive decision didn't help his cause. He turned and ducked. A lot of parents who said they weren't properly watching the game said they were alerted to the incident by the almighty thud of the ball rebounding off Brad's skull. He dropped to the floor and instinctively I ran to him from the boundary edge with several others following behind me.

Perhaps if Phillip Hughes, the Australian Test cricketer, had not tragically died in November 2014, after being struck by a cricket ball, I would not have felt so uneasy about the situation that was playing out before me. The father of one of Brad's team mates, Pete Baxendale, made the immediate decision to phone for an ambulance and I crouched over Brad's prostrate body and grabbed his hand. He was conscious but was initially just mumbling incoherently but once he started to speak, the words were not a great deal of comfort.

"I can't open my eyes," and "I can't feel my arms or legs," were the first two things Brad managed to say.

Thankfully, one of the Liverpool player's father's was a Doctor and he came over to check Brad over. He was actually an eye specialist so I wouldn't imagine blows to the skull were his particular strongpoint, but he was able to check Brad's pulse, open his eyelids and provide comfort that his heartbeat was normal and there was no other reason Brad couldn't open his eyes other than shock.

Unfortunately the paramedics who received the call to bring their ambulance and their expertise to us were in Ormskirk when they were notified, a good twenty minutes drive away, even with sirens wailing and blue light flashing. We just tried to keep Brad warm and from going into shock whilst we waited. One thing he said during the painful twenty minute wait, which he has no recollection of saying, still makes me smile now.

"Dad, can you do me a favour? Can you go in the dressing room and get me my mobile phone? I need to ring Mum and tell her what's happened."

Unable to see or move, he still wanted his mobile phone! It was heart warming that he wanted to speak to his Mum though.

Once the paramedics arrived, several parents helped them carefully lift Brad on to a stretcher. They put him in a neck brace and he was put into the back of the ambulance. John Harper, the manager of Brad's local football team, Croston Juniors and father of his team mate, Max, said he would take Brad's cricket bag back to ours later, so I just jumped in the back of the ambulance. I subsequently heard that everyone was very concerned that the ambulance did not leave the side of the cricket pitch for ten minutes, as they were worried that Brad may have taken a turn for the worse, but the delay was just caused by the paramedics relating his symptoms to the operative to get guidance as to where they should take him.

During the delay, I tried to phone Alison, my wife, at work to tell her what had happened. As you may recall if you have read the previous books within this trilogy, Alison is a midwife and was working at Preston hospital so, not surprisingly, her phone was off so I sent her a text. Brad is often melodramatic about minor injuries, so I had to let her know that this wasn't one of those moments, but at the same time re-assure her that he was now conscious and reasonably coherent. Five minutes later, Alison phoned me back. Having remained very calm throughout, this was the first time I could feel myself getting emotional when I had to recount the incident to Alison and explain that Brad was in a pretty bad way. Initially, it appeared that we would be bringing Brad into Preston hospital so Alison said to let her know when we arrived and she would come down to see him at the first opportunity.

The arrangements soon changed. The operative told the paramedics that after having checked, there was no paediatric unit open at Preston, so we would have to go to Alder Hey hospital in Liverpool. I tried to phone Alison back to tell her, but once again her phone was switched off, so I sent a text. When we were almost at Alder Hey, Alison phoned back to say she had spoken to the midwife in charge of the unit and she was going to be allowed to leave once she had finished looking after the lady she was with.

By the time we arrived at Alder Hey, Brad had tentatively opened his eyes but his vision was poor. He also said he was getting feeling back in one leg. We were immediately taken in to see a Doctor who checked Brad out, said he felt the lack of movement and vision were very likely to be only temporary but would arrange for Brad to have a brain scan. By now, Brad was talking normally and could accurately answer the questions he was being asked. The sense of panic I had felt was gradually subsiding and by the time Alison arrived midway through the afternoon, Brad was still in a neck brace but could see properly, had full feeling back in one leg and it was starting to return in the other. The brain scan subsequently came back fine and other than the whole of Saturday and Sunday, up until he was in the ambulance, being totally wiped from Brad's memory banks, he is absolutely fine.

On reflection, there is no doubt Brad was very, very lucky. He had severe headaches for a week afterwards, but within a fortnight he was playing cricket and football again. Matthew Ragsdale, the lad who threw the ball and was not surprisingly very shaken up by the whole incident, visited Brad the next day with his Dad, Colin. The Eccleston Cricket Club coach, Tony, who had been temporarily in charge of the District side that day also kindly called around. They were re-assured to see Brad getting back to his old self.

Prior to the cricket season, Brad had finished last season's football season on a high. He played for a local club, Croston Juniors, but for two years has also played for Chorley District's football side. In what turned out to be their last game of the season, they played Preston District in a Cup Semi-Final and lost 2-1, largely due to Preston's central midfielder, Elliot Watt, a Scotland schoolboy international who bossed the game and scored two goals from about twenty yards out that were perfectly placed in the top corners. Brad is a goalkeeper and in a game Preston dominated, he made a string of excellent saves that captured the attention of a Preston North End Academy coach, who spoke to Kev Keeley, Brad's District coach after the game and said he would make arrangements for Brad to go down for trials.

At the end of the season, Kev Keeley also had to nominate players from his squad to attend Lancashire trials. Brad was one of the players he nominated. This led to Brad being invited down to four trial sessions, after the cricket incident, in Blackburn and Preston. At the three training sessions in Blackburn, I didn't get out of the car. I wanted Brad to be focused and didn't want to cause a distraction by standing at the side of the pitch watching him. The fourth session was a trial match at the University of Central Lancashire, which I did watch and was pleasantly surprised by how well Brad did. He kept a clean sheet, distributed the ball well and made some good saves. About seventy lads trialled and the coaches told them they would initially cut the numbers to around thirty five, play a few games against North West Academy sides and then the squad would be trimmed further to twenty something. Brad was confident that he had done enough to be named in the initial squad and his confidence was justified as I received an email after a couple of days to say Brad had been selected in the squad of thirty five. The email confirmed that their trial games would be against Blackpool, Preston North End and Blackburn Rovers Academies, as well as a further friendly against Bamber Bridge Under 17s.

I actually missed Brad's first game for Lancashire. Having managed to get on our financial feet over the last two years, I wanted to take Alison down to London to see a West End show. I have been a fan of Carole King since my mid-teens so had booked tickets for the show about her life called 'Beautiful'. When the dates for the games were announced, I had a sinking feeling when I realised that the first one coincided with our trip to London, but my Dad stepped in as a very able replacement mentor for Brad and Brad's cousin, Max also went to watch. As Alison and I watched a superb performance of 'Beautiful' at The Aldwych Theatre, Brad was playing for Lancashire against Blackpool Academy at Squires Gate FC, Blackpool. The game finished 1-1. My Dad, not a man to dish out compliments, text me to say Brad had played well and as Alison and I were walking along Embankment on a perfect summer's evening, Brad phoned to say he felt he had played pretty well but more importantly Andy Clitheroe, Lancashire's Head Coach, had come over to shake his hand and had told him he had had a great game.

Forty eight hours later, the positivity about Brad's performance was rubber stamped when the Lancashire Schools FA Secretary, Mike Timberlake, phoned me to say a Blackburn Rovers scout had been at the game and they too, like Preston North End, wanted to take Brad for a trial period. Brad has been training on a Monday and Friday evening at Fleetwood for a few months and they had decided to retain him for the 2015-16 season but Fleetwood are only a fledgling Academy and both Preston North End and Blackburn Rovers would be considered a step up the footballing ladder if either wanted him to sign.

Brad spent half the summer holidays sleeping over at various friend's houses or camping out so when he came back home from one of his overnighters, I had a chat with him about Blackburn Rovers interest.

"See, I told you I'd had a good game. I wasn't just 'bigging' myself up," he said cheerily.

On this occasion, I hadn't doubted him because his performance had come with a rare seal of approval from my Dad. Brad knew though that sometimes I was sceptical about his self-analysis. I was the type of person who would play a game in goal, make four good saves and a mistake and dwell on my error. Nowadays, if I point out Brad's error, in similar circumstances, he will just shrug and say,

"Yeh, but did you see my four saves?"

I'm not saying my way is the right way. I'm just saying we are very different. At Brad's age I worried too much about what other people thought of me, sometimes Brad doesn't give enough thought to what other people may think.

With regards to Blackburn Rovers, however, Brad was unsure whether it would be a good idea to go. He was one of eighteen players at Fleetwood in the under 16's section and nine of them would be getting scholarships next season. A scholarship in football these days is like the old apprenticeship/YTS of old. Brad, despite being an intelligent lad, wants a football scholarship in preference to going to Sixth Form or subsequently University. I am happy for him to make his own decision on this, if indeed he has a decision to make, as a scholarship may not be offered. I went down the traditional Sixth Form then University route and ended up in my thirties and forties working for various bosses who had no formal qualifications.

GCSEs are forgotten about once you have 'A' levels. 'A' levels are forgotten about when you have a degree. A degree is forgotten about once you have experience. I think, therefore, if Brad has dreams of playing football professionally, we should let him follow those dreams until it gets to a point (if it happens) that those dreams do not become a reality. At this stage, Brad feels the pursuit of the dream may be better served at Fleetwood than Blackburn. I suggested he have a chat with one or two of the coaches at Fleetwood and gather their opinions on what they would do if presented with a similar set of circumstances.

The Fleetwood coaches could have acted in their own interests and told Brad to just stay put at Fleetwood but to their credit, they have encouraged him to go to Blackburn and give it a go for the six week trial. As a fledgling Academy they knew they couldn't offer the same short term opportunities as Blackburn and I had a chat with Fleetwood's Director of Football, Stuart Murdoch, who said they would welcome Brad back after six weeks if Blackburn didn't sign him. I contacted Blackburn and he will start there on Monday 7th September, two days after our first Vase game.

As for Lancashire Under 16s, when Brad played his second game, in a friendly against Bamber Bridge u17s at Preston College, I managed to get along to watch. Lancashire ran out comfortable 3-1 winners with Bamber Bridge scoring a late consolation goal. I couldn't fault Brad for the goal he conceded. The striker drove a low hard shot across his body and Brad managed to dive full length and get a strong arm to it, pushed the ball on to the post but the rebound fell kindly to an attacker who was following up and he guided it in to the empty net. Overall, Brad performed with credit and after two positive performances, I felt he had a very strong chance of making the final squad. At the end of August, after two further games that Brad wasn't involved with as the other two keepers played (a 3-0 win against

Blackburn Rovers and a 3-1 defeat against Preston), we received notification that Brad would be part of the squad for the season. They will play approximately a further ten games, depending on how they fair in Cup competitions. How many Brad will play in remains to be seen but it will be a great experience just to be involved.

On a personal front, the other major change in my life since the FA Trophy Final is that I have parted ways with 'World of Warranty', the company that provided me a lifeline during the depths of our financial crisis. I left at the end of May after twenty months as a car warranty rep. They are a relatively small firm with around fifteen to twenty staff at any given time so I found it very difficult to sell second hand car dealers a warranty proposition from a company they hadn't heard of when big players like AA, RAC and Warranty Wise were very prominent in the market. I had a small band of dealers who I got along very well with and stayed loyal to us because I got on so well with them but a lot of the more prestigious dealers were tempted away by the larger companies. As I had a new fictional book coming out and was in a much stronger financial position than when I started there, I decided to return to writing full-time. It wasn't the perfect job for me and although no-one put me under any great pressure, I strongly suspect I was jumping before I was pushed. I suspect, unless my new novel, 'Waiting For The Bee Stings' hits the Top100, that within a few months I will return to some sort of PAYE role, probably in my field of expertise, the mortgage industry, but for now I am just trying to see how long I can make a living from my writing.

So, that's you, the reader, updated with the main summer goings on for Alan and me. Let's get into the football and what we are calling 'The Unbreakable Vase'.

Chapter Two

Saturday 5th September 2015

The FA VASE – 1st Qualifying Round

Eccleshill United v Heaton Stannington

So what exactly is the FA Vase? It is a competition solely for teams from Steps Five, Six and Seven of the National League System that can adhere to certain stipulations, such as being able to play at a floodlit ground. The FA Trophy was for teams from Steps One to Four, so the FA Vase is for the lowest three tiers of the system. It replaced the FA Amateur Cup and theoretically is for teams who are unlikely to pay their players wages. The money received, both from the F.A and from gate money, for progression to the latter stages of the FA Vase could be vital for keeping a small club afloat.

The money paid to the winners in each round by the F.A is as follows:-

1st Round Qualifying Winners £600

2nd Round Qualifying Winners £800

1st Round Proper Winners £900

2nd Round Proper Winners £1,000

3rd Round Proper Winners £1,300

4th Round Proper Winners £2,000

5th Round Proper Winners £2,500

6th Round Proper Winners £4,500

Semi Final Winners £6,000

Runners Up £17,000

WINNERS £25,000

As you can see, there are ten rounds with two qualifying rounds followed by six further (proper) rounds, before a two legged Semi Final and the Wembley final. This season, for the first time, the FA Vase and FA Trophy are on the same day, the day after the FA Cup Final. In a perfect world, Everton and Manchester City will get to the FA Cup Final, North Ferriby United and Chorley will get to the FA Trophy Final and two North West clubs will reach the FA Vase Final and we will go to all three games!

Not all sides have to enter at the Qualifying Round stage. Teams that were relegated from Step 4 only have to enter at 1st Round (Proper) stage, as do teams that finished in the top five in Step 5 and were not promoted. Finally, teams that reached at least the 4th Round in last season's competition only enter this season's competition in the 2nd Round, so for example, last year's winners North Shields will only come into the competition in the Second Round (Proper). They will not have to get through the two qualifying rounds and the first round. Is that all clear? I hope so.

For the past two seasons in the FA Cup and FA Trophy, Alan hasn't had many opportunities to visit grounds that were new to him. In the FA Cup, I think only Guisborough Town was virgin territory and in the FA Trophy there was only Farnborough. As the FA Vase is from tiers of English football Alan has yet to conquer, it provides greater opportunities to visit unseen grounds. I hadn't even heard of Eccleshill United, let alone visited their stadium and pleasingly it was a new ground for Alan too.

Eccleshill United currently ply their trade in the Toolstation Northern Counties Eastern League Division One and prior to our visit had played five league games, winning two and losing three, with fifteen goals scored and fourteen conceded. Averaging almost six goals a game seems pretty common place in these lower leagues as defences are nowhere near as solid and well organised as in the higher tiers and players not as fit so lapses within a ninety minute game are common place. We saw 56 goals in the FA Cup and 43 in the FA Trophy, but we are hoping we might be in for a goal fest in the Vase. One thing is for certain, we'd be unlucky to come across a 0-0 game having avoided them in the higher competitions for the last two years.

Eccleshill United's Mitton Group Stadium is situated in Wrose, Bradford. As I live in Chorley and Alan lives in Failsworth, it wasn't exactly the game closest to home but Alan had chosen it for good reasons. As well as the opportunity to take in a new ground, it was a central point between the North West and the North East and Alan was wanting to incorporate a gentleman called Shaunee Smith into our adventures.

Shaunee is a groundhopper from Gateshead. He has been previously mentioned in my footballing trilogy as he is the author and creator of 'The 100 Grounds Football Club', a groundhopping blog and Facebook page. When Alan became a fully fledged groundhopper, Shaunee was on hand to offer advice and became something of an inspiration to Alan as he always wrote captivating and informative accounts of his journeys on his blog. For the last couple of years, Alan has been hoping we would cross paths with Shaunee at some point during our travels, but it had not been possible in the FA Cup or FA Trophy. This time around Alan had been discussing meeting Shaunee in the FA Vase for several months. I think it is unlikely that Shaunee will do the whole journey with us, but he is talking about doing the first couple of rounds and the final, at the very least. I am sure he will be an interesting character to have on board.

Talking about interesting characters to have on board, this season Gordon Johnson, who came to Farnborough and Wembley in the FA Trophy, has committed to doing as much of the Vase experience as possible. Gordon may actually end up going to more games than me, as I am definitely going to miss the First Round Proper game (the third set of games) as the Wade family are off to Lanzarote for eleven days in late October and early November.

Gordon is currently the County Welfare Officer at Liverpool County FA. As well as meeting Alan at Farnborough and Wembley, he also refereed Alan's latest charity football match at Droylesden in May between Manchester City legends and Manchester City Supporters Club. I went down to watch for the second year in succession and it was once again a brilliant afternoon out. The 'Legends' team included Peter Barnes and a surprise new recruit this year was Shaun Goater. Goater has piled on a few pounds since his playing days and more than one supporter was heard to utter that the 'Feed The Goat' comment may have been taken a bit too literally and he may have been fed a little too often. It was great of him to take part though and he lasted about half an hour before possibly feigning injury and heading off for a rest. Once again, the game raised several thousand pounds for 'The Christie'. Gordon refereed the game well, aided by his two assistants, his son Kieran and Leighton Baines brother, Dale. This year, the youthful supporters club side ran the legs off the legends and revenged the previous year's defeat, triumphing by more goals than anybody probably wants me to mention again.

For our trip to Bradford, like most previous 'F.A' games, I volunteered to drive. Alan can't drive and Gordon offered to, but I said I'd drive this time and perhaps Gordon can drive for one of the following rounds. I picked Gordon up from a church car park in Wrightington, which is roughly half way between Gordon's house in Ormskirk and mine in Euxton. We then drove over to Failsworth to pick Alan up.

After leaving 'World of Warranty' I obviously had to give back the BMW One Series company car I had, so I needed to buy a 'new' car. I had said to Andrew Gartside, a great car dealer and huge Manchester City fan from ADRG in Cheadle Hulme, that I would buy a car off him but unfortunately he was on holiday the week I decided to leave 'World of Warranty' and with our sons hectic sporting schedule, I had to act quickly so bought a '58' plate Vauxhall Astra from a local car dealers called Burnetts, who I also knew were great guys from my warranty dealings with them. I hate letting anyone down, especially as it felt to me like I was going back on my word to Andrew, so I was very apologetic when he arrived home. Thankfully he was very understanding. Hopefully there will other opportunities to buy a car from him. I'd like to think one day it will be a more expensive one than a '58' Astra but there are more important things in life than fancy cars.

Brad and Joel weren't overly impressed that a brand new BMW had been traded for a seven year old Astra with 71 000 miles on the clock, but for me it was a sign of progress. Last time I left a job with a company car, at Lloyds Bank, to go to work for myself, I had to share Alison's Corsa with her, which would have been a logistical headache this time around with Brad's increased footballing activities. This is the first time since I was in my mid-twenties that I have actually owned my own car so the Astra may not be anything spectacular but it is functional, so the boys will just have to get used to it.

On the way to Bradford, Gordon and Alan soon noticed that my Astra didn't move like the BMW and was giving out uncomfortable, strained noises, especially when we were going up steep hills.

"I don't think it has anything to do with the car," Gordon quipped, "I just think it's down to all the weight you're carrying in the back."

Alan, who was sitting in the back, didn't pick up on the fact that the joke was on him. He was in good spirits but wasn't as switched on as he normally is, with good reason. Jo, Al's wife, had initially responded very well to her chemotherapy but her temperature had spiked due to her white blood cells dropping so she had been admitted to hospital and had only been released on Tuesday. Overall, Alan said the Royal Oldham Oncology staff were really happy with Jo's progress and the side effects were just unfortunate indications that the chemotherapy was doing its job, as it tends to wipe out everything that gets in its way. Alan said after the chemotherapy, Jo has to have radiotherapy too, for a couple of weeks but they are hoping that will be the end of the treatment and Jo will subsequently be given the all clear. I know how much Alan wants to do every round of the FA Vase this season, but I pointed out that if Jo ever needs him to stay at home one Saturday, he really should give the game a miss. Alan replied by saying he would always put Jo first and other than the Vase and perhaps the FA National Sunday Cup, that Gordon has suggested would properly complete the set, he is cutting back on his groundhopping this season.

We arrived in the Bradford area within an hour of leaving Alan's but soon discovered a further drawback of not having the BMW – no SatNav. AA Route Planners are great if everything runs smoothly but they don't factor in a wrong turn. We ended up spending an hour circling Bradford City Centre before we eventually decided to ask for help. We pulled into a side street and Alan spotted someone who he felt looked like a football fan so told me to stop, leapt out the car and ran over to the passer by. The lad, who was in his early twenties, looked a little taken aback that this trench coated little bald bloke in his fifties was darting towards him and quickly switched off his iPod so he could ascertain what the hell was going on. It transpired that if the young man was a football fan, he would perhaps have been a Borussia Dortmund or Bayern Munich fan rather than a Bradford City or Eccleshill United fan, as he was a German tourist. He still had a better idea than us though how to get to the ground and tapped in Google Maps into his i-phone and then attempted to direct us in pigeon English to the ground. Three clueless Lancastrians being directed to the ground by a German would have amused any local Yorkshire men, thankfully there were none around.

Gordon latched on to the Google Maps idea and within ten minutes we finally arrived at Eccleshill United's elaborately named 'Mitton Group Stadium'. The ground is situated towards the top of a very steep hill and Alan was counting his blessings as we arrived that he hadn't had to make his way to this one on foot from the local railway station. From the outside, the ground looks far from impressive with a bumpy car park and what looks from the exterior like a very dilapidated club house, but once you go through the turnstile, the stadium is impressive. The playing surface looked flat, green and well cared for and there was a good sized stand with blue and white coloured seats on the half way line that could find room for 225 backsides. Early indications were that they would not be needing them all today.

In recent years, Eccleshill United have had a relationship with RIASA (Richmond Development Academic and Soccer Academy – not sure why it wasn't RDASA) who provided the team with a string of foreign players, mainly from the United States. They also appointed some well known managers including former Bradford City and Oldham Athletic player, Lee Duxbury but at the end of the 2014-15 season the club decided to cut their ties with RIASA and instead decided to try to nurture local talent.

After our unnecessarily long journey I was ready for a cup of tea, so headed towards the canteen that was housed within a portakabin. The entrance had a sign up that said it was purely for management and officials (corporate entertainment is pretty basic at this level, I am sure prawn sandwiches would not have been on offer) but there was a hatch at one end that had a gentleman serving refreshments. I was all set to order a cup of tea and a pie when the tea urn decided it didn't fancy the idea of providing hot drinks all afternoon and began to fizz out boiling water from the base at a dangerously quick rate. After gathering his thoughts for thirty seconds, during which time the boiling water had run across all his work surfaces and was beginning to spread itself across the floor, the bloke serving bravely decided he had no option but to pick the urn up, run the length of the cabin, screaming at all bystanders to stand clear and dump it outside to allow it time to empty itself of its contents. He came back (probably putting a brave face on his third degree burns) to tell me he was going to have to close for ten minutes whilst he cleaned the place up. There was no other option but to go to the social club for a pint.

To get to the social club, you had to get a pass out from the man on the turnstile, which we did, but they had run out of passes so told Gordon he would have to return with Alan and me to ensure he got back in, which wasn't a problem. The social club was more pleasant than it looked from the outside, it was old fashioned but homely. Clubs at this level are not going to spend thousands on sprucing up their social clubs, the very fact it is open is a bonus. It was very busy inside, boosted by about thirty Heaton Stannington fans who had come on the coach with the team. Their numbers had been boosted by an extra one, as Shaunee Smith had also arranged to travel with them.

I had heard a lot about Shaunee from Alan, but although I had seen many of Shaunee's blogs and Facebook posts, I hadn't really paid much attention to any of his photographs (other than the ones showing football grounds) so couldn't really recall what he looked like. He was more youthful than I had imagined (apparently he is around fifty but looks well on it) with a positive nature and a friendly manner. He will hate me for saying this, as he has a real musical passion and I can imagine he hates nothing more than 'The X-Factor', but he looks like he could be the father of that lad from North (or perhaps South) Shields who won the X-Factor, Joe McElderry.

Alan was chatting away with Shaunee so I went to get Gordon and me a pint and Alan a soft drink. Alan has been off the beers a few years now and has no desire to return. One of the Heaton Stannington supporters, who was an oldish bloke in his sixties or seventies came over to me and said he recognised me from somewhere and was trying to work out where it was from. I was hopeful that it might be the back cover of one of my football books but it turned out that he didn't know me at all and I obviously just have a common looking face!

After having our pint and resisting the temptation to smuggle a kettle out of the bar and over to the portakabin, to ensure we had a half time cuppa, we headed back into the ground. We got chatting to Shaunee and it transpired that as well as a groundhopper and administrator of an excellent Facebook site/blog, he was a fan of Newcastle United, Gateshead and Dunston UTS. Dunston actually won the FA VASE in 2012 when they defeated West Auckland 2-0 in the Final. Dunston are still a very strong team in the Ebac Northern League, so will be one of the favourites again this season to win the competition.

One of the other things that emerged from our conversations with Shaunee was that he isn't a fan of selfie sticks. I don't think I have ever taken a photo of myself in my life so I have been oblivious to the phenomenon, but when Gordon brought his recently acquired selfie stick into the ground with him, to take some pitch side photos, it appeared to me to be a good idea. At least it would stop us having to bother a random passer by to take a photo of us. Shaunee didn't agree.

"I hate those bloody things! I can't believe you are asking me to be on a selfie!" Shaunee said sounding exasperated whilst reluctantly managing a smile for the photo.

Little did Shaunee realise that Gordon is a bit of a wind up merchant and if he comes with us to several of these Vase games, Gordon will be following him around everywhere with the selfie stick. Anyway, once the obligatory selfies were out the way, we resumed the conversation and Shaunee was telling us that he is currently trying to get to the grounds of every former winner of the Scottish Junior Cup. I have forgotten how many winners he said there have been, but given the competition has been in existence since the late 19th Century, I am thinking a fair few.

As well as Shaunee's trips around the British Isles (and further afield) watching football, he is also trying to frequent as many Wetherspoon's pubs as he can. I was asking how this came about and he explained that it started mainly because of the local real ale selection, the history behind each pub building and his OCD of collecting things. When Shaunee began groundhopping in 2006, he began look for the local 'Spoons' on his travels, so the ticking off started then. Almost ten years later he has now visited 255 of the 900 or so Wetherspoons in the UK. I should have asked whether they do a loyalty card.

As the sides came out, Eccleshill United in their traditional blue and white and Heaton Stannington in a change trip which was a tangerine/orange colour top with white shorts, we took a guess at the result. We all opted for a narrow Heaton Stannington win, based on their Northern League pedigree.

"As long as we avoid a draw, especially a 0-0, I'll be happy," I announced.

"It won't be nin-nil," Shaunee announced confidently, "I've been to thirty games so far this season and seen 133 goals already. I had a proper look at it this morning and I've calculated a 3-1 win to Heaton Stan."

I'm sure Shaunee, like the rest of us, gets some of his result predictions completely wrong, but he knows his stuff at this level better than the rest of us, even Alan, so I cheated a bit and followed his lead going for 3-0 to Heaton.

Once the game kicked off, it was soon clear that this one wasn't going to be a goalless draw. It was an open, end to end game with forwards looking dangerous and defenders looking lethargic. Heaton Stannington centre forward, Jon Wright, had a manner that reminded me of Rushall Olympic's striker, Luke Benbow who we had come across playing for Stourbridge in the FA Cup. Wright, like Benbow, had a touch of class about him (I suppose at a higher level the comparisons would be Cantona and Berbatov) but didn't like putting a shift in until the ball came into his vicinity when he would come alive. Tracking across to snub out a run from a full back or chasing down a kick from the goalkeeper would not be high on his list of objectives in a ninety minute game.

It took only seven minutes for Heaton Stan to take the lead and it was Wright who began the scoring from the penalty spot after Lewis Burns was up ended in the box. The striker calmly slotting home from twelve yards. Eccleshill were soon on level terms though, when number ten, Luke Harrop got on the end of a right wing cross to fire home. There was no suggestion that the goal scoring would finish there. Heaton Stannington did look like they did have a bit more creativity in midfield and slightly more solidity at the back (but not much), so there was no surprise when Heaton Stan made it 2-1 after twenty six minutes when Ben Taylor squared from the right for Matt Hayton to neatly finish.

Both goalkeepers looked agile and good shot stoppers but the thing they lacked, which probably prevented them playing at a higher level, was height, so corners were particularly dangerous as neither keeper had the physical presence to dominate his area amongst a melee. Eccleshill's second equaliser came from one such corner when Jermaine Springer volleyed home. 2-2 before half time and Alan was rubbing his hands.

"I'm getting a pound a goal from Shaunee and the bloke who runs the 'Non League Crowds' site on Twitter! The Vase could swell the 'Christie' pot a fair bit, as no-one seems to know how to defend," Alan exclaimed with Mancunian delight.

It remained two-all until half-time and when the ref blew for half-time we wandered over to the portakabin with fingers crossed that the urn had been repaired and hot drinks were now being served. Thankfully they were.

We had watched the first half from the halfway line, in front of the Eccleshill United stand and as we made our way back there, with drinks in hand, the second half kicked off. Eccleshill United came out with fire in their bellies and dominated the early proceedings. After only two minutes, Eccleshill almost took the lead for the first time in the match, as a shot from distance hit the bar and a minute later Heaton Stannington's keeper, Dan Rule had to save well with his feet.

Heaton Stannington had never won a game in the FA Vase for 33 years as they had only entered it for the first time in 22 years last season and had lost 4-0 to Colne in their first game back (their record in the 1980's and early 1990's had been pretty woeful too). This seemed like an opportunity to re-write the club's record books for the better, but when Heaton Stannington's Andrew Weeks hit his own crossbar with a misplaced clearance in the 49th minute, it seemed like it was only 'Lady Luck' that was keeping them level. After a mad five minute spell straight after half time though, the Heaton Stannington nerves settled and they began to re-assert their surpremacy.

In the 56th minute, Brian Dodsworth sent a Heaton Stannington free kick into the Eccleshill United box and although it was cleared, it fell invitingly to Lewis Burns who sent a crisp right foot volley flying into the Eccleshill net. For the third time, Heaton Stannington were in the lead. Apparently Dekka Thompson, the Heaton Stannington manager had given out a rollicking to his players at half-time for twice squandering their advantage but once again they sat back and allowed Eccleshill to come at them.

Heaton Stannington had Dan Rule, their keeper, to thank for preserving their lead, as he made a number of top quality saves. The best of the lot came in the 74th minute when a shot was fired across his body and he dived full length to parry clear. Three minutes later, Rule showed he was prepared to put future generations of the Rule family at risk to help the Heaton Stannington cause, as he made a point blank save which unfortunately struck him in the 'crown jewel' area and he needed lengthy treatment to put the wind back in his sails.

As is often the case, when one side is forced to throw men forward seeking an equaliser, they leave themselves vulnerable at the back. In this game, both defences were already vulnerable, so when Eccleshill started throwing bodies forward there were huge spaces behind the front eight for Heaton Stannington to exploit. In the 89th minute, the Eccleshill United keeper, Joe Stead, made a great low fingertip save from a 25 yard strike, but he could do nothing to prevent Ben Telford scoring a fourth in the second minute of injury time and putting the game beyond doubt. 4-2 and we had started with a goal fest.

After the game, as Gordon, Alan and I headed back to my car for the journey home, Shaunee went to have a beer with Michael Swaffield from Saltaire, a member of his '100 Football Grounds Club' squad, who had approached him, with his mate Keith, during the game to introduce himself. After leaving the Eccleshill United clubhouse at ten to six, he travelled back with the Heaton Stannington coach, although they stopped in Boroughbridge on the way home for a few beers at Three Horse Shoes and The Crown, eventually getting back to their ground at quarter to ten. Hope Shaunee keeps coming to games on this FA Vase journey because not only is he a great lad but he is also someone I can have a few beers with if Gordon does some of the driving. I think hell will freeze over before either my Dad or Alan ever have a pint!

FINAL SCORE :- Eccleshill United 2 Heaton Stannington 4

Chapter Three

Friday 2nd October 2015

Having only ever missed one 'F.A' game in the last two seasons, I have a feeling this season is going to be far trickier as events in the last few weeks have suddenly conspired to make my life busier than it has been for a number of years. It is definitely an enjoyable form of 'hectic' though.

My latest fictional book, 'Waiting For The Bee Stings' has been selling steadily but not spectacularly and as I began to wonder whether I could be dragged back into financial difficulties in a few months' time, out of nowhere I was offered a job. To an extent, my football books played a part in the job offer.

When I was a 'Business Development Manager' for Yorkshire Building Society, Accord Mortgages and BM Solutions in the North West, I struck up friendships with several mortgage brokers, but I would say three in particular became good friends. They were Carl McGovern, a broker in East Lancashire and a big Blackburn Rovers fan who I ran a couple of marathons with, including New York. I briefly mentioned Carl in 'Another Saturday & Sweet FA', as we went to an Everton game together. There was also Dave Winnard, a real character from Leigh. Dave is a massive Manchester United fan, a season ticket holder for many years and also a lover of horse racing and was always the first to break into song on a corporate function. Dave is in his sixties now, but I used to call and see him for a cup of tea after visiting a car dealers behind his office in Leigh. He is still as much of a character as ever. He still likes a bet and can still belt out a great version of 'Danny Boy'. Finally, there was a broker from Southport called David Barron.

I've known Dave Barron for thirteen years now and there would be very few people in Southport who don't know him. As well as running a successful mortgage brokerage for the last thirteen years, he is very involved in the local community, is a key sponsor of Southport Football Club and has raised hundreds of thousands of pounds for charity through various fundraising events. For many years, he raised money for Claire House, the children's hospice in Bebington, Wirral and more recently he has founded and Chaired the 'Community Link Foundation' in Southport.

I have kept in touch with all three since I left the mortgage industry, speaking on the phone from time to time or catching up for a coffee or lunch. Whilst he was away on his summer holiday this year, Dave Barron read 'Another Saturday & Sweet FA' and I received a few texts off him saying we needed to meet up when he returned home as he had a proposal for me. A few days after he arrived back in the UK, we met up and Dave offered me a job in his mortgage office. I am a qualified mortgage broker, but the role he wanted me to do was more of an administrative role on his mortgage cases. Dave thought there was enough work for a full-time role, but with me still harbouring ambitions of making progress with my writing career, I explained three days a week would be ideal. Dave smiled and said he would rather have me there three days than none and he would go away and sort out a wage and a start date. I was flexible on both counts as I am happy to be getting a set wage each month (as the royalties on the books can fluctuate wildly) and could start as soon as he wanted me to. Within a few days, he rang to say 1st October would be ideal for him, which was absolutely fine with me too. I started yesterday and think I will enjoy returning to work in a mortgage office, on a daily basis, for the first time since 1998.

A regular income is a huge positive, but the slight negative is the knock-on effect it has on the FA Vase journey. The three days I work currently, whilst I am training, are very flexible but once I get up to scratch, I will be working Mondays, Wednesdays and Fridays from 9am to 5.30pm and once a month on a Saturday. Thus, if there is a FA Vase game on a Wednesday night, more than a couple of hours drive from Southport then I am going to struggle to make it.

On the family football front, Brad started training at Blackburn Rovers Brockhall training ground on 7th September and the first person we saw there was former Manchester City, Stoke City, QPR and Barnsley player, Mike Sheron, who is apparently the new under 16s Academy coach. Subsequently we were introduced to the Academy goalkeeper coaches Ben and Steve, who were very welcoming. In a strange quirk of fate, the regular under 16s goalkeeper is a lad called Joe Boyling and guess who his Uncle is? None other than Alan Oliver!

Alan has mentioned a few times that Joe was a keeper at Blackburn, and has been there for about eight seasons, but this had added significance once Brad was asked to go down to trial there. My impressions over the last month are that Joe is a very fine goalkeeper, a tremendous shot stopper with an excellent work ethic. The only negative I could come up with, in the ruthless world of professional football, is that he is relatively small for a keeper. He currently stands at around 5 feet 9 inches tall and unless he grows at least another three inches, no matter how good he is, I suspect he will be shown the door. This may seem harsh but I can't think of any recent goalkeeper at Premier or Championship level smaller than six feet tall and most nowadays are above 6 feet two. I hope he has a growth spurt because he seems like a good lad and has been very welcoming to Brad. His parents, especially his father, Lee, have had to make a massive commitment driving him up to between

Blackburn and Clitheroe several times a week for eight years from Failsworth, but for the large majority of dedicated parents there is no happy ending. You just hope it teaches your son some important attributes such as discipline, a strong work ethic and a sense of teamwork. I have to admit though, I am glad Brad has been a late arrival at this level of schoolboy football.

My observations on Brad over the last month, at Blackburn, are that for some reason he isn't shining. I suspect it is because he doesn't feel overly comfortable there. I am not quite sure why, because his first session went excellently but subsequently he has seemed a little outside his comfort zone. He has played games against Burnley and Everton, as well as in a tournament against Manchester United, Newcastle United and Sunderland but despite playing solidly in every game, he hasn't played as well as I know he can. He has kicked excellently, but his command of his area hasn't been what it normally is. Perhaps he is just being tentative because the quality of player he is up against is much higher than what he is used to. I can't quite put my finger on it, but we have been told he will find out whether Blackburn Rovers want to sign him in the next week or so and my gut feeling is that they won't. Brad has already said he doesn't want to go back to Fleetwood, as he feels their other keeper, Billy Crellin, is higher up the pecking order than him, so it may just be that a scholarship isn't going to materialise and he will have to put his footballing ambitions on hold and concentrate on his education.

I have enjoyed going down to Brockhall, Blackburn Rovers training ground though. It takes a large chunk out your week driving backward and forwards, as they train three times a week and then play on a Saturday, but the facilities are great and I have got to know a couple of the other trialists Dads. One father I particularly enjoy speaking to is Gareth Gray, who I already vaguely knew as Brad had played cricket and football against his son, Dan, for a number of years. Gareth works for the British Transport Police and formerly had a brief League football career at Rochdale, where he made a few first team appearances in goal. He now also helps out with the goalkeeping coaching at the Academy at Preston North End. Dan is a fine sportsman and has been picked in the Lancashire Schools Football Association squad too. Dan has been at Preston North End for a number of years but has been told he isn't going to be given a scholarship there, so Blackburn have decided to take a look at him. He is a versatile player who can play in midfield or in any position across the back four. His most natural position is centre back though and, like Joe Boyling, may suffer from the fact that he isn't the tallest. He is probably an inch or so smaller than Joe so again will have to have a growth spurt to be considered for that position. The days of 'if you're good enough, you're tall enough' are long gone and it's a case of whether he can slot in at full back or perhaps as a defensive central midfielder in a Claude Makelele type role. Dan is fast, has good feet and is intelligent with the ball, so he will find a decent team, it is just a case of whether he has to drop a level or two.

The Saturday after our FA Vase trip, my Dad came down with me to Brockhall as Brad had been picked in Blackburn's Under 16s squad to play against Manchester United. Having taken Everton's old 'A' and 'B' teams in the late 1970s and early 1980s, my Dad was amazed how the facilities had advanced. We were hoping Brad may get half a game with Joe Boyling playing the other half, but Blackburn were 1-0 up at half time, so perhaps sensing they may get a psychologically important victory, they kept Joe in goal for the whole game. United went on to win 3-2 but Joe wasn't at fault for the goals Rovers conceded. I couldn't help feeling a little disappointed for Brad though, if he is on trial he isn't showing anyone anything on the subs bench.

Once it had been established that Brad wasn't going to be coming on for the second half, my Dad decided to go over and watch the under 18s game on the next pitch, also between Rovers and United. He must have watched most of the second half and came back across just before the end.

"Spot any talent?" I asked.

"Blackburn are winning, but they don't have any particular stand out players but Manchester United have two kids up front who are excellent. Two black kids, a tall one and a small one, they are both quick and brilliant with the ball at their feet."

My Dad had a team sheet and we noted their names, Marcus Rashford and Angel Gomes. I'd never heard of Marcus Rashford but already knew a fair bit about Angel Gomes, which I will come to in a moment. A quick Google check when I arrived home revealed Rashford is seventeen and has represented his country at schoolboy level. It will be interesting to see if either of them make the breakthrough to senior level in the next few years. Brad and I have tracked Angel's progress over the last few seasons and I will stick my neck out and say I would be surprised if he doesn't make it at Premier League level.

The following week Brad was given an opportunity to come face to face with Angel Gomes himself. Joe was called up to the Blackburn under 18s squad so Brad was selected for the under 16s in a tournament against Middlesbrough, Newcastle United and Manchester United. Angel is the son of a former Portugese footballer, Gil Gomes, who played in a Portugal Youth team that won the World Youth

Championship before going on to play for Ovarense and Braga, amongst others. Gil played in England in the latter part of his footballing career, playing for several semi-professional clubs, including some in the Manchester area like Salford City and Hyde United.

When Brad had a six week trial at Manchester United when he was ten, Angel was already the stand out player in the squad. The coaches often used to refer to the fact that he was almost a year younger than some of the other lads, as he was born on 31st August 2000, the last day possible for their school year, but would win every sprint and had more technical ability than everyone else. Brad was excited to play against him in the tournament which was up at Middlesbrough's training ground at Rockcliffe Park. Parents were not allowed to accompany their children to this one, but Brad said the facilities were fantastic with top class pitches and Angel Gomes, not surprisingly, ran the show for Manchester United. United beat Rovers 2-1 with Gomes beating Brad from the penalty spot to seal victory. Brad was gutted about that as he said he wanted a penalty save from Gomes on his c.v! He said the constant advice to the United players from their coaches on the touchline was,

"Give it to Angel, give it to Angel," so no doubt big things are expected from the boy. I hope he goes on to fulfil his potential.

Tomorrow, we head up to the 2nd Qualifying Round of the FA Vase as Heaton Stannington face a tough away tie at Chester-le-Street who are currently top of the Northern League Division Two, with Heaton Stannington sitting in fifth spot. Gordon, Alan and I are all heading up together with Shaunee Smith meeting us there. We also have a returning guest as my Dad is coming along too.

If you have read the first two books about our FA travels, you will already know all about my Dad, Richard, but just to briefly summarise, he is a former FA Amateur Cup Finalist with Skelmersdale United, as previously mentioned is a former coach of the schoolboys at Everton and is also a football fanatic like the rest of us. He came along with us to all bar one of the FA Cup matches but last year decided going around the country for the FA Trophy wasn't for him and he only made one appearance for the North Ferriby United game against Ebbsfleet United. He will be 72 in February so I suspected he would not want to come along for the Vase games either but when I asked him if he fancied coming with us to a game at Chester le Street, to my surprise, he said he would love to. Gordon is driving this time, so he is picking my Dad up first and then picking Alan and me up from mine, with Al getting the train through to Buckshaw as he has done so many times before in the last three seasons. I am really looking forward to it. I just hope there are as many goals as there were in the last round.

Chapter Four

Saturday 3rd October 2015

The FA VASE – 2nd Qualifying Round

Chester-le-Street v Heaton Stannington

There may not always be huge amounts of quality in lower League football, but thankfully this gap is filled with passion, incident, enthusiasm and excitement. Today's game had an abundance of all four.

As arranged, I picked Alan up from Buckshaw Parkway train station and he came over to ours for a cup of tea, before Alison drove us over to Charnock Richard service station on the M6, which is only about three miles from ours, to meet up with Gordon and my Dad. Alison is a former Oncology nurse so was asking after Jo. Some of the conversation was a bit too in depth for a layman like me to follow but the gist of it was that Jo is taking two steps forward and one step back with her chemotherapy, but overall, Alan is very proud of the way Jo has dealt with the difficulties she has had to face.

Gordon arrived within minutes of Alison dropping us off at Charnock Richard, with my Dad in the passenger seat so Alan and I clambered into the back. Gordon is probably four inches and four stone heavier than my Dad and I am a foot taller than Alan but I still made the schoolboy error of sitting behind Gordon, so spent the journey reminding myself to sit on the other side or in the front on the way home! Gordon doesn't like to hang around when at the wheel of a car, so we were in the North East before I started to get pins and needles in my cramped feet.

As we were within half an hour of the ground even before midday, we decided to make a stop at Durham Service Station for a coffee. My Dad doesn't really get this 'Fancy Coffee For A Fortune' craze and it was amusing to go in to Costa with him. The service station was incredibly busy and there was a big queue at Costa so we patiently stood there for ten minutes before it was time to order. I went first,

"Could I have a medium skinny latte with an extra Espresso shot, please?"

My Dad went next,

"Coffee, please."

There was subsequently a conversation between a patient barista and my Dad to establish that he just wanted a standard, white coffee. When this arrived in a bucket sized mug that was large enough to fit a sponge to wash my car, my Dad's confusion was exacerbated and became even worse when he was asked to pay the grand sum of £3.50. Bewildered, my Dad sat down with Alan, Gordon and myself, shaking his head and complaining that when he first started work back in 1959, he was paid less than that for a week!

When we looked around Costa and the surrounding shops, we realised that a lot of the surrounding tables were filled with people wearing dark green Springbok tops. The Rugby Union World Cup is currently on but none of us footballing lads really know much about it.

"South Africa must be playing up North somewhere today. Anyone any idea where?"

"They're playing Scotland," Gordon answered, "must be at Murrayfield."

A quick Google check actually revealed they were playing at Newcastle United's St James' Park. A couple of weeks ago South Africa had lost 34-32 to Japan in one of World Cup rugby's greatest ever shocks. Despite not knowing much about rugby, we concluded they wouldn't allow themselves a repeat performance and Scotland were probably in for a difficult afternoon. We weren't far wrong. On our way home we heard Scotland lost 34-16. Later on in the evening, England also had a good hiding from Australia at Twickenham.

After our coffee we headed over to Moor Park. The ground is just off the A167, behind a pub called the Chester Moor. I think the ground is officially also known as Chester Moor, but widely referred to as 'Moor Park'. A bit like the West Ham United's ground being called both 'Upton Park' and 'The Boleyn Ground' (apparently it is 'The Boleyn Ground' in 'Upton Park'). With it only being about one o'clock, there were only half a dozen cars in the car park, so we decided to have a look around the ground. As we went in, the match officials were inspecting the pitch. It turned out Gordon knew two of the three, the ref Scott Henry and one of his Assistants, Christian Backhouse.

Gordon is a referee coach in the North West region for the National FA development programme and Christian is also a coach in the group. Scott, who is probably twenty years younger than Gordon and Christian (early 30s rather than early 50s), is one of the refs. They meet for sessions about four or five times a season. Apparently the North West group is led by Premier League referee, Anthony Taylor.

Christian and Scott seemed taken aback that Gordon should be at their 2nd Qualifying Round, FA Vase game up in the North East. After an explanatory chat we went over with them into the clubhouse for a cup of tea. Well, tea for the match officials, my Dad and Alan, a pint for Gordon and myself. Scott, Christian and the other Assistant referee, Tommy, all seemed like good lads who loved their football and a laugh. It's a real shame that refs aren't given more respect from players and supporters as the game wouldn't function without them. I know some local Leagues are struggling for refs now so are dependent on the old guys who have been doing it for years to keep going. A lot of enthusiastic teenagers who take it up for a bit of extra pocket money soon find themselves getting frustrated with the amount of stick they get from the sidelines. Unless there is a real change in attitudes, I can only see things getting worse. Scott, Christian and Tommy were probably just hoping for a quiet afternoon, but unfortunately it wasn't what they got!

Ten minutes before kick off we took our seats in the small stand by the half way line. The ground, much more so than Eccleshill United's in the previous round, looks old and tired, a victim of trying to maintain a stadium on a shoestring budget, but the covered stand, that has about 150 red, plastic seats with no back on, is fairly impressive and the pitch looked well maintained but a little bumpy. None of this is meant as a criticism of the club. The people who run clubs at this level of English football work tirelessly without pay to maintain good standards, it's just impossible for them to provide a surface like that of a Premier League club. Inevitably, this means the players are going to make more mistakes and today these errors led to another goalfest.

Alan had again arranged to meet Shaunee Smith and as the game kicked off, he was puzzled why Shaunee hadn't arrived. It turned out Shaunee was with a couple of his mates and they had been for a few pints in Chester-Le-Street and then had to wait for the Number 21 bus up to the ground which was running late. They turned up a few minutes into the game and as they took their seats in the row in front of us, Shaunee quickly introduced them. One was Darren Turnbull, who Shaunee calls 'Zippy' (apparently no-one else calls him that other than Shaunee). They became friends in 1987 when they were both Christmas temps working at Traidcraft on the Team Valley and have been best mates since. The other was Chris Riley, who Shaunee knew from the Gateshead games. I took this to mean the football matches at Gateshead that Shaunee goes to rather than the athletics annual event that Brendan Foster kickstarted in the 1970s, although maybe I should have double checked. Chris now lived in Chester-le-Street so told me he was a regular at Moor Park.

It was a dull, damp day in the North East but within a couple of minutes of kick off we could sense this was going to be a lively, entertaining encounter with Heaton Stannington going for the jugular from the off with Chester-le-Street looking bemused by the onslaught.

Jon Wright, Heaton Stannington's mercurial striker was showing the most class in an opening strewn with errors and after five minutes he was on the end of a good move involving Lee Johnson and fired 'Stan' into an early lead. The 'Stan' domination continued for the first quarter of the game and in those early encounters it looked like this was going to be a comfortable Heaton Stannington victory. None of our group of seven were at all surprised when 'Stan' made it two after twenty minutes. Matthew Hayton beat Chester-le-Street Town defender, Kevin Dixon, on the left and fired a shot towards the far post that keeper, Aiden Ames managed to flick on to the top of the bar and away for a corner. From the resultant corner kick, there was a goalmouth scramble which led to Ames making another save but the ball only rebounded to Lee Johnson who slotted home. 'Stan' had brought a decent away following and they were delighted to see such an excellent start from their side.

A third goal from Heaton Stannington before the break would, no doubt, have killed off the contest. There is a slight slope on the pitch which favoured 'Stan' in the first half, but a three-nil lead would have taken some pegging back. They continued to dominate proceedings without overly troubling, Ames in the Chester-Le-Street goal.

Five minutes before half time, the game was turned on its head. A Chester-le-Street free kick from the right wasn't cleared by the 'Stan' defence and it fell to Lee Mole on the back post, who brought the ball down, swivelled around and fired it high into the Heaton Stannington net to make it two-one. It was harsh on Heaton Stannington. When Scott Henry blew for half-time, it was probably the horizontal blue and white stripes of Chester-le-Street who were happier than the vertical black and white stripes of Heaton Stannington because they were only a goal behind at the break in a game they had been second best in throughout.

At half-time, as well as nipping to the loo and reflecting upon an eventful forty five minutes, I questioned why the Heaton Stannington players all had 'CHUF' on the backs of their kits rather than their names. It transpired it was in support of the 'Children's Heart Unit Fund' at Freeman Hospital in Newcastle, one of the world's leading specialist centres for children and babies born with, or who develop, heart conditions. I subsequently sent a tweet over to 'Heaton Stan' twitter page asking what the link was with 'CHUF' and was told a former player's son was treated there and subsequently as a club they have done what they can to raise the 'CHUF' profile. An excellent touch.

I think collectively we all expected Heaton Stannington would go on and win the game after the first forty five minutes. When the second half began, they were again in the ascendancy and when Lee Johnson pulled the ball back to Matthew Johnson, it seemed he had time to pick his spot, but his low effort cannoned back off the post. As is often the case on our FA travels, we can pinpoint a turning point in a match and this was certainly the moment that changed things for a subsequently resurgent Chester-le-Street. The home side started to creep into the game and after 58 minutes they were rewarded with an equaliser that was of the highest quality.

Danny Hepplewhite strode forward along the Chester-le-Street right. From at least 35 yards out, he struck a sweet shot that flew into the top corner beyond a helpless Lee Martin. The 21 year old centre back has probably never struck a sweeter shot and as soon as it left his boot, Gordon next to me said 'Effort!' It turned out to me much more than that and a delighted dugout raced on to the edge of the pitch including an unusually dressed coach in jeans and a hoodie who had obviously not played too much of a part in the prolonged pre-match warm up.

For the first hour, the officials had had a quiet day, but the next hour saw Scott Henry, largely not of his doing, become centre stage. Most decisions we felt he ended up getting right, but when Joe Hamblin was upended by a nasty looking tackle from Jon Wright, we felt he was lucky to escape with just a yellow card.

This tackle continued to be a talking point fifteen minutes later as a Chester-le-Street free kick was cleared and a good move that involved Dodsworth, Watson and Wright ended with the latter coolly slotting away his second of the game, to make it 3-2 to 'Stan'. With less than ten minutes left on the clock, it appeared that Heaton Stannington were going to grab an excellent away win.

Chris Riley told me that Chester-le-Street hadn't looked as strong as the previous times he had seen them this season and put this down to the absence of their missing 34 year old central midfield, Craig Marron, who he felt had the class and experience to get others playing around him.

Alan and I, always keen to avoid midweek replays were now settling for a 3-2 win for Heaton Stan. I was going to be in Lanzarote for the next round, but Alan had his eye on a trip up to Newcastle for the next game. This hope soon evaporated as four minutes later Chester-le-Street equalised again. 'Chester' captain, Kevin Dixon went for a run down the left wing before finding centre forward Scott Heslop. The striker is currently in a rich vein of form and is the Northern League Division 2's leading scorer with fourteen already in all competitions. Heslop looked supremely confident in front of goal and slipped the ball past Martin to make it three-all.

There were a number of disappointed Heaton Stannington fans behind the goal and whether or not they said anything to Heslop as he celebrated is immaterial, the striker should have known better than to do what he did next, which was aim a rude gesture at the 'Stan' fans, which we presumed was a one or two finger salute. The ref spotted this and rewarded Heslop with a red card for his exuberance/stupidity.

Our seven man panel all agreed that the sending off was justified but there was not as much agreement in camp when Brian Dodsworth of Heaton was sent off for a tackle that, to me, looked like a yellow at worst. If Jon Wright's tackle was a yellow earlier in the half then this one was barely a foul. I suppose Heaton deserved to be down to ten, but the wrong man was off the field.

The resultant free kick from the sending off tackle led to a comical couple of minutes when Chester-le-Street did everything but score. Kevin Dixon's effort following a knock down from the free kick looked like it was going to be the winner until it was scrambled off the line for a Chester-le-Street corner. When the corner was swung in, Mole climbed higher than the Heaton Stannington defenders but once again the Heaton Stannington rear guard held firm and the ball was cleared off the line. There were no further chances and after ninety minutes it was a three-all draw, with the sending off count equal at one-all.

Before each game the two teams can agree extra time rather than going to a replay and in this case, the two sides must have made the arrangement in advance as when the final whistle blew, both teams got together in huddles rather than head to the dressing room.

The thirty minutes of extra time continued in the dramatic fashion of the second half. After only four minutes of the first period of extra time, Chester's Lee Mole, an obvious threat from set pieces, got on the end of another corner but this time his header was slightly too high, clipping the top of the bar.

Early in the second period, Adam Rowntree, a Heaton Stannington substitute put a long ball over the top of the Chester-le-Street defenders for Jon Wright to chase on to. It landed smack in the middle of Jon Wright and Aiden Ames in goal and both sprinted towards the ball at full pelt. Wright, eyeing his hat-trick was marginally the quicker and struck a lofted shot over Ames head and towards the Chester-le-Street goal. He was about 40 yards out at the time but hit it powerfully and it was just a case of whether it would drop out of the sky in time to land in the goal. Everyone seemed to watch open mouthed as it began to drop and it looked for all the world like it was going to drop in but, agonisingly for Heaton Stannington, it hit the underside of the bar and rebounded to safety.

Chester-le-Street seemed to sense after this that luck was on their side and when Michael Scott, Heaton Stannington's right back, stretched into a weary tackle and missed the ball, he was given a second yellow card which took the player count to ten-nine in Chester-le-Street's favour. Once again, although you could have sympathy with Michael Scott, it was difficult to argue with the referee's decision. It seemed certain that Chester-le-Street would now go all out to make their numerical advantage count and for the last ten minutes it was always going to be a case of whether Heaton Stannington could hold out for a draw or whether Chester-le-Street could snatch a dramatic late victory.

The question posed was immediately answered. The free kick from Scott's foul was launched into the area by Michael Hepplewhite and substitute Andrew Grant-Soulsby, an experienced 29 year old, who formerly played for Birtley Town and Jarrow Roofing, headed the ball beyond the stranded Lee Martin to make it 4-3.

Heaton Stan's nine men mustered one last chance when substitute Ben Telford had a shot just wide but the dream of Wembley was over for Heaton Stannington. Chester-le-Street were through to the First Round Proper of the FA Vase for the first time since 2001 and they extended their unbeaten run to fifteen games.

The 1st Round Proper will see some of the teams with a realistic chance of winning the FA Vase entering the competition, including Northern League Division One sides, so a real test awaits Chester-Le-Street in the next round. On today's showing Chester-le-Street have an excellent team spirit and a never say die attitude but they will need to avoid the defensive lapses they displayed today (and perhaps get their talisman, Craig Marron, back) if they want to reach the 2nd Round Proper for the first time since Billingham Town beat them in 1998.

Our journey home was another speedy one with Gordon at the wheel. Alan was pleased with a Man City 6-1 win over Newcastle United which was part of a frustrating double defeat for Shaunee Smith's sides with Gateshead losing 3-2 at home to Dover Athletic, a game Shaunee had sacrificed to see the Vase game.

I will update you on the next Round draw for Chester-le-Street Town (and Brad's footballing progression/regression) before passing the note pad on to Gordon and Alan for the First Round Proper.

FINAL SCORE :- CHESTER-LE-STREET TOWN 4 HEATON STANNINGTON 3 (after extra time).

Goals so far :- 13 in 2 games.

CHAPTER FIVE

Monday 5th October 2015

Alan rang me when I was at work earlier to say that Chester-le-Street have been drawn at home against Newton Aycliffe in the 1st Round Proper. Newton Aycliffe are another Northern League side, but are a Division One side so will fancy their chances against Division Two, Chester-le-Street. In a selfish way, I was pleased that it was a return to Chester-le-Street as it would mean that I wasn't missing out on a new ground on our journey.

Newton Aycliffe aren't a team we are totally unaware of, as we have been following North Ferriby United's results this season, after their FA Trophy exploits last season. Ferriby were drawn against them in the FA Cup 2nd Qualifying Round with Ferriby travelling up the East Coast to Newton Aycliffe's Moor Lane Sports Club ground. From all accounts, it was a very tight affair with very little goalmouth action. Ferriby's huge centre forward, Tom Denton, came closest to scoring when powering a header on to the post in the 81st minute but the game finished 0-0. Back at Ferriby, in the replay, the home side dominated and came away with a 3-0 victory with a brace from Danny Clarke and another from Nathan Hotte.

We have continued to keep in touch with several North Ferriby fans and they have contacted us via Facebook following the draw to warn us that Newton Aycliffe are a very physical side and at times this spills over to being a little bit 'nasty'. We have decided to reserve judgement on this, as a few opposition supporters were saying similar things about Ferriby last season and we never thought they played in any way other than 'hard but fair'. North Ferriby fans may also have caught the worst of Newton Aycliffe, as they did have six players booked in an ill tempered second half at the Eon Visual Media Stadium.

I suspect that although I won't get to see Newton Aycliffe in the 1st Round, I may well get to see them subsequently as a side that can manage a draw against a strong Conference North side like North Ferriby United will be a decent outfit and will probably have too much about them for Chester-le-Street.

At this stage, however, I am unsure exactly how much of the Vase I will get to see. I started working for Barron Financial Solutions on Friday and trying to balance working there from 9am to 5:30pm, three days a week, with writing my fictional books (and running the one man band Limited Company that keeps the sales ticking over) as well as driving Brad to football four or five times a week (and our younger son, Joel a couple of times a week), may prove too much. Alan and Gordon are well aware of this and know they may be required to be the team sports writer more than just the one time when I am with the family in Lanzarote at the end of this month.

My participation in the FA Vase journey will depend a lot on a meeting Brad and I have with Ben Benson, Blackburn Rovers Academy goalkeeper coach, after Brad's training session on Wednesday. My gut feeling is that he will not be signing. Frustratingly, although Brad has looked a capable keeper in his six weeks at Blackburn, he hasn't shone. On the whole, he has a lot of confidence about him, which can sometimes tip over to arrogance at home, but whilst he has been at Blackburn, he has been subdued. If there is anywhere I want to see him look confident or borderline arrogant, it is on a football pitch, but to me he looks like he is holding back. Whether this is because he feels Joe Boyling, Alan's nephew, is a better keeper than him currently, is a distinct possibility. Joe has been at Blackburn's

Academy since he was a little boy, so has had professional coaching for years which has helped develop his game whilst Brad has largely been playing park football.

I have tried to drum into Brad's head that he isn't battling against Joe, he is battling against himself. Joe has issues with his physicality that he can't do anything about, whilst Brad's issues currently are mental ones, which I feel he can address. Perhaps it is just that Brad isn't comfortable at Blackburn or that he needs the certainty of a contract to build his confidence, but I fear he is letting the opportunity slip away. I have asked him how much he really wants a football scholarship, as I don't want to be encouraging him if he doesn't want it himself but he insists that he wants nothing more than a scholarship. At the moment, his body language isn't expressing that. We will see what Wednesday brings.

Wednesday 7th October 2016

After five weeks as a trialist at Blackburn Rovers, Brad and I had our anticipated meeting with Ben Benson and his goalkeeping assistant, Steve, tonight but it didn't go as we had expected. Just to summarise, following on from playing for Lancashire, Brad was asked to go to train with Rovers under 16s at Brockhall, Blackburn's fantastic training set up, halfway between Blackburn and Clitheroe. It was initially meant to be for a week, but after the first week, which saw him play a half in a 2-0 win against Burnley and be on the bench for a 3-2 defeat against Manchester United, he was asked to stay for up to a total of six weeks.

I would take him to Brockhall on a Monday, Wednesday and Thursday night for three sessions that started at 6.30pm and finished at 9pm. They were nearly always on the first team 4G surface. It's about a forty minute drive from our house when it's quiet on the roads but at half past five, it could easily take an hour so we tended to leave about twenty past five. Brad was always involved in some way (half a game, substitute or a full game) on a Saturday too, so that either involved me going and watching or dropping him off and picking him up later. Thus, it was four trips a week. It seemed like a massive commitment to do this for five weeks, but the likes of Lee Boyling, Joe's father and Alan's brother-in-law had been making the journey from Failsworth in Manchester to Brockhall for about nine years. For most of these young lads, there isn't going to be a pot of gold at the end of the rainbow, but if it teaches them about discipline, teamwork, camaraderie, fitness and effort, amongst other things, then it is worth the journeys.

After the Burnley and United games, Brad played in a four team tournament between Rovers, Manchester United, Newcastle United and Middlesbrough, up at

Boro's Rockliffe Park (parents weren't allowed). They lost 2-1 against United, drew 1-1 with Newcastle and 0-0 with Boro and then his final game was against Everton at Brockhall. Brad played the second half in a 1-0 win. After that game, I bumped into Ray Hall, former Youth Development Officer at Everton and an old friend of my Dad's, who was very disappointed that Blackburn had beaten Everton 2-1 in the u18s game on the adjoining pitch, as Everton apparently have a very rich crop of under 18s, the best, he believes, for about ten years. As an Evertonian myself, it will be interesting to see how many of them make the breakthrough.

Tonight, however, was decision time. They had seen enough of Brad to make a decision and as we sat outside the designated meeting room waiting to be given the instruction to go in, I quickly asked Brad,

"What do you think your chances are?"

"Absolutely no chance!"

"Why?"

"I've played two half matches in five weeks and not let any goals in and played in a tournament and let three in, in three games, two of which were penalties, but last Saturday, they picked a lad released by Preston to play a half in goal, as well as Joe, so it seems like they've already made up their mind."

I thought about what Brad had said and he was right. He had been asked down every weekend before the Saturday just gone, but hadn't really played much. From what I had seen, he had looked competent but not sparkling in those games and had trained similarly. Perhaps, if they were looking for someone to sign, he would have to set the world alight. Brad hadn't done that.

Minutes later, we were beckoned inside the meeting room and were sat down, facing Ben and Steve across a table. Ben Benson is only in his mid-20s but has a big, deep booming voice and a maturity that belies his years.

"Well, Brad, you've caused us quite a headache," Ben said to open the conversation.

As soon as he started with that sentence I knew for sure Brad wouldn't be signing for Blackburn. This isn't the X-Factor. They aren't pretending to give disappointing news to entertain the millions watching from home, then providing a twist. This is reality. The reality was that Brad wouldn't be signing otherwise Ben would have opened up with, 'We have some good news for you'.

Over the next ten minutes, Ben and Steve went on to explain why Brad wouldn't be signing for Rovers. He had done 'nothing wrong' they said, but having played in local Leagues for the past eight seasons, they felt there were flaws to his technique that needed ironing out. They said if he was thirteen and playing in the under 14s, they would have signed him, but at fifteen, playing in the under 16s, they didn't know if there was enough time before they would have to make the decisions on who would and who would not get a scholarship.

"I was at Carlisle previously," Ben explained, "and Steve was at Bury. Now if we were deciding on whether or not to sign Brad for Carlisle or Bury, we would have signed him after a week, but this is a higher standard. If we signed Brad, it wouldn't be fair on him. We have to look after Joe's interests too and we are still keen on looking at other keepers at this age who are getting told by the likes of Everton, Liverpool, United and City, that they aren't getting a scholarship. So, Brad would only be getting the odd half game here and there. It wouldn't be fair on him."

This was sounding like the similar patter of rejection that we had heard before. Brad had been at United under 10s for a trial and at that point, after six weeks, we were told he was no better than the two keepers they already had and it wouldn't be fair on Brad to be one of three keepers. The next thing they came out with at United, was to say they would keep an eye on his development and I sat there expecting Ben and Steve to say that next.

"What we would like to do, however, with your permission, is to see whether we can fix Brad up somewhere else. We have really good links with other teams in the North West and what we will do, because we think he is a great lad with good potential, is to speak to other clubs in the North West over the next 24 hours and see who might be interested."

Both Brad and I suddenly sat a bit more upright in our chairs. This wasn't turning out to be quite the brush off we had been anticipating.

"That would be brilliant," I said on Brad's behalf and Brad nodded in agreement.

So, on our way home, I had a chat with Brad. He had done well at Blackburn but if he wanted to make it, he had to come out of his shell and play with the confidence and exuberance he had when he played with people he knew. If he went on a trial somewhere else and wasn't signed after six weeks, he would have to put football on the backburner, return to playing local football at Croston Juniors and concentrate on his GCSEs.

We will find out tomorrow whether Ben and Steve are as good as their word. I don't see any reason why they won't be. They could easily have shaken our hands, thanked Brad for coming along and waved him off with good wishes. They have given him an opportunity. I am just hoping this time around he grasps it.

Thursday 8th October 2015

Next stop Rochdale! I've had three calls today from clubs in the North West enquiring about Brad – Bury, Carlisle United and Rochdale, but Rochdale rang first and neither Bury nor Carlisle said anything that made me think agreeing to take Brad down to Rochdale was a bad decision. I am sure the three clubs are of a similar standard but I agreed to take Brad to Rochdale based on logistics and opportunities.

The first call I received was from Rochdale Academy's Head of Recruitment, Ronnie Cusick. Ronnie immediately came across as a warm and friendly guy. He explained that Rochdale trained twice a week on a Tuesday and Thursday night at Matthew Moss High School on the all weather. Seven until half past nine on a Tuesday and half past seven until half past nine on a Thursday. The timings and days were ideal. I am due to work Mondays, Wednesdays and Fridays at Barron Financial Solution's once I am trained up into my role and even if these days swop, I can get home from Southport and over to Rochdale in time for seven. There was more encouragement to come. Rochdale had just released their under 16 keeper and their under 18s keeper, Johny Diba Musangu, had already signed professionally for the club and was often on the bench for the first team, so Ronnie said if Brad was good enough, he would get a chance at both under 16s and under 18s level. Ronnie also went on to say, as things stood, Rochdale would not have a scholarship keeper for next season, so if Brad came in and did well, not only would he have a great chance of signing, he would also have a strong chance of getting a scholarship. This sounded perfect.

A scout from Carlisle and the Bury goalkeeping coach, Ian Wilcock, rang subsequently but Carlisle is a nightmare to get to and Bury's training starts at

5:30pm, which would be tricky for me, so I felt that I had done the right thing in arranging for Brad to go down to Rochdale tonight. I told Brad and he seemed really keen once I told him that they currently didn't have an under 16 or under 17 goalkeeper. He wasn't quite sure where Rochdale was in the North West or what League they were in, so I informed him they were only a League below Blackburn but operate on more of a shoestring so not to be expecting facilities like Blackburn's when he turns up tonight. I have a good feeling about it all and will not give you a day by day update now, but will make sure I post an update before we go to Lanzarote.

Wednesday 28th October 2015

The 'Wade family' head off to Lanzarote tomorrow for 11 days but I wanted to write a few pages before we go. It's been a busy month once again for Brad but there has also been some very sad news for Evertonians and football fans around the world with the news that our most successful manager ever, Howard Kendall has died.

On the Thursday night of my last post, I took Brad over to Rochdale and we were introduced to the two under 16s Academy coaches, Chris Brown, who runs the team and Ryan Ball, the Academy goalkeeping coach. What was immediately striking was that they both only looked like young lads themselves. At a guess I would say they are both around 23 or 24. I had a good chat with Ryan before leaving Brad to it and going to sit in my car in the car park for a couple of hours. The car park is right next to the 4G pitch they train on, so I was able to watch from there. This has become a routine over the last three weeks and if I am not sat in the car park watching, I am down at Tesco's in Rochdale trying to pass some time. Realising I was not fully utilising my time, I have started to take a note pad down and have begun to write my next fictional novel.

After the first session, once they had established that Brad was a capable keeper, they asked if he would play on the Sunday against Blackpool. Rochdale's home games are at Hopwood Hall and when I went over to watch, I ran into Gareth Gray, father of Dan Gray, who had been on trial with Brad at Blackburn. He had also been released at the end of his trial and was trying his luck at Blackpool. Dan had a better game than Brad with Blackpool winning 5-2. Rochdale had about three stand out players, but the rest of the team looked weak and although Brad was only partially at fault for one goal and blameless for the others, I came away thinking he would have to improve if he wants to stay beyond his trial period.

Thus, Sunday morning had been a bit anti-climactic after a brilliant day, the day before. Next season (2016-17) will mark the 50th Anniversary of Skelmersdale United's first Wembley appearance in the FA Amateur Cup when they played Enfield. If you have read my previous football books you may remember my Dad played in this game, in front of 75,000 at the old Wembley, drawing 0-0 and losing the replay at Maine Road, 3-0. 'Skem' have lots of events planned to commemorate the 50th Anniversary and have been in contact with Enfield to arrange a pre-season friendly next season.

One of the things that came out in their talks with Enfield was that Enfield still had 'movie reel' highlights of the Final and the replay. 'Skem' asked if they could borrow it and were putting the recordings on a screen prior to their Northern Premier League game against Frickley. Several of the nine surviving players including my Dad, goalkeeper Terry Crosbie, midfielder Micky Worswick and forward Wally Bennett turned up to watch highlights of the game. None of them had ever seen clips from the games before.

There were probably no more than six or seven minutes of highlights from the two games, but it was fascinating to watch. My Dad was shown a couple of times, clearing the ball from a cross with a well timed header and playing the ball out from the back. 'Skem' missed their chance to win the Cup when they missed a penalty in the last minute when Alan Bermingham's penalty was saved by Enfield Town goalkeeper, Ian Wolstenholme. The highlights showed the penalty miss, struck waist high to the keeper's right and all the ex-players looked at each other when they watched it afresh after 49 years.

"I remembered it being a better penalty than that!" seemed to be the universal comment.

Still, it was wonderful to watch a few brief highlights at a full looking Wembley and a jam packed Maine Road for the replay. It was on rotation so I sat and watched it about five times! I never came anywhere near to emulating my Dad so my footballing ambitions are now passed to my boys, with Brad the front runner to play somewhere special. It may be that he is destined for a non-League career like my Dad, but I am still keeping my fingers crossed that he could still get somewhere with Rochdale.

Since the Blackpool game, Brad has played twice more, drawing 1-1 with Walsall and losing 3-1 at home to Preston. I would say he is improving game by game and at training. It appears that Rochdale see it that way too, as they asked him to go in to train with the under 18s from Monday until today which he has really enjoyed. I am hoping his progression continues once we return from Lanzarote.

The place we are going to in Lanzarote, Club La Santa, is a place I have been five times before, four times as a teenager as my Mum and Dad had a timeshare there. Set in the middle of nowhere, on the North West coast of Lanzarote, it is the biggest sporting holiday complex in the world. We took the boys there five years ago and they loved it, so now our financial difficulties are gradually becoming a memory, we thought it would be a great time to go back. I was hoping Brad and Joel would want to fully utilise the facilities, but Brad has already announced that he is 'shattered' and is wanting to chill out for his holiday!

On Saturday 17th October, I nipped into Chorley to buy myself some sports tops and shorts for the holiday and when I got back to my car, I switched on BBC 5Live and they were announcing the news that Howard Kendall had died aged 69. I didn't know him personally but he was the helm at Everton through my teenage years and brought a period of success to the club the likes of which I am unlikely to see again in my lifetime. Everton won the League twice in 1985 and 1987, the FA Cup once in 1984 and the European Cup Winners Cup in 1985, as well as appearing in countless other finals and winning the Charity Shield three times.

My Dad had worked at Everton in the late 1970s and early 1980s, so I immediately phoned his mobile but there was no reply. I started to drive home, listening to the radio in a stunned disbelief and after a couple of minutes my Dad phoned back. I parked up at the side of the road and took the call. My Mum and Dad were shopping in Ormskirk and had gone for a coffee. My Dad hadn't heard the news and was taken aback. Dad had known Howard Kendall pretty well and he said he had seen him at a Ken Dodd Charity lunch a couple of weeks earlier and had a good chat with him. It was no secret that Howard liked a drink, so my Dad said it had been good to catch up with him early on in the event as he was sober and good company. It is not known as yet what caused his death but he had gone to Southport hospital feeling unwell and had died whilst there. His funeral will be held at Liverpool's Anglican Cathedral tomorrow afternoon at 1pm.

One last thing before I pass the baton on to Alan, as Brad has been in training during the day for the last three days, I went down to Victoria Park, Chorley last night with my friend, Shaun McManus, to see if Chorley could beat Northwich Victoria in their FA Cup 4th Qualifying Round replay and reach the 1st Round Proper for the first time in twenty five years. Things were looking good when Andy Bond put Chorley one-nil up in the 41st minute when he scored directly from a free kick. It was one of those cross shots that the keeper anticipates someone will get a head to and when they don't, they are left stranded. The keeper in question was Mason Springthorpe. I spent the first half repeatedly saying 'I know that name' and put myself out of my misery by googling him at half time to discover he was a former keeper at Everton who had been bought for £125,000 from Shrewsbury Town when only 17. He had been released by Roberto Martinez twelve months ago and had dropped straight down to non-League level. He is still only twenty so perhaps he may rise back up the pyramid.

As for Chorley, everything went wrong in the second half. A debatable penalty was given against Chorley's centre back, Andrew Teague, in the 49th minute, allegedly for a trip (to universal cries of 'He never touched him ref!') and Richard Bennett fired home the equaliser from the spot. Ten minutes from the end, Northwich, who are two leagues below Chorley but are a team of giants, won it when the largest giant, substitute Aboubacar Sanogo, headed home less than five minutes after coming on.

Despite the result, I still always enjoy going to Victory Park and will hopefully be back before the end of the season. Anyway, time to get packing. See you in a couple of weeks!

CHAPTER SIX

Saturday 31st October 2015

The FA VASE – 1st Round Proper

Chester-le-Street v Newton Aycliffe

Written by Alan Oliver

Gordon picked me up in Failsworth at approximately 10.30am. He also picked up some picture frames he'd bought off me to mount two signed football shirts for his son, Kieran and his daughter, Heather. Kieran's frame was a Wigan Athletic FA Cup winners shirt from 2013 (can't think who they beat that day though, Gordon?) Heather's was a signed Wayne Rooney England shirt.

After the frames were carefully packed in Gordon's car, we set off for Chester-Le-Street, County Durham, for today's FA Vase 1st Round Proper match between Chester-Le-Street Town and Newton Aycliffe. However, given the speed Gordon drives, we had set off way too early and decided to stop off for a coffee break. We had the brainwave of killing two birds with one stone and doing a bit of a reconnaissance mission to find Newton Aycliffes' ground, just in case they proceeded to the next round (best laid plans)? We had a right performance finding it, first we had the coffee break just off the roundabout signposted Newton Aycliffe and then we drove around an industrial estate. We had almost given up but as we were heading back towards Chester-Le-Street we recognised the road it was off, Shafto Way. So we drove in to what we thought was the entrance. There was a rugby ground and the football ground was just behind the clubhouse. We thought the footy ground entrance must be behind the clubhouse so headed that way. How wrong were we? We ended up at a dead end near a path that led to a park and turned around. Gordon drove around in circles for a while, but whichever direction he drove in, we couldn't find the entrance to the football pitch. We gave up in the end and decided that you must enter both from the social club. If we end up going back there, we will have to ask someone in advance how to get in!

All we had to do now was get back on the motorway to make our way to Chester-Le-Street. When we got there the car park was already three quarters full. We started to think there was going to be a decent crowd and perhaps we had totally underestimated the fact that this was a local derby. The gateman put us straight though saying,

"Don't let the cars fool you! The majority belong to players and staff. We don't expect much more than 120 people through the gates."

He wasn't far off either the official attendance was 154.

Chester-Le-Street 0 – Newton Aycliffe 4

Chester-Le-Street were well beaten 4-0 by a well drilled Newton Aycliffe side. After taking the lead on nine minutes, from a Dennis Knight penalty, Aycliffe never looked back. They extended their lead after twenty nine minutes after good skill on their right wing from Matty Moffat, one of Aycliffes' stand out players on the day. Moffat crossed for Alan Harrison to head in past Chesters' goalie Aiden Ames. He would be picking the ball out of the net again a couple of minutes later, when a long kick by Aycliffes' keeper Winter found Dennis Knight who headed on for Matty Moffat to score their third. At half time, it remained 3-0 to Aycliffe.

Gordon and I decided to stay in the stand for the interval rather than grab a coffee. We didn't fancy the trek back to the clubhouse which isn't inside the ground perimeter and had already spotted a good few fans heading over there, so there would have been a bit of a queue and we'd probably miss the start of the second half.

One reason we particularly don't want to miss too much action is because we are doing this Chapter as Calvin is away on holiday. We'd been well drilled by Calvin on having a note book, pens and to get as much info as possible. It's rather like handing your English homework in on time for the teacher. In any case, Gordon was meeting a mate, Dave Ryan, one of his refereeing mates who he had met in Portugal in 2014 when Dave was Gordon's fourth official at the Iber Veterans Cup Final between Malaga and Sevilla. It's a competition for ex-professionals from Portugal and Spain usually held at the end of the season in May.

The second half had no sooner got underway when Aycliffe got their fourth goal, a superb bullet header from that man Moffat again from a Knight corner. Chester-Le-Street had very few chances, the most notable was a Matthew Smith free kick curled over the wall on 53 minutes which James Winter tipped over the bar. Matty Moffat was having an excellent game, as was Dennis Knight and on 83 minutes Moffat raced clear but Aiden Ames made a fine save to his left, to deny him his hat trick. The only other incident of note came midway through the 2nd half and was spotted by both my refereeing pals. The Aycliffe coach was making a substitution and put his board up indicating number nine, Matty Moffat, to come off, which we found odd as he was having a decent game. What actually occurred was number 10 Dennis Knight came off instead. This was missed by all the match officials.

All in all it was a pretty decent day, another £30.00 to my Christie cancer charity c/o Gordon (for the picture frames) and we found Newton Aycliffes' ground eventually for future reference (although we still don't know where the entrance is) and witnessed a decent (although a little one sided) game of football. This vindicated our tour of Newton Aycliffe. I also managed to remove the official team sheet which Chester-Le-Street pin up near the turnstile for fans to check their teams line-ups. That'll be another keepsake from the journey as well as the obligatory match programme.

FINAL SCORE :- CHESTER-LE-STREET 0 NEWTON AYCLIFFE 4

Goals so far :- 17 in 3 games

CHAPTER SEVEN

Monday 9th November 2015

The Wade family are back! After a great eleven days in Lanzarote, at a fabulously upgraded Club La Santa, we are back to normality. I had a few texts off Alan whilst I was away, the first couple were worrying, as Alan's wife Jo had been admitted to hospital. Despite doing really well with her chemotherapy, when her temperature spikes, Jo needs to go back in to hospital, so they can keep a close eye on her. She was only released in the early hours of the Saturday morning prior to the Chester-le-Street v Newton Aycliffe game. Alan has done every round of the FA Cup, FA Trophy and FA Vase so Jo understands he wants to make it to the end but Alan is also aware that if Jo was really unwell, his family would take priority.

I had texts off Alan after the game to say it was a comfortable four-nil win to Newton Aycliffe and that Gordon had pointed out that it seems to be the first team to four that wins. Hope we continue to see the winners scoring four in subsequent rounds but suspect the nearer we get to the final, the tighter things will be.

Last Monday lunchtime, I received a further text from Alan to say Newton Aycliffe had been drawn away to Colne in the next round. This is an easy one for us as Colne is only a few miles east of Burnley, about thirty odd miles from Chorley. The game is on 22nd November. Although Alan was a little disappointed that it wasn't a new ground for him, he was pleased that it would give him an opportunity to catch up with an old friend. Alan was formerly a security guard at Lewis' in Manchester and his former boss is now the security manager at Boundary Mills, Colne, so he said he will be jumping on the 'Pendle Witchway' bus from Manchester (£6 return) and going to visit his mate before kick off. I will probably travel across with Gordon and see if my Dad fancies coming too.

With regards to family life, Brad did use the opportunity to chill out in Lanzarote. I know he is having to work harder, football wise, than he has ever done before, so far this season, but I thought he would still be up for playing a lot of sport whilst he was away. In the biggest sports complex in the world, he spent more time utilising the free Wifi than he did playing sport. He did join in a bit with tennis, swimming, paddle boarding, badminton and a few other things, but nowhere near as much as Joel.

I found it a bit frustrating that he wasn't keen to participate but Alison is often very level headed when she sees me getting annoyed with him and quietly pointed out it is natural for a fifteen year old boy to have their lazy moments! He still has the utmost faith in his own ability to get a contract from Rochdale but from what I have seen so far, he will have to improve. He also seems very laid back about his GCSE work and I pointed out that although it would be great if he became a professional footballer, there is still a long way to go.

"Currently Brad, you have become third choice Lancashire goalkeeper at under 16s. Now, if that means you are the third best goalkeeper for your age group in the whole of Lancashire, then that's fantastic, but you will have to go from where you are now to being one of the best fifty goalkeepers in the country, in all age groups, if you want to be a professional goalkeeper. That's a hell of a lot of improvement!"

I don't really know why he is slipped down to third choice keeper at Lancashire. He has played well in both friendly games he has played for them but the coach seems to prefer the other two lads, which is obviously his prerogative.

"Why only fifty keepers?" Brad asked.

"Well, at least half the keepers in the Premier League and the Football League are foreign."

"True."

"So you need to go from maybe being in the Top 100 keepers in your age group in the country to being in the Top 50 between the ages of 18 and 38. It's a big ask."

"I can do it."

"I hope you can but you need to have a Plan B and that Plan B involves you studying."

To be honest, I really hope he does get signed and then does get a scholarship. Brad is a social butterfly and if he doesn't get a football scholarship, I can see him partying hard and studying very little over the next two years. He is bright but certainly no genius and it isn't as if he will be giving up the chance to go to an Oxbridge University or a career as a barrister. He would thrive with the discipline needed at a football club but he is going to have to play well over the next few weeks to earn himself that chance. He was improving in the last couple of weeks before our holidays so I hope that progression continues from tomorrow onwards.

Sunday 15th November 2015

This weekend started in the most horrible of ways. I woke up on Saturday morning, stumbled out of bed and went down to put BBC News and Sky News on, as I do every morning. Normally, if there is nothing really going on in the world, I soon switch over to Sky Sports News but unfortunately yesterday morning there was too much news to switch over.

On Friday evening, several terrorists had gone on a killing spree in various parts of Paris, shooting and bombing hundreds of innocent people before killing themselves. Over a hundred people died and several hundred were injured. The majority of the deaths were at the Bataclan Theatre when gunmen stormed a concert by an American rock band called 'Eagles of Death Metal'.

This is a football book and I don't want to write too much about tragic news events but in a weekend that was filled with personal joy, it would be wrong not to acknowledge the tragic events that had taken place in Paris. As each year goes by, the human race seems to find more barbaric ways to treat each other.

The reason I was actually up early on Saturday morning was partially football related. I have to work one in four Saturday's at Barron's as they open from 10am to 2pm on a Saturday, largely to accommodate people who cannot get in to see a mortgage broker during the week. I had managed to get out of working in October, due to being new and having a holiday, but it was my turn this weekend. I am really enjoying the job, so didn't mind anyway, but yesterday there was the added bonus that David, my friend and boss, was the Match Sponsor of the Southport v Cheltenham Town game, so as a company we had about forty guests coming for a meal in the lounge before kick off, so I was going into work early as Dave and I were heading over to Haig Avenue (or The Merseyrail Community Stadium, as it is now called) for just after one o'clock. I had to drive, but I go to most games without having a drink these days so didn't mind at all.

Cheltenham are currently top of the Vanarama National League and Southport are third from bottom and on yesterday's evidence, they are both where they deserve to be. Cheltenham won 4-0 without needing to get out of first gear, they were 3-0 up within the first 15 minutes and coasted after that, scoring a further goal early in the second half. I fully expect Cheltenham to be back in the Football League next season and unless things change quickly at Southport, I expect them to be battling to avoid the drop to the Conference North.

When we were handed the team sheets for the game, I was interested to note that Cheltenham's substitute goalkeeper was a lad called Rhys Lovett. Rhys had spent several years at Walsall's Academy but despite getting a scholarship, he wasn't getting enough game time at Walsall so in the second year of his scholarship, he went to Rochdale and played a lot of games last season for their under 18s. Rochdale's Academy goalkeeping coach Ryan Ball said he was a really good lad and a strong keeper but with the emergence of Johny Diba, there wasn't an opportunity for him at Rochdale. Steve Collis, the Rochdale first team goalkeeping coach recommended him to Gary Johnson at Cheltenham and as a consequence, he was given a trial and obviously impressed as they signed him. I was hoping they might give him a run out at 4-0 up, but unfortunately it wasn't to be.

Today, Rochdale under 16s played Shrewsbury under 16s on the all weather at Hopwood Hall. Brad has had a good week training (they asked him to go in on Saturday morning to do an extra session with the under 18s) and seems to have come back with a steely determination to do well. During the warm up and in the first five minutes of the game, I could tell he was brimming with confidence and although I normally have a sense of nervousness when I watch him play, today I had the feeling everything was going to go well.

My sense of confidence was dented slightly midway through the first half. Brad had started well, made a couple of tidy stops and had come off his line to collect a corner, something I feel he doesn't do often enough, but then a through ball was played into the box and he underestimated the speed of the centre forward and raced out his six yard box only to be beaten to the ball and upend the striker for a blatant penalty. Thankfully the Shrewsbury player was heading away from goal otherwise it might have been a sending off, but I could tell once Brad took himself back to his line that he fancied himself to save the penalty.

Despite not being the greatest watcher of football, Brad reads a game well and can often pick where a penalty taker is going to put the ball from his run up and body shape. The penalty was struck firmly, high to Brad's right but Brad reacted quickly and lunged to his right, getting a strong right hand to the ball and parrying it to safety. After that, he continued to play well and I heard satisfying mutterings from various spectators saying how well he had played. It was the first time since he had started at Blackburn (prior to Rochdale) that I had seen him play to the level he had played at for Croston Juniors, his local side. Week by week, he was improving at Rochdale and growing with confidence and I could tell the coaches were impressed.

Rochdale had realised a lot of the lads within the under 16 squad were not going to make it as footballers so had released several of them. They were therefore playing with several under 15s, who were very good players and gelling much better as a side. Rochdale ended up winning 3-1 with Brad and a relatively new centre back, Isaac Ward, who had joined from Hull City, particularly impressing.

After the game, I went back to my car and rang Croston Juniors manager, John Harper. Brad had played a couple of games for Croston early in the season, when he hadn't had a game for Blackburn on the Saturday and back in his comfort zone, had really shone. I knew John had mixed feelings about Brad's progression. He really wanted Brad to do well, but knew it would mean he would have to find another keeper and would struggle, at local level, to find someone as good as Brad.

"John, I don't think Brad is going to be coming back," I said, trying to balance out my enthusiasm with a sense of decorum, "he keeps improving week on week here and I get the feeling they will want to sign him."

John was delighted that Brad had done well and if he was disappointed, he masked it well, saying the Croston situation was insignificant, as this was a potential career for Brad. No sooner had I put the phone down from speaking to him, there was a knock on my window It was Ryan Ball, the Academy goalkeeping coach.

"Can you come in for a few minutes?"

I like Ryan a lot and more importantly Brad really likes him. With him only being in his early twenties, he is young enough to feel like a mate to Brad. He is calm, doesn't shout a lot but is analytical and is wise enough to be able to converse with Brad on his level one minute and then move on to speaking on my level the next.

"We're going to sign him," Ryan said as we headed across the car park towards the College, "he's done really well and he keeps getting better."

When we were inside the College, Ryan led me through to a room where Brad was chatting to the under 18s coach, Rick Ashcroft about certain aspects of his kicking. At local league level, we always thought Brad had a tremendous left foot for a goalkeeper but at this higher level there are some aspects of his distribution that they want to work on. They feel when he receives a back pass, he doesn't get it out of his feet quick enough and he doesn't pinpoint who the weakness is in the opposition back four when he hits it long. There is no doubting he can ping a sixty yard ball, but who he kicks it to and how quickly he does it are what they want to improve.

After his chat with Rick, Brad sat down with Ryan and me and we begin the process of signing several forms. Euphoria is spread across Brad's face. When we complete the signing process, Ryan delivers another bombshell.

"We have a FA Youth Cup 2nd Round game on Tuesday. Johny Diba isn't fit at the moment and we're not sure how he'll be. We'll need Brad to come with us and if Johny's not fit, he'll be playing."

"Where's it being played?"

"Notts County's first team pitch, Meadow Lane."

I think my heart skipped a beat at that point. It was a mixture of delight and trepidation. Brad had only just found his feet at under 16s, at this level and now he might have to take a big jump up to under 18s, not just for a friendly either, for an important FA Youth Cup game. He was only fifteen in July, some of the lads he would be playing against would be eighteen. It would be a great experience, but I was just a little bit concerned it would be too much too soon.

When we got back to my car, Brad punched the air and let out a celebratory, 'YES'!

"Congratulations, son. Now the next step is making sure you keep improving so you get a scholarship. How would you feel about playing on Tuesday?"

"I'm not sure. I might be happier being on the bench and just getting to know everyone."

"True, but opportunities to play at places like Meadow Lane aren't going to come around every week."

"I know, but I'd be crapping myself!"

"I'm sure you would, but you need to keep pushing your boundaries if you want to be a footballer."

"Yeh, I know."

"Anyway, enjoy this moment for now. We'll see what happens on Tuesday. You've at least got the rest of the season to show them you're good enough to get a scholarship. Give your Mum a ring and let her know what's happened."

Monday 16th November 2016

I was working at Barron's today. At lunchtime, my phone rang. It was Ryan Ball. He knew I was at work so kept it brief.

"Johny's not fit, Calvin. Brad will be playing. I'll text you the details about what time he needs to be at Spotland."

I had been to Meadow Lane once before. On 10th March 1984, as a thirteen year old, I went there with my Dad to see Everton beat Notts County in the FA Cup. Extended highlights of the game are still available on 'You Tube'. Kevin Richardson and Andy Gray (with a header about six inches off the ground) scored for Everton in a 2-1 win. We were supposed to be picking up complimentary tickets that day, but although the late Everton coach Mick Heaton (Mick tragically died in a car accident in Haslingden in April 1995 aged just 48) left tickets for us, someone had nabbed them by the time we came to collect them from the ticket office, so we went on the terraces. It bucketed down all game but we went home drenched but happy.

Back then the ground was more than a little dilapidated. The side of the ground where Neville Southall was in goal in the first half was little more than a few metal bars and about four rows of terracing with cars parked behind it. I googled to see what the ground looks like now and was blown away. Meadow Lane has been extensively modernised since the 1990s and is now a 20,000 all seater stadium. There are grounds in the Premier League that are not as good.

I rang Brad after work, on my way back to the car to tell him he was playing and the nerves seemed to ooze out the earpiece on my mobile phone.

"Just enjoy it!" I urged.

Easy for me to say though, I won't be playing. I don't even think I am going to enjoy watching this one. I will have a mixture of pride and pain for ninety minutes tomorrow night. Can't wait though!

CHAPTER EIGHT

Tuesday 17th November 2015

FA YOUTH CUP – 2nd Round Proper

Notts County v Rochdale

As far as days that will lodge in the memory for the rest of my life go, this one will be right up there. Dropped Brad off at lunchtime at Spotland as they were travelling down on a coach normally reserved for first team travel and I headed down to Nottingham on my own, unfortunately Alison couldn't come as she was working. It was dry and breezy when I dropped Brad off but the forecast was for gale force winds and heavy rain later in the day, not perfect conditions for a goalkeeper.

One of my mates, Andrew Elkington, still lives in Nottingham having gone to University there. He is originally from Lincoln, but we became mates as he was in a house, during his time at Nottingham Polytechnic, with a couple of my friends from Ormskirk, including my 'Best Man', Andrew Berry and we shared a love of horse racing, cricket and beer so hit it off straight away. For many years we picked two horses each for a Saturday Yankee but that fell apart when my finances were stretched. 'Elks' was one of several friends who offered help to me when things were difficult and I will always appreciate that. Anyway, I called him yesterday and we are going to meet up for a pint before the game. 'Elks' works within half a mile of Meadow Lane but has a one year old son, Joe, so isn't coming to the game as he wants to get home and see his little lad before bedtime.

I stopped for a coffee on the way down and when I text Elks about a meeting place, he suggested 'Hooters'. From memory, I thought 'Hooters' was an American bar with scantily clad waitresses with big boobs and short shorts. Was I getting confused?

"No, you're spot on," Elks confirmed, "but it's a Sports Bar first and foremost these days and does allow kids in, so not the place it was. I am happy to suggest somewhere else if you want though?"

"No, Hooters will be fine. As long as it's not £8 a pint, I'm sure I'll cope."

It wasn't and I did. Elks didn't hang around much more than half an hour but it was great to see him. I text Brad to say we were in some bar called 'Hooters' and he said the coach had just driven past it and when all the lads spotted it, they cracked up.

When I left 'Hooters' it was only about six o'clock but had nowhere else to go, so just headed over to Meadow Lane. The gates didn't open until half six, but as soon as they did, I was straight in. By this time, the forecast high winds and driving rain had arrived and I was keen to get some shelter. I bought a pie and a coffee and then went into the Main Stand to take some photos of the ground. It is a fantastic ground, the pitch looked amazing and all four sides of the ground have top quality stands. It is a travesty that they are in the League Two and along with Portsmouth's Fratton Park, they must have the best ground at that level. The weather was my main concern for Brad, as the rain was coming in horizontally and the corner flags were almost being blown out from the base.

When Brad and Ryan came out to warm up ten minutes later, I was still the only person in the stands and was cowering behind the wall to the directors box to try to keep out of the wind. I watched Brad warming up for ten minutes and he wasn't catching a thing, which wasn't doing my nerves any good, so I went down to grab another hot drink. Brad has never been the best at warming up, he plays much better once the adrenalin is pumping, so I tried to reassure myself that he would be alright.

Forty five minutes later, the game kicked off with 'Storm Barney' swirling around the pitch and making it difficult for both teams, especially both goalkeepers. Notts County started the brighter but I relaxed a little as I noticed that Brad was playing with a bit of swagger and, although he was probably incredibly nervous, was giving off the impression that he was enjoying it. He was distributing the ball well with his feet and looking neat and tidy. The other thing I was pleased about was that he was being positive with corners, punching clear when called upon.

The rest of the half went well for Brad, he made a good save with his feet from a deflected cross shot but wasn't called in to play too often. He isn't far short of six feet tall now but still looked physically weaker than a lot of the other players on the field, including two big County centre forwards. He wasn't looking out of place but the big positive was that if he could play at this level now, he would look even better in a couple of years time.

The half finished on a high for Rochdale, Brandon Smalley whipped in a free kick from Rochdale's right and Jack Stewart, who had looked one of the better players on the pitch ghosted in to head home. Jack isn't one of the taller players at Rochdale but he timed his run well and powered a header past Joe Searson-Smithard in the Notts County goal.

Rochdale's first team manager, Keith Hill and his assistant, Chris Beech were at the game to see how their crop of youngsters were performing. Until a couple of years ago, Chris used to live down our road in Euxton, Chorley so I know him reasonably well. His children went to the same primary school as my boys and although Chris's son, Brandon, is a couple of years younger than Joel, he would often be amongst the lads playing out in the road.

Chris played for several clubs during his football career, amongst them Blackpool, Hartlepool, Huddersfield and Rochdale and was always good to listen to with his memories of his footballing days as he played for several well known managers amongst them Steve Bruce, Lou Macari and Sam Allardyce.

I had stood up at half time to try to move around a bit, to get some warmth into my body. Chris spotted me and came across to say 'hello'.

"He's doing well," Chris observed, "he's not had a great deal to do but he's looking composed and kicking well. We like to throw them into the deep end sometimes and see how they cope with it and so far he's looking like he's enjoying it."

I was pleased Chris had judged Brad's first half performance in a similar way to me, but I was well aware the first half would soon be forgotten if he had a stinker of a second half. As soon as the second half kicked off, Notts County pushed forward and were immediately rewarded with a free kick in a dangerous position after a cross from their right was only partially cleared and Rochdale centre back Kisimba Kisimba was adjudged to have fouled five yards outside the box to the left of centre. The resultant free kick was curled powerfully around the four man Rochdale wall and was heading just under the bar, but Brad was well positioned and dived full length to get a strong right hand to the ball and push it over the bar. It was a fine save and I was feeling really proud of how well he was coping. If he could keep a clean sheet it would be the icing on the cake after a brilliant experience.

After that incident, the game was very end to end and Rochdale had a couple of chances to snatch a two goal lead. Brandon Smalley forced an excellent save out of County's keeper, Searson-Smithard, when a fizzing strike from just outside the box went low to the keeper's right and then soon after Matt Gillam hit a sweetly struck effort that caught the wind a little which took it over the bar.

Rochdale had looked slightly the better side in the second half but in the 71st minute, Notts County equalised. County had been given offside just outside the Rochdale box and Brad cleared upfield into the County half. The County centre back won the aerial duel and the ball landed in the centre circle and was lofted upfield between County centre forward, Montel Gibson and centre back Kisimba Kisimba. Brad came towards the edge of his box to offer a pass back option but Gibson managed to get to the ball in front of Kisimba and lobbed the ball over Brad into the empty net. 1-1.

Every time Brad concedes a goal, I always analyse it to see whether I think he could have done better. If I was being hyper critical, he could have sent the free kick a bit wider and perhaps could have stayed on his six yard line as the ball bounced around, but if he had done that, I would have probably complained that he wasn't being positive enough. Overall, I concluded it would be harsh for me to attach any blame to him. I would perhaps suggest on the journey home, he tried to kick a little wider, but overall he kicks a hundred times better than I ever did so I wasn't in a position to criticise. Plus, these days, I let Ryan, the goalkeeper coach, do most of the analysis and just pass on the odd comment on car journeys, trying on the whole to be positive.

With just under twenty minutes left, I began to consider the implications of a draw. I was pretty sure these games didn't go to a replay and instead headed to extra time and penalties. Having saved a penalty at the weekend, I knew Brad would fancy his chances if the game went to a shootout.

These thoughts were premature. Straight from the kick off, Rochdale surged forward and some clever interplay down the right hand side saw the ball laid back to Tyler Berry on the edge of the box. With acres of room, he had time to have a free run at the ball and pick his spot and he drove the ball hard and low to the keeper's right. Once again Searson-Smithard was alive to the danger and made another smart save, palming the ball away and it was then scrambled away for a corner.

Unfortunately, Rochdale's corner came to nothing and Notts County pushed forward, going for the winning goal themselves. A cross in from the County right was cleared for a corner. From the resultant corner kick, the ball was driven high and hard towards the back post. There didn't seem any immediate danger, but Storm Barney played its part as the ball hung in the high winds and as it did, Montel Gibson closed in on Rochdale centre back, Louis Coyne. Louis is a very solid defender, good in the air and with his feet, but perhaps lacking a little bit of pace to make it in the higher levels of the game. As Gibson closed in on him, Coyne tried to loop the ball over the bar for another corner but didn't get a strong enough connection and agonisingly for him and the rest of the Rochdale team only managed to divert the ball into the net. 2-1 to County.

Once again, I analysed the goal. Could Brad have done better? His starting position had perhaps been too close to his front post and he had to scurry across when the ball went deep but it was a horrendous night and in a swirling wind it would have been difficult for him to get the ball. He could also perhaps have communicated better with Coyne as the defender didn't seem to get a shout but they were minor errors rather than significant ones and I suppose just part of the learning process. He was a fifteen year old lad playing with much older lads for the first time.

There were still fifteen minutes left for Rochdale to grab an equaliser. They dominated the closing proceedings with Brad only called upon to make a few kicks up field. It wasn't until the last two minutes though that a golden opportunity came Rochdale's way. Brandon Smalley fired in a shot from the edge of the box and Searson-Smithard parried it to his right. The ball dropped invitingly for Rochdale substitute, Jordan Prescott, who had come on in the 80th minute to replace Tyler Berry. Sensing glory, Prescott ran in to meet the ball which was sitting only ten yards out with just a prostrate keeper guarding the net. Perhaps Prescott was not fully attuned to the game having only been on a few minutes as he didn't get a good connection on his shot which allowed the rising keeper to parry once more. By this time, County defenders were arriving on the scene and although Prescott managed to gather the rebound and round the goalkeeper, the ball was then booted to safety in no nonsense style by County's Jordan Richards.

When the final whistle blew soon after, I felt sorry for Jordan Prescott and Louis Coyne. Through the game, Rochdale had missed several chances, free headers from six yards out had gone over the bar, strikers and midfielders had struck the ball into the keeper's midriff when it had been easier to find the back of the net but the own goal and the missed late chance were the two stand out memories from the game. From Brad's perspective though, he had made the step up well. He had kicked well, commanded his box well for the most part and made a few decent saves and one very good one. It was a strong debut that had been a little spoilt by the defeat.

After the game, I went around to the player's entrance to collect Brad. As I was waiting Chris Beech and Rochdale's manager, Keith Hill came out and they came over to me to have a chat. Overall, they felt the team had played well on an atrocious night and felt Brad's performance had been 'really encouraging'. Soon after their departure, Brad and goalkeeper coach, Ryan emerged. To say Ryan was delighted with Brad was an understatement as he was bubbling over with positivity.

"He's done brilliantly," Ryan enthused, "I couldn't have asked any more of him. My first step was to get Brad to a level which ensured that we signed him and now the next step is to make sure he gets a scholarship. Putting in a performance like that tonight in front of the first team manager and assistant won't have done him any harm at all."

Brad came home with me in the car rather than get the coach back to Rochdale, as he is back in school in the morning. He had loved the experience of playing at Meadow Lane and said all the lads were encouraging and welcoming. I hope it is the first of many such experiences for him and who knows, maybe it won't just be the roads of this FA experience that will lead me to Wembley!

FINAL SCORE :- Notts County 2 Rochdale 1

Wednesday 18th November 2015

What a week this has been! After Brad's experience of playing in the FA Youth Cup yesterday, today I have had my best ever day of e-book sales. Amazon contacted me about six weeks ago to say they wanted to include my latest fictional book, 'Waiting For The Bee Stings' in their 'Kindle Daily Deal' offers in November. A few weeks ago, I heard that it would be promoted today at 99p and I excitedly watched its progression through the day as more and more people downloaded it. Previously, my first book had once sold 841 copies in a day and reached number nineteen in the UK Kindle Charts but as I write, 'Waiting For The Bee Stings' has just finished its promotion having sold more than 3,000 copies today (the figure keeps growing as Amazon catch up with the downloads) and reached Number TWO in the UK Kindle Charts. I doubt very much it will stick around in the Top 10 for long once the price returns to £2.99 but it has given me a pleasant financial boost and more importantly it has introduced me to a lot of new readers. I am chuffed to bits.

Thursday 19th November 2015

Someone (a lady called Justina Loughlin) posted on my Facebook site after the news about Rochdale's FA Youth Cup appearance and my ebook selling well, that these things tend to come in threes. She was right! As I arrived at Matthew Moss school tonight to drop Brad off at football training and begin two and a half hours of waiting around, Ryan Ball came out into the car park and tapped on my window.

"Have you got a few minutes, Calvin? Tony Ellis would like to have a word with you and Brad."

Tony Ellis is in charge of the Academy at Rochdale. I also remember him from being a goal scoring centre forward who played for several clubs in the 1980s and 1990s. I remember him at Preston North End and Blackpool, but a quick check on the internet after our meeting revealed he played over 600 first team games scoring over 200 goals for the likes of Oldham, Preston, Stoke, Blackpool, Bury, Stockport, Rochdale and Burnley. I'm guessing on that basis he knows the North West football scene better than most.

Tony wouldn't be the tallest of former strikers but he's quite an imposing figure, largely because he comes across as a tough Mancunian with a stern expression and a dry wit. I think a lot of the lads are a little bit scared of him and I get the impression he likes it that way. He's like a tough, old school PE teacher.

Ryan introduced me to Tony outside the entrance to the 3G pitch where the lads train but he wanted to go through to the school, so I had a chat with Tony as we walked across with Brad and Ryan following behind. It was a bitterly cold evening with an icy wind blasting against our faces. Tony was saying Rochdale was the coldest place in England and when I said memories of watching Oldham Athletic in January at Boundary Park during Joe Royle's managerial reign were even worse than this, Tony revealed Joe was the manager that signed him out of non-League football, a fact I was unaware of.

Once inside, Tony cut to the chase and said Brad's performance at Notts County on Tuesday had impressed everyone at the club and personally he had been impressed with Brad's composure. The coaches all felt Brad had a huge amount of potential and on that basis, he wanted to offer Brad a scholarship at Rochdale for the next two seasons.

I am 44 now. Age generally erodes the ambition of youth. I know I'm never going to play for Everton, never going to be the Chief Executive of a bank or Building Society, never going to have that six figure salary and to be completely honest, I don't care. All I want to have each month is enough money to pay the bills, with hopefully a little left over for an annual holiday. I would love to be able to make this amount of money through my writing but I have no desire to be the next JK Rowling. I understand that I don't have her creative genius.

When it comes to my children though, the ambition within me is very much alive. I want the best for them. This doesn't necessarily mean I want to see them financially rich, I just want them to have the life they want to have. Brad would love to be a footballer and this is a step towards that goal. I know how pleased this will make him, particularly because as yet only one other lad has been offered a scholarship. Like me, Brad performs better when he feels he is appreciated and this will be a huge boost to his self-confidence.

For the next ten minutes, I chatted with Tony and Ryan about what a scholarship looks like. It would mean Brad being in Rochdale six days a week, four for training, one for College and Saturday for a match. Realistically getting him across a few evenings a week is a logistical test but getting him across for six days would be impossible. This isn't an unusual predicament and Tony and Ryan explain that most lads live in 'digs' with a landlady who lives within a couple of miles of Spotland. Brad chips in to say he would like that, so by the time we leave the room having signed a few preliminary forms, it is all sorted. After his GCSEs, Brad will be leaving home. He isn't sixteen until 3rd July, so will be moving out when he is still fifteen. It's a big step but he's a sensible lad and wants to chase his dreams so there is no way I will be trying to hold him back. Over the next couple of years, we will just have to make sure he has a Plan B, because not every lad who signs a scholarship for a football team subsequently becomes a professional footballer. It's all good news though so I will let him rejoice in his success for now and will have the 'planning' talks further down the line.

After training I took a euphoric Brad back home and he chatted all the way about what the next two years would bring.

"You keep telling me that not many lads make it as professional footballers, Dad, but I might just be one of the ones that does."

"I hope you are."

"I'm playing for the 'eighteens' on Saturday too. Jonny still isn't fit."

Saturday is the next Round of the FA Vase at Colne, so this news both pleased and concerned me. If there was ever a choice to be made between following the FA Vase and following Brad's game, the latter would win hands down.

"Where are you playing?"

"At Man City's old training ground at Carrington."

"Against Man City? No, against Bury, they use it since City moved out."

"Well, I'll have to see if Gordon, Alan and 'Pop' fancy going there first before we go to Colne."

I've subsequently spoken to my Dad, Gordon and Alison and we have a plan in place for Saturday. Alison is going to drive me and Brad to Carrington and Gordon is going to drive too, picking my Dad up. After the under 18s game, Alison will take Brad back home and I will jump in Gordon's car with my Dad and head up to Colne. It should be a great day. Colne are currently top of the North West Counties League with Newton Aycliffe seventh in the high quality Ebac Northern League Division One, having only lost two games from their fifteen played. Colne have only lost one in sixteen, so I am expecting a tough game between two teams who are likely to be of a similar standard. My gut feeling is that Newton Aycliffe will edge it.

Brad's game should be interesting too. Bury are top of the North West Youth Alliance with Rochdale sitting in a lower mid-table position, so Brad is likely to be tested even more than he was on Tuesday. Should be a good test for him and at least he can play without pressure as he knows he has two and a half years ahead of him at this level.

CHAPTER NINE

Saturday 21st November 2015

The FA VASE – 2nd Round Proper

Colne v Newton Aycliffe

This morning, before the FA Vase game at 3pm, we had the Bury v Rochdale under 18s game. Overall, at Academy level, the attitude of the players, parents and coaches, that I have witnessed, has been excellent. A few of the Manchester United under16s parents were a little over exuberant and argumentative, but this wasn't replicated by their children on the pitch. Today though, it was the Bury players (not their parents) that I was disappointed with. The game finished 1-1 which was probably deemed a poor result for Bury so perhaps this contributed to their agitation, but they were very quick to surround the referee en masse when decisions didn't go their way and, although I have decades of experience of hearing a few choice words on the football pitch, the Bury players bad language was constant and intimidating. In the FA Trophy, I felt the need to criticise Shaun Reid, Warrington Town's manager, for his language and attitude, today Bury had half a dozen of a similar ilk. If Brad ends up behaving like that, even when he is seventeen or eighteen, I would still have a stern word after the game. I am hoping the Bury parents did the same.

With regards to Brad's performance, after an exciting week, it was back down to earth with a bump. I am not saying he played poorly today, he didn't, but whilst he seemed to take Meadow Lane in his stride on Tuesday, today, especially in the first half, he seemed to look uncertain. I guess one thing that dented his confidence was his choice of footwear. Manchester City's old training ground looked a bit like a ghost town training complex with the main building deserted and just a couple of security guards and Bury FC officials milling around but the pitches are still first class. The ball zips off them though and Brad's cheap boots that have always done a job at local League level are now starting to look like Bambi's hooves on ice. At half time he swopped boots with Ryan, the goalkeeper coach and looked much more comfortable in the second half but it means we now need to fork out on a new pair of boots (thankfully Alison's Mum and Dad have stepped forward and said they will contribute).

As soon as the final whistle went, we headed back to the cars. Alison was desperate to get back into hers and get the heating on, whilst she waited for Brad, as it was a bitterly cold day. My Dad and I joined Gordon in his car and we headed up to Colne.

For the second Vase trip of the season, like our trip to Eccleshill, we spent ages trying to find the ground once we reached the town. The reason for this is because the ground is a mile or two outside the town centre and you have to get up a bloody big hill to get to it. It wasn't too bad for us sat in the comfort of Gordon's car, but as Alan was going to be heading there on foot following his trip to see Alan Hodges at Boundary Mills, it was going to be a knackering walk for him. I must confess we laughed all the way up the almost vertical slope picturing Alan's short, stocky frame clambering up the hill mumbling swear words to himself about the injustice of it all.

Once you reach the car park of the Holt House stadium (now rebranded as the 'XLCR' Stadium, due to the sponsorship by a local vehicle management company) there is a spectacular view down to Colne and the surrounding snow capped hills on the edge of the Pennines. For those of you who don't know, Colne is in East Lancashire, six miles North East of Burnley. It's an old Lancastrian cotton mill town and its population and prosperity diminished as the twentieth century progressed and memories of the industrial revolution faded. The rows of terraced housing that spill down the slopes from the town centre look fabulous from a distance though. I can mentally picture it having been a bustling, thriving town back in the nineteenth century.

When we got out the car, Gordon went straight to the boot to find his trusty selfie stick. Shaunee Smith would not be here today for Gordon to terrorise with his close up photographs but he still wanted to take as many photos as he could for posterity.

I have probably been to the ground before, with my Dad, many moons ago, when it was the home of Colne Dynamoes. They went bust in 1990, but had previously enjoyed a successful progression up the non-League pyramid, significantly helped by some major investment from their Manager/Chairman/Owner, Graham White. They won the Northern Premier League in the 1989-90 season but were refused entry to the Conference, I think due to the ground not meeting Conference standards and they subsequently folded. During their successful late 1980s run, I remember seeing them at Marine and amongst their players that day was double European Cup winning ex-Liverpool player, Alan Kennedy.

Once we entered the stadium, the probable reason for the Conference disdain back in 1990 was immediately apparent, as there is a large slope down from one goal to the other. One corner flag to the right of the bottom goal as you look down from the top end, is particularly low. I've played on hundreds of pitches like it at lower non-League level, but I can understand why the upper echelons of the Non-League may not have viewed it with any degree of romanticism. It will be interesting to see what the Evo Stik Leagues make of it, if Colne are promoted, but hopefully, they should be alright. Colne FC were only formed in 1996 and they are pushing boundaries never previously reached.

As ever, the first place we looked to find Alan was the pie shop/refreshment stall and sure enough he was walking away from there with a pie and a coffee. After our greetings, Alan's pie and drink were dispatched and his complaints about the walk up the 'BAS***D hill' were out the way, it was 'selfie' time. Gordon wanted to ensure there was photographic evidence that a Scottish £10 note donated to 'The Christie' from his friend Kath, on the Isle of Skye, was passed over to Alan rather than used for liquid refreshment. He also wanted to take some group photos of us standing in front of a Colne FC flag with the words 'Red Army' emblazoned on it. I think this was just to wind me, my Dad and Alan up, as we are two Evertonians and a Manchester City fan.

Alan enjoys nothing more than a quirky photo or two to post on social media himself, so when he spotted the Colne fancy dress mascot, which was a six foot tall cockerel or rooster or something of a similar ilk, partaking in the pre-match warm up on the pitch, he shot off like the Road Runner, towing Gordon along with him. Alan must have had a handful of corn feed as the mascot was soon over to the side of the pitch, allowing Alan to cuddle in to his furry costume. No sooner was one novelty photo out the way, Alan went in search of another. He had discovered that Newton Aycliffe's former manager and now Chairman was also called Allan Oliver, so he went to seek him out so Gordon could take a photo of the two 'Alan/Allan Oliver's.

They duly found him and after an introductory conversation, the desired photo was taken.

After the photographic frenzy, the next item on the agenda was for Gordon to see whether he knew any of the match officials. Not surprisingly, he did. Umar Ahmed, one of the Assistant referees is from Yorkshire, but he went to study at Liverpool University for three years so registered as a referee with Liverpool County FA so Gordon got to know him. We went over and had a chat with him and he seemed to be a good lad. Most officials I've met have been friendly, decent types. It's a shame fans like to treat them as the pantomime villains. Personally, like most fans I would imagine, I much prefer a low profile ref to a ref who wants to be centre stage in proceedings with twenty two players playing a supporting role to his lead.

Half an hour after our chat with Umar, the game was underway with Newton Aycliffe kicking down the slope in the first half. Newton Aycliffe were in blue and Colne in red. At kick off, I had no preference who won, but by the end I found myself favouring Newton Aycliffe, largely because of the behaviour of the Colne manager, Steve Cunningham.

Cunningham took charge of Colne in November 2013 as a 33 year old, which only makes him thirty five now, a mere youngster for a manager. When the ball is not being kicked around the football pitch, he is no doubt a really sweet man, who dotes on his family and helps old ladies across roads, but through the course of this match, he was a nuisance to the officials and also dampened the enjoyment of a terrific game for the spectators on our side of the pitch.

We had taken our seats in the stand opposite the dug outs, but unfortunately for us, Steve Cunningham, and possibly his assistant too as he was with him, were serving touchline bans and were not allowed to coach from the dugouts. This sort of ruling is very difficult to police at non-League level, as it isn't as though the banned coach can be sent to the second tier stand. Cunningham and his assistant ended up walking along the front of our stand throughout the course of the match, challenging every decision, barking instructions and shouting abuse. I'm sure a lot of managers don't behave impeccably, in fact I'd guess the majority don't, but given they were on a ban, you would have thought they would have been wise enough to tone it down a little. They weren't that wise, so although Colne is far more convenient for us than Newton Aycliffe, I ended up willing Newton Aycliffe to win. I am all for managers showing some passion, but there is a line and Cunningham jumped over it with both feet and all studs showing.

Early in the game, it very much looked like I would get my wish without too much trouble as Newton Aycliffe dominated the early proceedings. I am sure they would have been instructed to take full advantage of the slope and from the very start they took the game by the scruff of the neck. After eleven minutes, Newton Aycliffe's early domination was rewarded as Stuart Banks was tripped in the box, the ref pointed to the spot and Dennis Knight, with his sweet left foot, converted from twelve yards. One-nil Newton Aycliffe.

My Dad is often critical of referees for not having the bravery to award penalties as they feel the severity of the foul has to be of a higher nature inside the eighteen yard box before they point to the spot. This was not a criticism he could level at Colin Whittaker as he went on to award four penalties in the course of this game!

The second penalty went, against the run of play, to Colne. Whittaker spotted a handball in the box and Danny Boyle stepped up to take it. James Winter had looked a big, strong keeper in his limited involvement in the early encounters and our impression of him was raised a notch when he dived spectacularly to turn Boyle's effort around the post. For several minutes, Colne asserted some further pressure with Chris Anderson forcing another save out of Winter and Michael Morrison shooting over the bar following a Colne corner. In his earlier days, Winter had been with Middlesbrough and Hartlepool United and had only recently signed for Newton Aycliffe from Durham Alliance League side, Sherburn Village. It looked like an astute signing.

With the first forty five minutes up, we were all ready to go for a half-time drink when we were surprised by a second goal. After defending solidly, Newton Aycliffe cleared the ball up field and down the Colne slope. After a defensive slip up, Dennis Knight picked the ball up and ran menacingly at the Colne defence, breaking clear and finding himself one on one with the advancing Colne keeper, Chris Thompson. Knight took the ball around him, but still did well to steer the ball into the back of the net from a tight angle. Two-nil to Newton Aycliffe. In a game and a half of FA VASE football, Gordon and Alan had seen Aycliffe score six goals without conceding and although Colne would have the advantage of the slope in the second half, we expected the task of scoring at least two, without reply, would be too much for them.

We headed to the bar for hot drinks for everyone in our party other than me, as I decided to have a pint. We got talking to another groundhopper from Liverpool who had missed the second goal as he had headed to the bar early to get a beer in. Like us, he could see no way back for Colne.

When we re-emerged outside for the second half, the temperature had seemingly dropped from freezing to Siberian levels, only previous matched on our FA travels in the Stevenage-Everton FA Cup 4th Round match. Steve Cunningham had probably warmed the Colne players up with a bit of a half time Fergie-esque hairdryer treatment, as they came out in the second half with a lot more pace and determination and this was rewarded on the hour mark when Danny Boyle redeemed himself for his penalty miss by turning sharply inside the box and firing past James Winter to bring the score back to two-one.

"Game on!" Alan commented, but no sooner had he said it, Newton Aycliffe had gone back up the other end and scored a third. Winger Stuart Banks struck a curling shot past Thompson and into the far post. Three-one.

"It's going to be first to four wins again!" Gordon said, as all three previous rounds had been won by the victors scoring four.

As we watched the action continue, partaking in our usual good humoured footballing banter, a photographer came over to our section of the stand to take some action shots. We got talking to him and he seemed like a great bloke. His name was Colin McNeillie and he was taking photos for his Facebook page 'Korhna Imaging Sports & Concert' photography. He takes photos on a match day for Newton Aycliffe and their independent supports club. Like many of the North Ferriby fans we met last season, Colin came across as a passionate, enthusiastic non-League football supporter with a cheery disposition. He was very impressed with the Colne fans and commented that it was a really friendly club. He went to the same barbers as Alan (the invisible one) and at a guess was in a similar age bracket to him too (late 40s/early 50s). He said he'd been watching Newton Aycliffe for seven years, but it was on and off for the first couple of seasons and then he became properly involved after that.

We told Colin about our recent footballing journeys (Alan doesn't let many people who engage with us in conversation escape without hearing our tale) and he decided to take pen profiles of each of us. As the youngest of our group of four, it could be surmised that I would have looked the best in those close up photos, but as an overweight, lanky chap, I don't take well to cold weather and the subsequent photos tell the story of someone who has lived a life indoors. My Dad, as a painter and decorator, is a much hardier soul and he was positively glowing on his photo. Anyway, after that interesting diversion we all got back to the job in hand of watching a fascinating game.

With fifteen minutes left, a game that looked like it had been heading to a relatively comfortable away victory sprang back to life. The ref spotted a handball in the crowded Newton Aycliffe area and pointed to the spot for the third time in the match. Danny Boyle, having missed one earlier, passed on the spot kick duties to Jason Hart.

Earlier in the game, Alan had pointed Jason Hart out as the former Clitheroe player who had earned himself a bit of tabloid notoriety after he had been filmed in a drunken post-match sexual encounter in the dugouts after a game at Mossley last season. Clitheroe Football Club had not taken kindly to this sort of unsavoury publicity and had sacked Hart and Alan mentioned that he had heard he had been given a chance to re-build his football career at Colne. He was a small, lively forward and had played well and tucked the penalty away with aplomb to bring the score back to 3-2.

Despite it being an entertaining match, I have to confess I didn't want Colne to equalise. Steve Cunningham's previously mentioned front row of the stand theatrics had become increasingly difficult to tolerate and by half past four the temperature up a huge hill in Colne had dropped to levels eskimos would struggle to tolerate so I had begun yearning for the moment that I was back in Gordon's car with the heating on. I think the correct word to describe me at that point was 'nesh'. There was obviously no long-term planning in my desperation for a Newton Aycliffe victory though. A win for them would increase the likelihood of further trips up to the North East in the depths of winter. I didn't care. At that moment, I would have agreed to a final in mid-January within the Arctic Circle if it had meant this game would finish after ninety minutes. 'Sod' obviously heard me whining and pleading and once again his Law came into effect.

In the 84th minute, to my annoyance, Colne equalised. A free kick from just inside the Newton Aycliffe half was swung into the box. The Newton Aycliffe defenders failed to deal with it and Christopher Anderson directed a well placed header beyond Winter and into the back of the net. 3-3. Several of the Colne players headed towards a jubilant Steve Cunningham, which suggested he may have been a well liked and respected manager, from his players perspective, despite being a bit of a nuisance from a neutral supporters perspective.

With the slope to aid them and Newton Aycliffe players now looking tired and disillusioned, Colne pushed forward sensing an unlikely victory. By this point, with frost bite beginning to kick into my fingers and toes, I would have settled for a Colne victory. Despite the pressure, however, Colne were unable to create any clear cut chances and the ninety minutes came to end with the sides level at three-all. On the balance of play, it seemed like a fair result although Newton Aycliffe will have been annoyed with themselves for not closing out the game and squandering their two goal lead.

Colne played the first half of extra time down the slope once more and it seemed important to us that they took advantage in the first fifteen minutes. It was Newton Aycliffe though who pressed forward at the start of extra time, probably after receiving a few choice words from their manager, Peter Dixon. In the second minute of extra time, the ball was played into the crowded Colne box and the Assistant referee spotted an infringement by a Colne defender, pointing his right elbow out and his flag across his chest, to give the referee the penalty signal. It was the fourth penalty of the game, two for each side, but from our vantage point it was difficult to spot and Steve Cunningham was livid.

Dennis Knight stepped up to take his second penalty of the game and it was duly dispatched to secure his hat-trick. 4-3 to Newton Aycliffe.

Steve Cunningham must have recognised Gordon from his many years of officiating and decided to vent his frustrations to us.

"You lot are referees, aren't you?" he said.

"Only Gordon," we replied.

"That was never a penalty, was it?" he asked.

"We couldn't really tell from here," Alan responded.

Steve Cunningham took that as a sign that we were backing his judgement. He continued to rant but to be fair to him, he came across as a decent guy just with a blinkered view of proceedings. There are millions more like him amongst the managers, coaches, players and spectators of Great Britain.

"We play good football though, don't we?" he said, as he departed up the touchline to moan some more at the nearside Assistant ref and to be fair they did.

For the remainder of the first half of extra time, Colne were bossing proceedings and it took two outstanding saves from James Winter to keep out Hart and Taylor.

"I am starting to get the North Ferriby feeling about Newton Aycliffe, Cal," Alan commented, as the half time whistle blew with their lead preserved, "they look solid, hard working and have an excellent keeper. Adam Nicklin played a huge part in getting Ferriby to the Final and maybe Winter can do the same for Newton Aycliffe."

With the slope to aid them, we thought Newton Aycliffe might go for the fifth goal to ensure victory, but they sat back and let Colne come at them. With five minutes left though, Newton Aycliffe broke out of defence and found themselves with a two on two attack. Alan Harrison, the Newton Aycliffe 17 year old substitute was put through on goal and he produced a sublime chip from outside the area that found the top corner of the goal. 5-3 and victory was secured.

It had been an enthralling encounter, packed with incident and some well taken goals and for the fourth successive round, the first team to score four had won, this time with Newton Aycliffe adding a fifth for good measure. Five minutes later, it was all over and Newton Aycliffe would be heading back to the North East with a place in the next round and dreams of Wembley still very much alive.

As we headed towards the exit, in a barely lit stand, all the seats had been put back up to the upright position with the exception of one which I failed to spot as I headed merrily, at pace, towards the warmth of Gordon's car. I rammed my left shin straight into it and felt like rolling around on the floor clutching it like a Premier League footballer, but as I had already done my fair share of moaning about the cold, concluded that I had to 'man up' so just hobbled back to the car, making a mental note to wrap up better and watch where I am walking in the next round.

I headed home from Cone with frost bite, ear ache (courtesy of Steve Cunningham), a bruised shin and some great memories of a thoroughly entertaining game. Would I swop it for a heated Executive Box in the Premier League? Not a chance.

FINAL SCORE :- COLNE 3 NEWTON AYCLIFFE 5 (after extra time)

FA VASE GOALS :- 25 in 4 games.

CHAPTER TEN

Sunday 22nd November 2015

My youngest son, Joel, has been doing a paper round for about 15 months now. Initially, I used to help him along, driving him around on cold or wet days but over time, I have phased my involvement out. From helping him several days a week, it became helping him at weekends and now it is just taking the occasional paper if he is running late for school. What I look forward to on a Sunday morning though, is giving him £1.50 and seeing him return an hour later with 'The Non-League Paper'.

'The Non-League Paper' is forty eight pages packed with match reports and stories from the Non-League level of English football. If I've been at a game on the Saturday, I often haven't had time to catch up with all the Non-League results so Sunday morning is spent watching one of my boys play football, but for the hour before kick off, I sit and digest the Non-League news.

This week, as well as catching up on the excellent job Mark Beesley, the former Cambridge United player, and local Burscough lad, is doing managing Burscough and reading about a fine 3-0 North Ferriby United victory over AFC Fylde, which sends them up to second place in the Vanarama National League North, I had the opportunity to catch up on other FA Vase results.

The current favourites to be holding the FA Vase aloft at Wembley in May are Hereford. In front of a massive crowd for the FA Vase of 2,170 they saw off Haughmond 4-1 and in doing so, secured their nineteenth straight win in all competitions. Hereford FC were founded last year following the demise of Hereford

United and they have taken over their Edgar Street stadium. They have a long way to climb back up the English league pyramid, as they are currently in the Midland Football League Premier division, which I think is the ninth tier of English football. The old Hereford United never made it to Wembley and given the new Hereford FC will be facing a lower standard of opposition than Hereford United did in their heyday, they fancy their chances (as do the bookmakers) of getting there this year. It will be interesting to see whether they make it and an extended run in the Vase will certainly raise the profile of the competition as no other club in it are capable of getting such big crowds.

One club Alan Oliver has been saying to watch out for is Newport (IOW) with the IOW standing for 'Isle of Wight'. If they make it to the latter rounds and have a re-arranged game on a Tuesday evening (and they become the team we are following) even Alan may struggle to make it along although I would still expect him to engineer a way. Yesterday, Newport beat Abbey Rangers 3-1.

The other thing I noted from yesterday's games was that the bad weather in the North East led to a series of FA Vase postponements with games at North Shields, Morpeth Town, Consett, Marske United and Guisborough Town all victims of the weather. The North East has some of the best teams in the Vase but also has some of the worst weather so without undersoil heating and expensive drainage systems, there tend to be several postponements. Alan and Gordon know that with me having to take Brad over to Rochdale three or four times a week and with my work commitments, my involvement in the Vase may have to become intermittent, especially if fixtures get moved due to postponements, but they are both determined to make every Round, especially Alan who is wanting to complete the FA Cup, FA Trophy, FA Vase and FA Sunday Cup foursome of following the winners of each round through from start to finish. We will see who Newton Aycliffe get drawn against next tomorrow, but if they are drawn at home, I think the logistical problems may really start to kick in.

Monday 23rd November 2015

Thought that might happen! Newton Aycliffe have been drawn at home in the Third Round of the Vase. They have been drawn to play one of two North West sides either Atherton Collieries or Chadderton. The game between Atherton and Chadderton takes place tomorrow night after having been postponed on Saturday due to a waterlogged pitch. My gut feeling is that if Colne couldn't beat Newton Aycliffe then neither of these sides will. Colne are top of the North West Counties Premier Division whilst Atherton Collieries are currently in seventh place whilst Chadderton are languishing in fourth to bottom spot in North West Counties Division One. It would be a big shock if Atherton don't beat Chadderton tomorrow but I'm sure Alan will be hoping for a Chadderton victory as their ground is only a mile or two up the road from Alan's house in Failsworth and he could probably jump on the team bus up to Newton Aycliffe.

Talking about Alan, yesterday he went to the next round of his FA Sunday Cup adventure. He went to Allerton FC and saw them lose to West Bowling AFC 3-1. The victors are from the Bradford/Leeds area so he will be following them now until they get knocked out. They play in green and white so comparisons are being made to North Ferriby United once again. In the next round, they have been drawn against Hardwick Social up in Stockton upon Tees in the North East. All roads seem to point there at the moment.

This was the Second Round of the FA Sunday Cup, a competition Alan didn't even know about until he got chatting with Gordon about it, after Gordon had refereed the Man City Legends game. The First Round game Alan chose was Allerton FC v Pineapple FC at South Liverpool's ground at Jericho Lane. He chose this game as it was a new ground for him and if South Liverpool ever make it back to the North West Counties League, Alan already has the ground ticked off. Allerton won 2-1 in front of a hostile crowd. Alan said he hadn't done his homework and wasn't aware that these sides didn't get on. There are seven rounds altogether and Al is doing it all by train. Last year's final was at Ewood Park, Blackburn but I think the location is dependent on where the teams are from, for example if two sides from the North East get there, there is no point having the final at Brighton or vice versa. Gordon and I are now thinking of other competitions that are linked to the FA that Alan can go to next season. The FA Youth Cup and the FA Women's Cup immediately spring to mind. I will keep you posted as to how the next five rounds go.

Tuesday 24th November 2015

Atherton Collieries beat Chadderton 3-0 tonight so will face Newton Aycliffe in the next round of the FA Vase (Third Round). It would be great to see a North West club do well in the Vase this year but I think the smart money will be on Newton Aycliffe to progress.

Sunday 13th December 2015

It is two and a half weeks since I last wrote and I should now be reporting on the Newton Aycliffe v Atherton Collieries FA Vase Third Round Proper game but it was postponed yesterday. I have a feeling this is going to turn into a real saga now as the weather is either bitterly cold or incredibly wet and neither will lead to this game taking place.

Brad didn't have a game for Rochdale u18s this weekend (he played for the u16s today in a 2-1 defeat against Preston North End) nor was I due to work yesterday, so I said I would drive up to Newton Aycliffe for this one. Gordon was going to come to our house and I was going to pick Alan up from Leyland train station. On Friday, when I was at work, I had a text from Alan saying there was due to be a pitch inspection at 8.30 am on Saturday morning, but the weather forecast is not good with snow forecast in the North East. By nine o'clock yesterday morning, I had a text from Alan simply saying 'It's off – Replay Tuesday.'

If the game does go ahead on Tuesday, I won't be able to go. Brad is involved in a football match (thankfully on a 4G pitch) which has to take priority. The weather forecast isn't a lot better for the next few days anyway, so in all likelihood the Newton Aycliffe game will be off again.

I am not alone in having difficulties getting up to the North East. I mentioned on Sunday 22nd November that there were several postponements the previous day and one of the ties between Morpeth Town and 1874 Northwich Football Club was re-arranged for the Wednesday night. This night, however, unfortunately coincided with several 1874 Northwich players having work commitments in the South of

England and as they were going to struggle to raise a team of eleven, 1874 Northwich were forced to make the painful decision to forfeit the tie.

There has been quite a lot of debate on social media where the blame lies for 1874 Northwich's withdrawal from the competition. In total, it is a 400 mile round trip from Northwich up to Morpeth and it has been suggested that perhaps the replay could have been arranged for the Saturday which would not impact on the players working lives but realistically if every postponement and replay had to be re-arranged for a Saturday there could end up with a massive fixture backlog. I think the only way around it really is to widen the football season in the lower tiers as they are, in effect, getting a winter break anyway, especially in Scotland and North East England when football struggles to go ahead on pitches without specialist facilities like top class drainage and undersoil heating. If that doesn't happen, teams withdrawing from competitions because they cannot raise a team for long distance midweek travel, is always going to happen.

Despite most Vase games in Northern England being postponed due to waterlogging in the North West and snow in the North East, several games in the South did go ahead. Vase favourites Hereford won again, this time beating Brocton in a 2-0 home win with goals from Mustapha Bundu and Joel Edwards. This was Hereford's twenty second consecutive win and I have a feeling our paths will cross with Hereford at some stage as it has a feeling of inevitability about it. I will stick my neck out though and say I don't expect them to win the competition. They are not playing really tough opponents week in week out like they have to in the Northern League so I anticipate that if they have to face a Northern League side in the later rounds then they will come a cropper.

Amongst the other noticeable results in the Vase yesterday, Bristol Manor Farm of the Western League beat Hengrove Athletic 7-1 with Pete Sheppard scoring a hat trick. Salisbury (another Phoenix club) had a comprehensive 5-1 victory at Highworth Town and Newport (IOW) are still in the competition with a two-all draw against Tadley Calleva (after extra time).

Monday 14th December 2015

The FA Vase draw has taken place for the last 32 (4th Round) whilst we have yet to see our Third Round game. With the wet weather continuing, the draw for the last 16 may even take place before the Newton Aycliffe game takes place against Atherton Collieries. Tomorrow's scheduled replay has already been postponed and it has been moved to Saturday. I can't go on Saturday as I am working at Barron's from 10 until 2 so it will be left to Alan and Gordon once more. I wanted to do every round of the FA Cup but the journey through the FA Cup, FA Trophy and FA Vase is really Alan's (with Gordon doing the Vase with him) so if I can join them for a game or two more and the final, then I will be really pleased. As things stand, Brad's football at Rochdale, my family life and my job at Barron's are my key priorities.

Before I forget though, Newton Aycliffe or Atherton Collieries were drawn against Marske United or Team Northumbria in the Fourth Round.

With regards to Brad's football at Rochdale, I am taking him over there for two training sessions a week on Tuesday's and Thursday's and also for games on a Saturday (under 18s) and Sunday (under 16s) – if they are away then obviously I go to wherever the away game may be which is generally in the North West of England or in the Midlands to the likes of Shrewsbury and Walsall. The 18 year old keeper, Johny Diba Musangu has been back playing for the u18s recently so Brad has generally been on the bench. The training sessions during the week last two and a half hours on a Tuesday and two hours on a Thursday so with the hour journey there and the hour journey back, it pretty much wipes out the whole evening. Football is going to be Brad's livelihood for at least the two seasons after this one though, so it all serves a purpose. Ryan, the goalkeeper coach, has hinted that they are also going to introduce a goalkeepers only training session on a Monday night in the New Year, so that will be three evenings a week sat in a car park in Rochdale or venturing over to a local pub near where they train. During the six weeks Brad was at Blackburn, there was a really nice pub within a mile of the training ground but in Rochdale the local pubs are a bit more rough and ready. They serve a purpose though which is usually to watch a game of football on Sky Sports, if there's no game on in the pub, I will sit in the car or venture down to Tesco rather than pubbing it.

I mentioned the other day that Brad is involved in a game on Tuesday but did not go on to mention that it's a Lancashire Schools FA game rather than a Rochdale game. Brad's hasn't been involved in the Lancashire Schools squad after playing in a couple of pre-season friendlies. Brad played well in both games, but he felt, rightly or wrongly, that the fact that, at the time, the other two keepers were listed as Academy goalkeepers at Fleetwood and Blackpool and he was listed as a Croston Juniors goalkeeper, having not signed for an Academy club at that point, may have gone against him. To be fair, that may just be a bit of a teenage mentality, as from what I've seen of the Fleetwood keeper, Billy Crellin, he is tall, commanding and impressive. I haven't seen much of Aiden Whitehead, the Blackpool goalkeeper, as the only time he has played against Brad, Blackpool dominated the match (against Rochdale u16s) and he wasn't called upon to do much. No doubt he is a strong keeper too though.

Andy Clitheroe contacted me last week and said he wanted to bring Brad back into the squad. They have played a total of eight games now, six friendlies and two competitive games, the ones that mattered were a one-all draw with Merseyside in a Northern Counties Championship Group game and a ten-nil win over Derbyshire in the National Inter-County Trophy. The game tomorrow night is the second Northern Counties Championship Group game against Cheshire. Andy said Billy Crellin would be starting in goal but he would try and give Brad a game if he could. I guess by that he meant if they were running out easy winners (or getting beat heavily), then they would have the chance to bring Brad on.

When I spoke to Brad about his re-selection in the squad, I was anticipating that he would be delighted, as he knows all the lads at Lancashire well and I think it is a great honour to be selected for your county but Brad saw it a bit differently. Brad knows Billy Crellin is first choice for Lancashire so he is reluctant to miss training at Rochdale, which he really enjoys, to warm the bench up at Lancashire. The other issue he pointed out is that Johny Diba Musangu is often asked to be the substitute Rochdale first team keeper so, on that basis, Brad will be called up to play for Rochdale Youth Team. He doesn't want to be involved with Lancashire as a sub on a Saturday when he could be getting valuable under 18s experience at Rochdale.

I understood Brad's logic. He feels his first loyalties are to Rochdale and in six months' time they would be the team who would be paying his wages and Lancashire would no longer be an option for him. I did feel however, that if Lancashire games clashed with Rochdale training, that Lancashire should take priority but if it meant missing a game for Rochdale to be a sub for Lancashire, then Rochdale should be priority. Brad agreed with this logic so I said I would speak to Ryan, Rochdale's Academy goalkeeper, about it.

Ryan was fine about Brad not going to tomorrow night's training, but, like Brad, was a bit concerned that Saturday games may clash with opportunities for

Brad for Rochdale's Youth Team (under 18s). I said if that was the case, I would have a chat with Andy Clitheroe, but for now it is just one game.

Tuesday 15th December 2015

Both Brad and I enjoyed out trip over to Skelmersdale tonight for the Lancashire Schools under 16 game against Cheshire but we both also came away a little puzzled as to why he had been asked to go down as he was one of three Lancashire goalkeepers there. As anticipated, Billy Crellin played the whole game in goal and did what he had to do very well but wasn't greatly tested in a 3-0 win. Brad enjoyed seeing a lot of footballing friends though and I enjoyed watching a good quality game. Most of the Lancashire players are affiliated to North West clubs, namely Preston North End, Accrington Stanley, Blackpool and Blackburn Rovers.

Andy Clitheroe said after the game that they have a National Cup last sixteen game against Worcestershire coming up early in the New Year and they would like Brad along for that too. As Worcestershire have a long journey, it will be a late afternoon kick off rather than an 8pm kick off, like tonight, which means Brad will have to miss an afternoon of school. This time around, almost certainly because it involves missing an afternoon of school work, Brad was keener to be involved. Hopefully Rochdale won't mind him going down again but it will be dependent on what their plans are.

Wednesday 16th December 2015

I had a text off Alan today to say the Newton Aycliffe v Atherton Collieries game has now been re-scheduled for next Tuesday night, 22nd December. For some reason, a reason that Alan isn't very happy about, League games are getting played on Saturday and the FA Vase has been put back to Tuesday. To add a bit of extra fuel on to Alan's flames, Newton Aycliffe are at home on Saturday, so Alan is already complaining that they will 'F##k the pitch up for Tuesday' (you are wrong if you thought the missing word was 'fork').

From a personal perspective, as I am not working at Barron's next Tuesday, this means I can go to the game whilst unfortunately the re-arrangement means Gordon can't go, as he is going to Poland for a few days and he isn't home until next Wednesday. An evening 300 mile round trip the Tuesday before Christmas is already rekindling memories of last season when Alan and I were amongst a handful of North Ferriby supporters at Boston, the Tuesday before Christmas. Really hope it's on as I fancy a pre-Christmas evening adventure.

Sunday 20th December 2015

Ironically, Newton Aycliffe did play yesterday. They warmed up for their FA Vase clash by losing 1-0 at home to North Shields. Atherton Collieries also played, winning 3-0 at away at Silsdon. Atherton are now only six points behind Colne with a game in hand so the Vase clash is likely to be another close encounter, as Colne and Atherton Colleries are obviously similar standard sides. I'm just hoping now that the Newton Aycliffe pitch is up to two games in 72 hours.

Before I go on to mention other club news, yesterday marked the passing of another footballing legend, as Jimmy Hill died aged 87. Throughout my childhood, (as anyone over 35 will also recall) when there was no Sky television and Sky Sports News talking about football 24/7, there was a fraction of the football that's on TV today. ITV had a Granada regional programme called 'Kick Off' presented by Gerald Sinstadt and Elton Welsby, their national football programme called 'The Big Match' which was presented by Brian Moore (and for a while a Saturday lunch time programme with Ian St John and Jimmy Greaves called 'Saint and Greavesie'). The BBC football highlights always seemed slicker and more impressive though. They had 'Football Focus' on a Saturday lunchtime, which was predominantly presented by Bob Wilson and then on a Saturday night it was 'Match of The Day' presented by Jimmy Hill. Hill presented the programme over 600 times before leaving to join Sky Sports in 1999. He stayed with Sky until 2007, presenting a Sunday lunchtime programme called 'Sunday Supplement' until Brian Woolnough took over from him (Woolnough has also died now, he passed away from bowel cancer in 2012). Hill was a much more opinionated and controversial presenter of 'Match of The Day' than Gary Lineker is these days and although not everyone would agree with his points of view, no-one doubted his football knowledge. He was a strong advocate for all seater stadium long before the Hillsborough tragedy and was also instrumental in dispensing with the maximum wage for footballers as he campaigned for its end when Chairman of the PFA. At that point (in the late 1950s/early 1960s), the maximum wage was £20 per week. How things have changed!

Rather than go through a whole host of results from yesterday, I thought I would do a quick update as to who is leading in a few Leagues at Christmas. Non-League wise, the National League is being led by Cheltenham, who I fully expect to go back into League Two next season, their closest pursuers are local rivals, Forest Green. In National League North, Nuneaton Town are top, with North Ferriby United, Solihull Moors, AFC Fylde and Boston United snapping at their heels. My money would be on Fylde (as they are the team with the most money). Then in National League South, Ebbsfleet United are top, with Maidstone United, Oxford City, Sutton United and Whitehawk the closest behind. With this one, although admittedly my knowledge on this League isn't the greatest, I predict Ebbsfleet United will go up into the National League.

I appreciate this book is largely about non-League football, but I just wanted to spend a little time commenting on the Premier League as this season seems to be an unusual one. Yesterday, Leicester City beat my team, Everton, 3-2 at Goodison Park to take a five point lead at the top. Leicester, managed by Chelsea's old boss, Claudio Ranieri, were one of the favourites for relegation at the start of the season and a few optimistic Leicester fans put the odd fiver or tenner on them to win the League at ridiculous odds of around 5,000-1. It is still unlikely that they will go on to win the League, as Arsenal, Manchester City, Tottenham Hotspur and Manchester United will probably go past them in the second half of the season, but even a Top Four finish and a place in the Champions League next season would have been beyond their wildest dreams back in August. Anyone like me, who doesn't have a side in the Top Five, is willing them to win it.

Although we have been struggling to get up to the North East for the FA Vase, Alan has been up there today for the FA Sunday Cup Third Round Game. He followed Yorkshire side, West Bowling AFC through as they were handed an away tie against Hardwick Social who play at Stockton-on-Tees. Alan was untroubled by the distance he had to travel as it was another new ground for 'The Casual Hopper' and he saw Hardwick Social emerge victorious after 120 minutes. Alan said it was one-all after ninety minutes but West Bowling AFC wilted visibly in extra time on the heavy pitch and Hardwick Social ended up winning 5-1. All paths seems to lead to Newton Aycliffe for Alan right now, as Hardwick Social will now play away at the winners of Newton Aycliffe WMC or Burradon & New Fordley in the next round. Alan said he hopes it is Burradon & New Fordley who win as he has heard they play at Morpeth and he hasn't been there yet.

Monday 21st December 2015

This is getting ridiculous now! Newton Aycliffe have had to postpone their game against Atherton Collieries again today, so we won't be venturing up there tomorrow night. Alan is seething about the fact that it wasn't played on Saturday, as there was a brief sabbatical from the almost constant rain that has blighted the football season in Northern England this winter.

If the game does finally take place on 5th January, it rules me out as that is the confirmed date of the Lancashire Schools game against Worcestershire but it does give Gordon the opportunity of continuing his 100% attendance in the FA Vase. Another piece of FA Vase news, I've just been reading that Newport (IOW) beat Tadley Calleva 4-2 in extra time in their replayed Third Round game. A trip over to the Isle of Wight is still not beyond the realms of possibility!

CHAPTER ELEVEN

Sunday 27th December 2015

Another Christmas comes and goes. We went over to Alison's Mum and Dad's on Christmas Day and had a nice family day as Alison's sister, Jenny was there and her husband, Jon and their young daughters, Chloe and Emily. On our way around we went to see Alison's grandparents in a care home. They are 92 and 91 now and although Alison's Grandad, Michael, lives with her Mum and Dad, Paula and Barry, his wife, Joan, isn't in the best of health either physically or mentally now so had to move into a care home. They have been married an amazing 68 years. Michael is still sharp as a button and still enjoys a good chat about football, especially Chester FC.

Yesterday, we were due to go to my Mum and Dad's and meet up with my sister, Lisa and her husband Vin, and their daughter and son, Olivia and Max, who are eighteen and fifteen. We got there eventually but our arrival was significantly delayed as our little area of Euxton, Chorley had become a small island as we were surrounded by flood water. If you turn left at the top of our road, the road runs under a railway bridge and because of torrential downpours over the last twenty four hours, the standing water was about 6 feet deep. If you turn right, it takes you through a road that cuts between two fields and the water had blocked that way too. The rain eventually eased by midday and we managed to get out mid-afternoon but it was quite a hairy drive and certain routes had to be avoided.

One of the routes avoided was through the village of Croston. It is a quaint village about five miles from here and a place we know well as Brad played his football there for four seasons, the last two of which, I helped run the team. Croston has been severely hit by floods as the River Douglas, which passes close to the village, burst its banks and the flood waters swept in, leaving the main road through the town two feet deep in water and sadly ran into the ground floor of many surrounding homes.

It is not just our area that has been hit by the floods. A lot of Britain has been hit, particularly in the Lancashire and Yorkshire regions. Alan posted a photo on Facebook of Colne's ground and the bottom corner, where the pitch slopes down to, was about three feet deep in water. The bad weather is just an aggravating inconvenience for me, but for families forced out of their homes at Christmas or people who see their business premises under several feet of water, it must be heartbreaking. The forecast is for the rains to ease for a while and then come back before the New Year so I hope the severity of what arrives in the second band is nowhere near as bad.

Monday 4th January 2016

Happy New Year! The rains have now eased and the recovery for the places most severely hit continues.

Alan and Gordon are preparing to go to watch the next round of the FA Vase at Newton Aycliffe tomorrow (whilst I head to Lancashire Schools FA v Worcestershire Schools FA). Alan has been in touch today to say he has been in contact with Newton Aycliffe's secretary and their pitch is still saturated and he thinks the chances of a game tomorrow night are very slim. If it is postponed, it is due to be Saturday which brings me back into contention. The Lancashire Schools game will definitely go ahead as it is on a 4g surface in Skelmersdale at 4pm. My Dad is coming to watch with me.

One other piece of footballing news is that Joe Boyling, Alan's nephew who was the other goalkeeper at Blackburn Rovers under 16s when Brad was there, was released by Blackburn before Christmas and is now trialling at Port Vale and Oldham. Apparently Blackburn's scientific checks indicated that he was unlikely to grow much taller than 5 feet 9 inches (his current height) and as a goalkeeper, they decided that would be too small. It seems very frustrating for the family that after having traipsed up to Blackburn for many years, several times a week, that they could not have come to this conclusion sooner. I am not sure what percentage of these scientific checks prove to be wrong but in Joe's case, I hope they are, as he is a very strong keeper.

Tuesday 5th January 2016

For what seems like the hundredth time, the Newton Aycliffe against Atherton Collieries game was postponed after an inspection at ten o'clock this morning deemed the pitch unfit. I will go if the game is on this Saturday, but according to Alan, Newton Aycliffe are already in contact with other clubs in the North East with 4g surfaces to see if they can play the game at their ground. Next Monday, the draw for the Fifth Round (two rounds ahead) will be made, so they need to get this game played now.

Newton Aycliffe are not the only North East time in the FA Vase struggling to fulfil their fixture. The winners of Newton Aycliffe and Atherton Collieries are due to play the winners of Marske United and Team Northumbria in the next round. On Sunday, with their pitch heavily waterlogged, Marske announced that to get the game played they would be playing the match at Billingham Synthonia's ground. At five o'clock this afternoon, it was announced that Billingham's pitch was waterlogged too, so the game was postponed once more.

On a brighter note, my Dad and I went down to a chilly JMO Sports Park in Skelmersdale this afternoon, to see Lancashire Schools FA beat Worcestershire Schools FA 4-0 with two goals from Dan Gray and a goal each for Newton and Garstang. Brad was one of two keepers there this time and with Lancashire having a comfortable lead, Andy Clitheroe took Billy Crellin off with about five minutes left to give Brad a bit of time on the pitch. I understand it is a competitive environment and Andy has to play what he sees as his strongest team, so I have no issues with this. My Dad enjoyed the game and was impressed with the quality of the Lancashire side. He was intending on going back home, having his tea and then returning to

Skelmersdale to see Skem United against AFC Fylde in the FA Trophy but we found out during Brad's game that Skelmersdale United's game had been postponed.

Brad had very little to do in his five minute cameo appearance. He made one routine save and took a couple of goal kicks but that was about it. Billy Crellin did well again. I must admit I am a glass is half empty type of guy sometimes and during my more negative moments, when I watch the likes of Billy Crellin bossing his area and looking extremely accomplished, I do worry that Brad has to find a lot of improvement in the next two years to make it as a professional goalkeeper. I do keep telling myself though, he has only had specialist goalkeeper coaching this season and he has improved a lot, so perhaps with specialist training every day, he will come on leaps and bounds. Time will tell.

Wednesday 6th January 2016

No further news on Satuday's Newton Aycliffe match but I have been given an added complication as I've been told by Rochdale that Johny Diba will be with the Rochdale first team squad so Brad will be making his third appearance for Rochdale u18s against Tranmere Rovers at Hyde United's ground. Rochdale u18s play their home games at either Hyde United or Radcliffe Borough (depending on if the parent club are playing at home) so I will look forward to Saturday's double header.

I have text Alan to see if he fancied coming to Hyde first and then making a dart up to Newton Aycliffe on the final whistle, but Alan is concerned that if Brad's game only finished at ten to one, it would be too tight. I have said I will go to watch Brad and follow them up to Newton Aycliffe, even if that means missing the kick off. I have long since decided Brad's football needs to be my priority now.

Thursday 7th January 2016

I spoke to Alan again this evening (whilst at Brad's football training) and he has been in touch with Newton Aycliffe's secretary again. Apparently they haven't been able to reach agreement with any other North East club about playing the game on their ground on Saturday so if it is on, it will be at Newton Aycliffe. It's less than forty eight hours before kick off and the pitch is currently waterlogged so Alan is pretty convinced it will be off again. On a more positive note, Brad's game against Tranmere Rovers looks likely to go ahead.

Friday 8th January 2016

Alan text me today at work to say there was a pitch inspection due at 5.30 pm to make an early decision on the FA Vase game. Not surprisingly, I subsequently received another email to say the match was off. This saga seems to go on forever. Personally, having conceded that I am just going to go to the FA Vase games when I can, I am not going to get too concerned about it, but for Alan, who is very driven in ensuring that he maintains his 100% attendance record in his FA Cup, FA Trophy, FA Vase and FA Sunday Cup challenge, all these postponements are really getting to him. He is still shaking his head and moaning that this fixture wasn't fulfilled on the 19th December when both Newton Aycliffe and Atherton Collieries played League games.

The fixture has now been re-arranged (yet again) for next Tuesday 12th January. Alison is working nights next week and Brad has a match for Rochdale u16s on Tuesday night on the 3g so I can't go up to Newton Aycliffe. Alan is looking into train details but Gordon says he will go as long as he can leave Liverpool County FA at a reasonable time. Alan has already researched train times and will be getting the 22.25 from Darlington back to Manchester if Gordon can't make it! If the game is unplayable on Tuesday, they have a Plan B of playing at Atherton Colleries on Wednesday night. That would suit me fine. I must admit, our neutrality on this one has well and truly gone and for logistical convenience, we are all now hoping Atherton Collieries win this game once it finally takes place.

CHAPTER TWELVE

Tuesday 12th January 2016

The FA VASE – 3rd Round Proper

Newton Aycliffe v Atherton Collieries

Written by Gordon The Ref

So can they get the third round game between Newton Aycliffe and Atherton Colleries played at the sixth time of asking? Fingers crossed. A pitch inspection had been scheduled for 1.00pm at Newton Aycliffe's Moore Lane Ground. Already we knew that the winners of this tie will be at home to Marske United from the Northern League. On Saturday, Marske United had finally managed to get the go ahead to play their tie against Team Northumbria and there was a dramatic climax. With the scores level at 1-1, Adam Preston of Marske had scored the winner five minutes into injury time to secure a 2-1 win, ensuring a place in the Fourth Round against the victors of our tie.

Yesterday, the Fifth round draw was made and the triumphant team out of Marske United, Newton Aycliffe and Atherton Collieries (together with our band of three), will face a long trip to Surrey to take on Camberley Town from the Combined Counties Football League at their Krooner Park ground, with Saturday 30th January being the scheduled date of that round of the FA Vase.

9.15am and word comes through that the game is on. The pitch at Newton Aycliffe's Moore Lane ground is once again unplayable so the game has been switched to Durham City's New Ferens Park ground which is a 3G playing surface and will almost certainly get the nod no matter what the weather in the area for the rest of the day. What followed was a frantic round of mobile text messages, email, Twitter and Facebook updates before arrangements are made to travel up to Durham later in the day. Unfortunately, due to work commitments and the need to get Brad to a game for Rochdale FC under 16s versus Curzon Ashton FC u16s, Calvin is going to be unable to make the trip, but Alan and I were able to make arrangements to get away early from our respective workplaces in plenty of time to make the trip.

At two o'clock, I left a wet and windy Liverpool County FA office at Walton Hall Park, Liverpool, to make the short journey home to Ormskirk and pick up appropriate wet weather and warm clothing for the evening ahead and also check up on my daughter, Heather who was laid up at home suffering from glandular fever.

By quarter to three, I was off on the road to Prestwich, Manchester from where previous arrangements have been made to pick up Alan. Approaching Eccles on the M62 motorway and the sky was actually brightening up and the rain stopping. Who says it always rains in Manchester? Perhaps this was a good omen for the evening ahead.

Forty minutes later, as I was entering the Irwell Valley on the M60 Motorway, approaching Prestwich, I phoned ahead just to check that Alan had made it on time to the agreed rendezvous point, just off the motorway at a Shell garage in Prestwich. Worryingly, the call went to voicemail as there was no reply from Alan. My initial thought was, "Has Alan managed to get away from work on time? Is he going to make it? It's not like Alan not to answer his mobile".

I tried again and thankfully this time there was a response from Alan who had already arrived at the agreed pick up point. Five minutes later, I arrived at the garage too. Alan has just been offered a lift up to the north east by a car full of Manchester United fans who were off to St James Park, Newcastle to watch the FA Premier League game between Newcastle United and Manchester United. I am sure a great deal of football pleasantries would have been exchanged between City fan, Alan and a car full of United fans if he had jumped in their car rather than mine.

Before the journey actually continued it was into the garage shop to stock up with supplies for the trip ahead and also to purchase a note pad to record details of the evening's events for Calvin.

 "He's asked you too, has he?" chirps up Alan, "He doesn't trust me to do it after last time does he?"

I try to be diplomatic and replied that maybe more information and different views on the game may be better as it would give Calvin more to work with. Alan is going to go back and add to his notes from the Chester-le-Street v Newton Aycliffe game as he forgot to take any notes at the time and originally came up with 'Newton Aycliffe strolled it and took the wrong player off. 4-0'. Alan is not normally a man of only a few words so he will probably change it to something of biblical proportions.

By five to four, we are back on the road towards Leeds on the M62 Motorway and then onwards up the A1(M) towards Durham City's New Ferens Park.

Although I am saying the game is being played at Durham City's New Ferens Park, it isn't actually their ground any more as the club actually left the ground in October 2015 after a dispute with the landlord and since that time have been ground sharing and playing their Home games at Consett, which as it would happen, also has a 3G playing surface.

The dispute between Durham City and their landlords made the national newspaper's sports pages because, since December 2013, the club's owner and Chairman has been Olivier Bernard, the French defender who played over one hundred times for Newcastle United. In October 2015, Olivier Bernard said the club were given a week's notice to leave by the co-owners of the ground, who included Austin Carney, a former Chairman of Durham City himself, who stated the club were being asked to leave due to a 'financial dispute'. The deadline expired without resolution on Monday 19th October 2015 and the club had to cancel the following evening's game against Jarrow Roofing. Subsequently, the pitch has been available for games, such as tonight's, but recently it has not been Durham City's ground.

Tonight's visit was my third to New Ferens Park having previously been referee for two of Durham City's Northern League games on the ground in 2005 and 2007. This had come about during my time as Secretary of the Greater Manchester Police Federation prior to my retirement from the police in April 2013. Colleagues of mine at the Durham Police Federation, annually held a black tie charity fund raising dinner at the Ramside Hotel, which is situated very near to the then Durham City FC's ground, a function which I regularly attended with my wife, Jackie. Being the football fanatic that I am, I always informed the Football Association's referee appointments secretary if I was ever travelling to other parts of the country in the hope that I might pick up a game in that area and get to visit a new club or ground. Consequently, on my visits to Durham Constabulary's Charity Dinner events over the years, I have managed to referee games at Ashington FC, Newcastle Benfield FC, Shildon FC, Ryton FC and of course Durham City FC twice.

My first visit to New Ferens Park was on Saturday 19th November 2005 for a Northern League game between Durham City and Tow Law Town. The game ended in a 0-0 draw and my performance during the game was assessed by former Premier League Referee Alan Wilkie. Small world, as on our first visit to Chester Le Street FC earlier in this season's FA Vase journey, we had been looking at Alan Wilkie's collection of football shirts that he had amassed during his time as a top flight referee, which are proudly framed and displayed around the Chester Le Street FC clubhouse, where Alan is the club President.

My second visit to New Ferens Park had been on Saturday 24th November 2007 for a Northern League game between Durham City FC and Dunston Federation FC. This visit was a bit more of an eventful game ending in a 2-0 victory for Durham City and with three players being cautioned (booked) and one from Dunston being sent off. On this occasion, my performance was assessed by a Peter Ramsey, who must have been happy with what he witnessed, as he awarded me an overall mark of 80 out of 100 with the expected mark, at that level, around that time being between 70 and 73. I remember the visit well, as does my wife Jackie, not for the football or the Charity Dinner event in the evening, but more so for events prior to the game itself.

As it was late November and approaching Christmas, the plan for the afternoon was that Jackie would drop me off at the game and then head off up to the Metro Centre, in nearby Newcastle, to do some Christmas shopping. So, after checking into the Ramside Hotel, I drove across to Durham City's ground with Jackie as my front seat passenger. On arrival at the ground, I retrieved my referee's kit bag from the boot of the car and Jackie climbed across from the passenger side into the driver's seat and set off en route to the Metro centre. Problem was that my car of choice at that time was a Suzuki SX4. For those of you who know your cars you'll know that the SX4 is one of those keyless cars that can be started as long as the key fob is inside the vehicle. Obviously this had been the case when leaving the Ramside Hotel but on jumping out of the car, with the engine still running, I still had the key fob in my suit pocket. Jackie merrily jumped across to the driver's seat and then set off on her journey. Fifteen minutes later and a good few miles up the road the reality dawned on Jackie who frantically phoned me to point out that I still had the key fob in my pocket.

"Don't worry" I said, "just head back to the ground and I'll come outside to meet you with the key, but whatever you do don't stall the car!"

The response from Jackie and the exchange of words when she safely arrived back at Durham City's ground would not really sit well on these pages so is probably best left out.

So we continued on our way to the North East discussing the possible options and permutations after the game had been played. Would it be a replay to follow at Atherton Collieries Alder Street ground, a game at Atherton Collieries versus Marske United or a game between Newton Aycliffe and Marske United, in which case at what ground and when? What was also discussed was the high scoring games that we'd seen already during the course of the FA Vase journey with the victorious team always managing to score at least four goals.

"Maybe not tonight though", I thought, having only seen a total of two goals in two previous visits to New Ferens Park.

During the course of our journey, we also heard from Colin McNeillie via Facebook, stating that he couldn't get away from work in time, so he wouldn't be able to make it to the game and meet up once again. We'd previously met Colin at the Colne versus Newton Aycliffe game during the previous round. Colin, a football blogger and Manchester City fan, now lives in the Newton Aycliffe area and consequently has become a keen follower of his local side.

"Oh well, maybe we'll catch up with him at the replay or next round if Newton win," piped up Alan.

By quarter past six, having made good time on our journey, we stopped off at Durham services, a few miles short of our destination, for a leg stretch, toilet and refreshment break. So Costa Coffee at the Durham services got its third visit of the Vase journey having previously been our watering hole on the two earlier visits to Chester Le Street in the earlier rounds. Suitably refreshed, we then headed on up the A1 to Durham arriving at the ground at 7.00pm. On arrival, we headed on to the car park where three young lads, one in a Hi-Vis yellow coat, charged us £1.00 to park the car. Were they official car park attendants or three young lads who identified the chance of making a few quid, who knows? A £1.00 coin was duly handed over to save a long walk back to the ground if parking elsewhere.

A few pictures were taken outside the ground, including the now mandatory selfie stick shot, and then we headed inside at a cost of £6.00 per head. No programmes for sale at the turnstile or inside and so questions were asked of the Newton Aycliffe volunteers on the gate to see where we could get them.

"We haven't done one", was the reply.

"What about from the original game?" asked Alan.

"We didn't do one then 'cause we knew it wasn't going to be on", came the reply.

Disappointment etched on our faces, we carried on in to the tea bar to get some food.

"I'm Hank Marvin" chirped up Alan, not for the first time.

Whilst waiting in the queue at the tea bar a Newton volunteer carrying A4 team sheets was spotted heading to the turnstiles and so three team sheets were grabbed, one each and one for the absent Calvin.

£4.20 for a cheeseburger and chips and we then headed on up into the 300 seater stand to shelter from the now torrential rain that was coming down. Alan, of course, couldn't resist seeking out Newton Aycliffe's own Allan Oliver, their Chairman, who we'd also previously met up with at the last game between Colne and Newton Aycliffe. Allan wasn't too difficult to find and once we found him he led us through via the players tunnel and dressing room area into the ground's boardroom. A lengthy pre match football chat about both the FA Vase and the FA Sunday Cup competitions then took place with the Newton club secretary, Stephen Cunliffe, and the FA delegate at the game, Northern League Secretary, Kevin Hewitt joining us.

With five minutes to kick off, we headed out into the stand and took up two seats just above the players tunnel, right on the half way line, sitting down next to two guys who were wearing red and white North Shields scarves and who had a camera and tripod already set up, obviously going to record the evening's proceedings.

Almost immediately the two teams were then led out onto the field of play by match referee, Tony Peart, from North Allerton. I had previously met and officiated with Tony during my time as an Assistant Referee on the Football League. 22nd January 2011 to be precise, on a League Two game at Edgeley Park, Stockport, between Stockport County and Lincoln City. It was a relegation battle at the time with the two teams occupying the bottom two places in the Football League. The match ended in a 4-3 victory for Lincoln City but this wasn't enough to save Lincoln in the long run and at the end of that season both of the teams were relegated from the Football League.

After many false dawns, this long awaited FA Vase game eventually started with Atherton Collieries in change yellow shirts, as opposed to their usual black and white tops, getting proceedings underway. The game was played at quite a frantic pace between, what appeared to be, two very evenly matched sides. There were two lengthy stoppages early on in the game, after 8 minutes for a head injury to Newton's No8 Stuart Banks and after 14 minutes for a similar injury to Newton's No5 Ashley Coffey. Neither occurred as a result of unfair challenges merely accidental collisions between players making genuine efforts to win the ball.

Nineteen minutes in and the referee played advantage as Atherton have a promising attacking phase of play following a bad tackle by Newton's Alex Kitchen on Atherton's Mark Battersby.

I leant over to Alan saying, "I think that could be the first caution of the game in a minute", expecting the referee to go back and deal with the offending Newton player at the next stoppage in play.

Much to my surprise though, this didn't actually happen, with referee Tony Peart choosing to have words with the Atherton player about his reaction to the challenge, as opposed to speaking to or dealing with the offending Newton player at the next stoppage in play.

Whatever the calming words the referee had with Atherton's No9 Mark Battersby, they didn't appear to have the desired effect, with him cutting down Newton's Alex Kitchen with a retaliatory challenge after 26 minutes of the game and rightly receiving the first yellow card of the game from referee Peart. The game at this stage seemed to be getting a little out of hand with lots of niggling and off the ball challenges being exchanged. After 28 minutes, Atherton's Mark Battersby intentionally kicked out at Newton's No7 Paul Garthwaite, which went unseen and consequently unpunished by the match officials. Had they seen it, this incident would undoubtedly have led to Battersby being sent off the field of play. Immediately after this, Atherton's No8 Bradley Cooke received the second yellow card of the game, for a reckless challenge on Newton's Ashley Coffey and the game continued in a bad tempered manner for the next few minutes.

After 42 minutes, following treatment for an injury, Atherton's No9 Mark Battersby left the field of play and was waved back on a short time later by match referee, Mr Peart, having changed into the No16 shirt. This was another puzzling decision by the match referee. The perception was that there was blood on the Atherton No9 shirt as a result of his injury, necessitating the change of shirt. If that was the case, I pointed out to Alan, then he should not have re-entered the field of play until a stoppage in the game, for him to be checked by the match referee – oops!

Only a minute later, I was commenting on the referee's performance to Alan again when a bad tackle by Atherton's No4 Josh Messer, on Newton's No10 Denis

Knight, did not receive the yellow card (caution) that I would have expected if I had been the match assessor on the game. Half time then arrived after three additional minutes had been played on top of the normal 45 minutes with the score still at 0-0. Not much goal mouth action but plenty of fouls and tackles which made the game interesting for me from a refereeing perspective.

During the half time interval we struck up a conversation with the two North Shields supporters who had been recording the game. They turned out to be Craig Lilley, North Shields FC Lottery Manager and Russell Wynn, the social media and website editor for North Shields FC. Craig explained to us that the two of them attend all North Shields games, home and away, recording the matches and publicising highlights on websites and social media. Whenever North Shields did not have a game, as was the case tonight, the duo regularly attended other Northern League grounds offering the same service for other clubs. The lads also went on to explain how they had both enjoyed a memorable day at the 2015 FA Vase final at Wembley stadium when their team had come from a goal behind to beat Glossop North End FC from the North West Counties League by two goals to one.

Before long it was time for the second half to get under way with the first opportunity of the half falling to Newton No10 Dennis Knight who, when played through one on one with the Atherton goalkeeper, Danny Taberner, by team mate Zak Boagley, struck his shot straight at the Atherton keeper who saved easily.

Three minutes later Dennis Knight lost possession on the half way line to Atherton right back, Jake Kenny, who immediately played a promising ball forwards down the right flank to Atherton No7 Ben Hardcastle. As Hardcastle cut inside Newton No5 Ashley Coffey, he was intentionally tripped by Coffey, resulting in a free kick being awarded to Atherton just to the right hand side of the Newton penalty area and a yellow card (Caution) for the offending Ashley Coffey, the third one of the game.

The resultant free kick was lofted into the Newton Aycliffe penalty area but easily cleared up field where the ball fell to the Newton No9 Matthew Moffat. Moffat using his skill and experience from previously playing at a higher level with Gateshead, drew two Atherton defenders towards him before playing a great through ball to No8 Stuart Banks, who coolly slotted the ball past the out-stretched Atherton goalkeeper to give Newton Aycliffe a 1-0 lead.

After 61 minutes, a promising attacking move down the left, saw Mark Battersby cut inside for Atherton and force a great save from Newton goal keeper, James Winter. From this save the ball fell to Atherton No10 Jordan Cover whose shot on goal was also blocked by goalkeeper Winter, completing a fabulous double save. On 65 minutes, Newton Aycliffe's Dennis Knight gave away a needless free kick just inside the centre circle tripping Atherton's No5 Mark Ayres. As he did so, and the referee Mr Peart blew his whistle stopping play, the ball fell to goal scorer Stuart Banks, who needlessly kicked the ball forty yards high over the Atherton goal and as a result, quite rightly received the fourth yellow card of the game from referee Tony Peart, for delaying the re-start of play.

The game became niggling again with Newton's Matthew Moffat using all of his experience in winding up the Atherton players. Consequently on 72 minutes two attempted trips were made on Newton No10 Denis Knight, neither of which were penalised by referee Peart who, it has to be said, was having an indifferent game. The ball spilled free into the Atherton penalty area where Newton's N11 Zak Boagley put in a heavy challenge on Atherton No5 Mark Ayres that was penalised by referee Peart. This sparked a mass confrontation involving the majority of the players from both sides and ending with all three match officials gathering in the Atherton goal area to consult on the incident after it had all calmed down. After what seemed like an age a red card was brandished towards Newton Aycliffe No4 Alex Kitchen for, what we could only presume, was for running from the half way line to get involved in the brawl. To be fair to the player, Kitchen, after his obvious initial shock at being sent off the field of play, duly turned and ran towards the tunnel without making any undue protestations or further obvious outbursts of dissent or unruly behaviour. What was surprising, certainly from my perspective, was the lack of disciplinary sanctions taken by the referee against the two instigators of the ugly scene, one from either side. So Newton Aycliffe were reduced to ten players for the last quarter of an hour and a string of substitutions were then made in the following few minutes, with Atherton bringing on No12 Kristian Holt and No15 Jacob Jones, pushing both substitutes forward, in effect playing with four up front, as they chased an equalising goal.

On 79 minutes, Newton's Matthew Moffat and Atherton's Mark Battersby squared up to one another in an aggressive manner, again with no action being taken by referee Peart!

Sixty seconds later, Atherton's No15 Jacob Jones broke down the right and cut into the Newton Aycliffe penalty area, as two team mates waited for a square ball across the penalty area, Jones chose to shoot towards the near post and yet again Newton keeper James Winter was up to the challenge, diving to his left to save and hold the ball. Atherton though continued to press and on 87 minutes were awarded a corner kick. They introduced their third and final substitute, No14 Matt Grimshaw, before the corner kick was again lofted high into the Newton Aycliffe penalty area but it ran harmlessly out of play for a goal kick to the home side. As the corner kick had been lofted into the area there had been a coming together between Atherton No6 Callum Jones and Newton No9 Matthew Moffat. Whatever happened between them it resulted in the Atherton player running back towards his own half threatening the Newton striker so loudly and aggressively that everybody in the ground could hear and was aware of the incident. Consequently it was no surprise then that the final yellow card (Caution) of the game was given to Atherton's Callum Jones before play was re-started with the Newton goal kick.

Three minutes added time was indicated by the match officials but the game was certainly not yet over. Well into the three minutes Newton Aycliffe's goal scorer, Stuart Banks, was again put through on goal by, man of the match, Matthew Moffat but this time he ballooned his shot high over the Atherton cross bar. From the re-start Atherton immediately lost possession with the ball falling again to Matthew Moffat who, with a chance to confirm the victory, shot wide. That wasn't the last chance of the game though and after 95 minutes Atherton had their final opportunity to grab an equaliser but this time it was No11 Mark Truffas who again forced a great full stretch save from Newton goal keeper, James Winter. Referee Peart blew for full time immediately afterwards. So Newton Aycliffe march on to the fourth round with a home tie against Marske United the next hurdle.

FINAL SCORE :- NEWTON AYCLIFFE 1 ATHERTON COLLIERIES 0

FA VASE GOALS :- 26 in 5 games.

CHAPTER THIRTEEN

Wednesday 13th January 2016

I spoke to Alan and Gordon on their way back from Durham last night and they sounded like they had a good evening despite it being a tight game with little goal mouth action. Gordon is more interested in how the ref deals with the ninety minutes of football than anything else and once I get his notes, this will no doubt be evident. He looks at everything from a referee or Assistant referee's perspective, including how they warm up, what they wear (especially if they are wearing the right badges) and how tackles and confrontations are handled. A sending off and a few bookings will give him plenty to write about.

Annoyingly, when we arrived at Spotland last night, for the lads to do gym work before the match, we were told the game was off as Curzon Ashton couldn't get a team, so it would just be training. It was disappointing, but realistically, with Alison working, I couldn't have gone to the Newton Aycliffe game even if I had known from the start that Brad would only be training.

The Fourth Round game between Newton Aycliffe and Marske United has been hastily organised for this Saturday, so I have swopped the Saturday I am due to be working from this week to next. Brad's under 18 game is apparently very doubtful, but if they aren't playing, he has to go to train at Soccer City, an indoor five a side place, in Rochdale, from nine until eleven on Saturday morning. If the Newton Aycliffe game is on, which I am guessing is always doubtful at this time of year, unless they arrange to play on 3G again, then I will either have to persuade Brad to come to the Vase game with me or drop him off at a train station with the money to get home.

Saturday 16th January 2016

As anticipated Brad's under 18 game was postponed, so we had to be at Soccer City in Rochdale at nine for indoor training. Once again, I was spending a couple of hours in a car park in Rochdale, this time reading a paper and texting around to see what the chances were that I would be heading straight up to Newton Aycliffe.

Alan had sent me a photo of Consett's 4G pitch last night, covered in snow, leading to the postponement of the South Shields v Morpeth Town game. We had heard from Colin McNeillie though, in Newton Aycliffe, to say all the snow in the North East had evaded them and there was a chance it could be on. Where there wasn't snow overnight though, in the North East, there was frost and as we had heard the pitch was like a paddy field earlier in the week, I couldn't see there being much chance of them playing on a frozen paddy field. Still, where there is life there is hope and I clung on to the hope that they may announce last minute that the game would be moved to a local all weather pitch – not one as snowy as Consett though.

Fate was against us though and before ten, I had a text from Alan to say it was off and was being re-scheduled for next Saturday. This was particularly annoying as I had swopped from this week to next at work and will now have to miss it, if it does go ahead, which must, as ever, be doubtful. Alan tried to make alternative plans to go to Daventry Town or Charnock Richard today (only a couple of miles from my house in Euxton) but Charnock Richard was soon postponed too and Daventry Town had a midday pitch inspection so Alan didn't want to risk getting half way down before finding out it was off. It was the right call as their game against Coalville Town didn't pass the inspection.

According to Alan, Gordon can't make next Saturday either so he'll be heading up to Newton Aycliffe alone. If we ever do the FA Vase again, we need to start in the Southern section.

Sunday 17th January 2016

With most of Northern English football falling victim to the weather yesterday, it was good to at least get 'The Non-League Paper' this morning to catch up on what has been happening in Non-League football, both on and off the pitch, around the country. There was an interesting article about Steve Claridge, the former Pompey and Leicester City striker (to name but two of his many clubs) who is now manager of Salisbury. As Hereford have been formed out of the ashes of Hereford United, Salisbury have risen from the ashes of Salisbury City and are currently scoring goals for fun, having bagged sixty in their last twelve games. Apparently there is much talk about it being an all 'Phoenix' FA Vase Final between Salisbury and Hereford, but as Claridge rightly pointed out in the article, the Northern League teams are pretty good!

A few FA Vase games did take place yesterday, with Hereford keeping alive the aforementioned 'Phoenix' final as they put six past Leicester Nirvana without reply at Edgar Street, in front of a mere 2,842 at Edgar Street! Thankfully for Alan, Newport (IOW) also played but they went out 2-1 after extra time to Ashford United, meaning Alan will not have to venture over to the Isle of Wight. I am saying 'Alan' rather than us now, as I will have missed three games if Newton Aycliffe v Marske United goes ahead next week and have conceded that 'The Unbreakable Vase' has become just that for me, 'Unbreakable'.

There was a total of six Vase games yesterday with Dunston UTS, Hartley Wintney, Hereford, Kidlington, Bristol Manor Farm and Ashford United progressing. There are twenty two teams left in the competition now but with some better weather over the next two weekends, this could be down to eight in a fortnight.

With regards to Alan's FA Sunday Cup adventures, he is still awaiting the tie between Newton Aycliffe WMC and Burradon & New Fordley to take place so the winners can play the team he's following, Hardwick Social. It was due to take place today, but, surprise, surprise it was postponed.

Monday 18th January 2016

The FA Sunday Cup Quarter Final draw took place today. Alan's quarter of the draw looks like this:-

OJM (Willenhall) or Mayfair Liverpool (Marine) v Newton Aycliffe WMC or Burradon & New Fordley or Hardwick Social.

Straight forward enough! Actually, Alan says that he's quite relieved because this means that once it eventually gets around to the Quarter Final, he knows he is out of the North East which seems to be getting the most postponements (closely followed by the North West). Marine is in Crosby, Merseyside and Willenhall is in the Wolverhampton area of the West Midlands so he's hoping for a bit of drier weather.

Friday 22nd January 2016

The torrential rain/freezing temperatures/snow have all been avoided this week in the North of England and Alan is once again clinging to the hope of getting to a Saturday FA Vase game in the North East . He kept texting me at work this afternoon asking me what the weather was like as it had stopped raining in Manchester! Not sure dry weather in Southport will help too much but he seemed to be taking re-assurance from the fact that the sun had come out in Failsworth. Anyway, given he is the only one going, I will pass the baton on to Alan for tomorrow's game. Alan's a more than capable writer when he sets his mind on it, but he is also a prolific talker and social butterfly and tends to neglect his writing duties because he is too busy telling everyone his groundhopping stories. He is under strict instructions not to come home with an empty note pad tomorrow, so ladies and gentlemen, I give you Alan Oliver. For those that know him, don't worry, he has been warned the 'C' and 'F' words are out!

CHAPTER FOURTEEN

Saturday 23rd January 2016

The FA VASE – 4th Round Proper

Newton Aycliffe v Marske United

Written by The Casual Hopper

When Gordon and I managed to get up to New Ferens Park to see the Newton Aycliffe versus Atherton Collieries game finally take place, on a 3G surface, I had said to (my namesake) Allan Oliver and Steve Cunliffe, Aycliffe's Chairman and Secretary,

"Will you be playing Marske here?"

"Oh, we won't be playing them here," they replied, "it'll be at our place."

I can understand their keenness to play a big game at home, but we already know from experience, it's a home that retains more water than a leaky boat. The pressure to get this game on is growing too, as the next round is to be in Surrey next Saturday. As I am writing this, it is lunch time on Friday and it is doing what Manchester does best – absolutely pissing down. I hope it's drier up at Aycliffe's Moore Lane ground.

The fact it is pissing down in Greater Manchester might actually help me. I already knew Calvin was ruled out for tomorrow due to work commitments but Gordon, who has a 100% Vase record so far, was a question mark. He has a referee's course to host in Litherland tomorrow morning and only a fully qualified ref can take it. The only possible referee who can stand in for him, is due to be officiating at Eagley in the West Lancashire League tomorrow, but has said he will stand in for Gordon, if the Eagley game is off. I spoke to Gordon earlier and he was thinking this rain might lead to a postponement at Eagley, but I reminded him that the forecast was for rain until now (midday) and then dry weather until tomorrow evening…

It is now 9pm on Friday evening and Gordon has just phoned. Sure enough, it has been dry all afternoon and tonight and Gordon has said what I was thinking,

"It doesn't look good mate, this Eagley game looks likely to be on."

I told him that with the sky being clear it might freeze but he said he wouldn't know for sure until 8.30 tomorrow morning, but to plan to get the train because as things stand he won't be able to give me a lift. There were no issues there, I'd already got my trains sussed out.

Now I can explain – this FA adventure has been fantastic but it's been a bit diluted for me in respect of the amount of times we've gone in the car. Don't get me wrong, I've enjoyed the company, but being a ground hopper these last ten years has taught me that it's not just the grounds you visit, it's the people you meet along the way.

When we did the FA Cup journey, for the Workington-Stourbridge game, Calvin didn't have room in his car as he had already had five in, so me, Jordan and Phil Cooper had to arrange a train journey that circumvented Northumbria. We travelled from Manchester to Workington via Carlisle, where we met a single mother, her daughter and the daughter's friend who was travelling to meet her Dad in Glasgow. We also got chatting to a bloke on his own, who can only be described as 'quirky' who was going up to the Lake District to teach a rock climbing class. He was into extreme sports, studying Law and was eating sugar snap peas at 6am. He said he either gets the train or hitchhikes and when I asked whether it was dangerous to be hitchhiking in this day and age, he said it wasn't because he took a photograph of the number plate and text it to his parents. Very strange!

It's therefore not alien to me to arrange a train journey as it's something I've been doing most Saturdays for the last ten years. One of the trickier ones looked like being Boston just before Christmas last year in the FA Trophy when it looked like I was going to have three train changes after the match and arrive back in Manchester at 7am. Luckily, Calvin was able to give me a lift so I avoided that one.

Tomorrow, I am getting the 9.57am, Manchester to Thornaby where I will change and get the train to Newton Aycliffe, arriving at 13.08 with a two and a half mile walk to the ground which will be no problem.

Saturday 23rd January 2016

When I spoke to Gordon last night, I said I'd make it to Manchester Piccadilly before he was due to ring me at half past eight. That would mean that I would have the option of jumping on a train and meeting him in either Liverpool or up in Darlington.

At Piccadilly, I bumped into some City old boys who were going to West Ham's Boleyn ground for the last time. They were heading down on the 8.45 train to London Euston – pretty good, eh, since we (City) weren't kicking off until half past five! Plenty of time for more than a few scoops and a chance to visit numerous boozers before the match. I have to say, the City away days were always a bit special. I think we all know the proper fans can be found on these away days and I'm proud to say that I was one until I left to take up my Non-League journeys. I must admit I do miss it sometimes. Well, not so much City as the people, the supporters, the lads so to speak. So, it was great to bump into them every now and then.

Anyway, 8.30 my phone goes and it's Gordon. The tone of his voice gives it away, he can't make it. I'm genuinely gutted his 100% Vase record has gone. He reminds me to take notes and get the programmes. Bloody Hell – him and Calvin are like two old women sometimes. I know mate, I know!

With Gordon not coming, I was now an hour in front. I know, I'll get the 8:57 to Thornaby from Platform One, so I went and got my customary Latte from the little coffee shop near Platform Ten which sells them for only £1.50 and then headed back to Platform One in good time for the TransPennine to Thornaby via Stalyvegas, Huddersfield, Leeds, York etc. It tickles me people boarding these trains stand up instead of checking the reserved ticket that's displayed on the seat. For example, mine read reserved from Leeds to Middlesbrough – that'll do me, table seat as well, with mains connector to charge my mobile whilst updating my Facebook/Twitter accounts – hey, listen I'm @thecasualhopper you know!

It was only when we arrived in Leeds that I twigged that Aycliffe is an infrequent service and I'm between times now. Do I carry on to Thornaby or get off at York and get another brew, then get back on the right train? I decided to get off at York as Thornaby's not got much to offer. I spent roughly forty minutes in York station making a Caramel Latte last in the Pumpkin Patch rail bar. Oh and I found a pound on the floor as well – hey, it all adds up.

I boarded the 11.15 to Thornaby, got a table seat again, plugged my phone in and then a voice said,

"You're in our seats, mate!"

"Sorry," I replied, "I'll move opposite."

Thing is, I'll only ever travel facing forwards on a train. Don't ask, it's a travel sickness thing from when I was a kid. The two seats opposite weren't taken so after an explanation, the two lads/men agreed to sit facing me, travelling backwards. Once they settled into their seats, I noticed a red scarf peering through one of their jackets,

"Ahh, you're off to the Middlesbrough match then?"

"No mate, we're Bournemouth. We're playing Sunderland, where are you off to?"

"Newton Aycliffe," I replied.

"Newton Aycliffe???"

Puzzled looks, ha ha! It baffles them all the time. They hear my broad Mancunian accent and it gets them guessing everywhere I go. They get the story…the three FA Cups, Non-League, 404 grounds groundhopping, Man City etc. They love it, they all do. We exchange stories of Luther Blissett's equaliser at Maine Road that meant we had to get something at Bradford to be promoted in '87. We then talk about Ian Bishop and Dean Court, me doing the '92' and then before you know it we are at Thornaby. I wished them good luck and then I'm on Platform One waiting for the 12.26 to Newton Aycliffe. I arrive at my destination along with two cyclists who point me in the direction of the town centre and inform me it's a twenty five minute walk to the ground. It would have been too, if I hadn't turned right instead of left on Shafto Way. Luckily, I realised soon enough and doubled back making my two and a half mile walk a three mile one. Fortunately for me Aycliffe is flat, unlike Colne, which is an uphill hike to their stadium. It's alright sourcing directions on the AA AutoRoute but it doesn't tell you about hills.

A short walk to Creighton Road and I'm here, Moore Lane Park, home of Newton Aycliffe. Rugby ground to my left and football ground behind the Social Club. I get my customary picture uploaded to let my social network know I've arrived. I enter the club just as the massive Marske contingent arrive, two coachloads of them. I was later informed that Newton Aycliffe's secretary, Stephen Cunliffe, had misjudged his programme print by a mile and had only had fifty printed. I'm glad that my three are reserved. I head left out the Social club to the turnstile, paying my £6 entrance fee. As I step through, an elderly gent stops me,

"Are you the groundhopper?" he asks.

When I tell him I am, he presents me with my three programmes and I give him £3. A pound each – bargain. I ask where Steve Cunliffe and Allan Oliver are and I'm directed towards the dressing rooms. When I arrive, it's handshakes all round and quizzical looks from Aycliffe's manager and assistant, as I am introduced as the groundhopping Alan Oliver. I think it's lost on them as they are too wrapped up with the job in hand of progressing to the next round to try to understand my mission/exploits. Allan and I get a coffee each and he invites me to his office. He's surprised to see me on my own and I explain Calvin and Gordon's positions and we start to talk football. He was wanting to avoid Marske although he thought if his team were up for it, they would give Marske a good game. It wasn't that he was nervous of them, just cautious, over cautious as it turned out.

The conversation moved away from today's game and on to football in general. We talked about Sunderland and City, about Dennis Tueart, Dave Watson, Colin Bell and Colin Todd, his passion for football, Aycliffe and his hopes and aspirations. We talked about Aycliffe's manager and how his ideas mirrored Allan's and how they both lived and breathed the game. We then walked halfway around the ground and it suddenly became clear why they wanted the tie here. The pitch was very heavy and sanded near the dug outs. I could only think that Marske are a footballing side and the pitch was going to be a good leveller. Having said that, Aycliffe can knock it around well too. They were pretty decent on the 3G against Atherton Collieries in the previous round.

It was getting around to half past two, so I let Allan get on with his pre-match business and I had a wander to decide where it would be best to watch. I usually watch from somewhere near the dugouts but I'd noticed that the vocal Marske contingent had adopted the whole of that side as their own. This was unusual in non-

League as a lot of fans normally congregate behind the goal their team is attacking then swap sides at half-time. So I ended up opposite the dugouts, on the Aycliffe side, if you like. I position myself just to the right of the two stands, level with the eighteen yard box, at the end Aycliffe decide to defend in the first half. Marske are defending the turnstiles/changing room end in their red and white hoops. Aycliffe are in all blue. After handshakes from the teams and a shout of 'seasiders' from the Marske fans, we are off.

    In the early stages it seemed that the Marske fans were more up for this game than their players who seemed subdued and couldn't string any passes together. I think it was a combination of the pitch and Aycliffe's defence, well marshalled by their impressive keeper, James Winter. Aycliffe, in contrast, seem well up for it. It's a proper Northern League duel with some hard but fair challenges going in from both teams. Having said that, some of the Marske challenges were a bit niggly and were getting punished by Mr Sowerby, the referee, much to the annoyance of the Marske fans. The majority of overly physical tackles were going in on Aycliffe's number ten, Dennis Knight. The Marske contingent were bellowing, 'Dive, dive, dive!' as if he was a human submarine, but he did take some hefty challenges and he didn't come across as a diver to me.

    Overall, the first half was a bit scrappy but Aycliffe were becoming more confident and dominant as the half progressed. They were unlucky too when winger Stuart Banks cross-come-shot evaded the keeper and came back off the post. When mentioning the Marske keeper, Rob Dean, I have to mention his pink goalkeeper kit, a brave choice in this gritty Northern League encounter.

Allan Oliver had earlier pinpointed Marske's centre forward, Jamie Owens, as their danger man. He had had a couple of half chances in the half but generally the Aycliffe defence of Brown, Pattinson, Kitchen and Mitton had kept the Marske forwards quiet with Brian Close in Aycliffe's midfield having a decent game too. Just before half time I moved behind the goal Aycliffe were attacking, so I was near the hospitality room at half-time so I could nip in and see Allan. More by luck than judgement, I was in the ideal place to see Aycliffe take the lead just on the stroke of half time. It was coolly put away by Matty Moffat who controlled the ball on his chest then thigh before shooting into the net. He jumped over the barrier by the goal to celebrate, nearly knocking Aycliffe's photographer, Colin McNeillie, off his feet.

The half-time whistle went soon after and I went to see Allan Oliver, thinking a one-nil lead was no more than Aycliffe deserved.

"Well, are we alright?" Allan asked when I saw him in the hospitality room.

"Alright?" I said, "I think you know you are, mate. Marske haven't turned up.

Allan wasn't counting any chickens and was expecting a different Marske in the second half.

A coffee and a sandwich or two and it was back out for the second half, once again adopting a position near Colin, the photographer. The game almost restarted how the first half had finished too, with Moffat going close again. The second half turned out to be similar to the first in many ways with Marske having some possession but no shots of note to test Winter in the Aycliffe goal. It was Newton Aycliffe who were posing the greater questions with Brian Close again running everything. Aycliffe sensed another goal would seal it and sure enough in the 76th minute Moffat won a tackle near the right corner flag, right in front of us. Moffat entered the penalty area unchallenged and squared the ball to Stuart Banks who put the game to bed with a deft finish. Aycliffe's fans were in raptures and Marske's vocal support were finally muted. 2-0 was how it finished with Brian Close my 'Man of The Match' with Moffat running him close and notable performances from Aycliffe's back four. In fact, the whole of the team put a performance in. It was very reminiscent of North Ferriby United in our FA Trophy adventure last season.

Allan Oliver, Aycliffe's Chairman was well chuffed, as was everyone associated with the club. I ended up in the clubhouse with them as I waited for a taxi to Darlington. I struck up a conversation with a Marske fan who was very gracious in defeat, concurring with me that his team had left their performance in the dressing room, to his bemusement. Take nothing away from Newton Aycliffe though, they were outstanding from start to finish. So it will be Newton Aycliffe who will be heading down with us to Surrey next week to face Camberley Town of the Combined Counties Premier in the 5th Round. I headed home glad that I had actually managed a visit to Moore Lane Park, as with postponements, bad weather and the likes, there were times I thought it may never happen.

FINAL SCORE :- NEWTON AYCLIFFE 2 MARSKE UNITED 0

FA VASE GOALS :- 28 in 6 games.

CHAPTER FIFTEEN

Wednesday 27th January 2016

I received a lengthy email tonight from Alan with his notes from Saturday's game. I think he must have been getting sick and tired of me and Gordon mithering him about taking notes and thought 'I'll bloody show them!' Glad he did though.

One thing Alan didn't mention, which I will just touch on briefly, was how his wife was getting on since her breast cancer diagnosis. Last week, Jo reached the halfway mark in her radiotherapy sessions. She has now completed ten sessions with ten more to go. From an outsiders perspective it is impossible not to admire how Jo, Alan and their daughter, Jordan, have dealt with the adversity fate has thrown their way. They remain positive, strong and resilient and determined to look on the bright side.

You might think that with everything going on in his home life and with his commitment to doing the FA Vase and FA Sunday Cup games that Alan may have lost a bit of focus on his fundraising campaign for 'The Christie', but typically he has recently agreed to take part in a new challenge. On 2nd July 2016, he will, along with several close friends, be trekking 26.2 miles over hill and dale in Glencoe, Scotland, as they attempt to complete 'The Glencoe Challenge'. Alan isn't the tallest or leanest of men, so walking a marathon distance on undulating hillside, isn't going to come easy to his fifty-plus year old frame, but I have no doubt he will rise to the challenge. I don't think I have ever met anyone in my life who enjoys a challenge as much as Alan!

With this final part of the trilogy being mainly focused on the Vase with some side stories about family (both Alan's and mine), I have tried not to get too sidetracked by incorporating the teams we support. Tonight, however, Alan's team, Manchester City played my team, Everton, in the Second Leg of Football League Cup Semi Final at the Etihad. Everton were 2-1 ahead from the first leg and despite this I did not feel confident at all. Everton are having a very indifferent season under Roberto Martinez and the positivity about my club expressed during the writing of 'Another Saturday & Sweet FA' has sadly evaporated as we seem to be getting worse and worse under his stewardship. I think one of the main issues for me is that we have two goalkeepers who are not good enough to represent a side looking to finish in the 'Top Six' in the Premier League. Tim Howard has had a fine career and until twelve months ago, I thought he did a good job for Everton but he was always more of a shot stopper than a keeper who commanded his box and now age is starting to catch up with him, he needs to be replaced. In my opinion, Martinez has taken too long to appreciate a fact that most Evertonians were blatantly aware of and even more concerning was that he did not have a top class replacement prepared. Joel is no more than adequate and a long way from top class.

Tonight, Everton went 1-0 up on the night and 3-1 on aggregate when a dangerous run by Ross Barkley was ended with a cool, low finish but Everton only held on to the lead for a few minutes before City equalised. It stayed 1-1 until the 70th minute when Raheem Sterling took the ball to the byline (and beyond it) before pulling the ball back for De Bruyne to make it 2-1 on the night and three all on aggregate. The ball must have been a yard out before the cut back and although it was a ridiculous decision, City were completely dominant at that stage and I don't think we (Everton) would have held out for another twenty minutes. We may have managed extra time though, which didn't happen after De Bruyne's goal as Aguero took City to Wembley with the tie winning goal six minutes later. They will play Liverpool in the Final.

Martinez is under a lot of pressure currently and when the first waves of discontent began towards the end of last season, I thought they were ridiculous but now, if we don't finish the season strongly, with at least an appearance in the FA Cup final and much improved League form, then I think Martinez should depart at the end of the season.

With regards to Saturday's FA VASE trip, I am currently 99% sure that I won't be going. When we did the FA Cup journey, there was very much a team feel to it with both Alan and myself going to every game, but my Dad and Phil Cooper also went to most games and Alan's daughter, Jordan, went to several. The FA Trophy was more just Alan and myself, with guest appearances from time to time, especially from Jamie Lowe at North Ferriby, but the FA Vase has been Alan's journey ably supported by Gordon Johnson and with me playing a peripheral role. On Saturday, it is my 45th birthday, Brad is playing for Rochdale u18s against Accrington Stanley u18s and then has to go to Rochdale's Spotland ground, along with all the other Academy players, as it is Academy Day. They will all go around the edge of the pitch at half time of Rochdale's game against Burton Albion. As Alan and I have said to each other a lot over the last three seasons, the football is great but family is the most important thing. Having already missed three of the six Vase games, it doesn't feel right to be spending every waking hour of my birthday going to and from Camberley Town against Newton Aycliffe when my son has an important game in his own football development. I also want to spend the evening with Alison, my wife. Thus, once again writing duties will pass to Gordon or Alan.

Before I pass writing duties on, in the FA Sunday Cup Alan was awaiting the victors from the game between Newton Aycliffe WMC and Burradon & New Fordley. It was Burradon that emerged victorious, winning 3-1. After five postponements of this tie, Alan is delighted he can finally go to his next FA Sunday Cup game, which will be Burradon & New Fordley versus Hardwick Social, on Sunday 7th February at Bedlington Terriers for a place in the Quarter Final.

CHAPTER SIXTEEN

Saturday 30th January 2016

The FA VASE – 5th Round Proper

Camberley Town v Newton Aycliffe

Written by Gordon The Ref

So, after the usual pre-match phone calls, Facebook and Twitter exchanges yesterday, arrangements are all sorted for the trip down to Camberley's Krooner Park ground in Surrey. The home club had certainly pushed the boat out in the week leading up to the game with a number of match day sponsors secured and a bumper crowd expected. Camberley had highlighted the fact that they last made it through to the FA Vase Quarter Final exactly thirty years ago, in 1986, at which point they were beaten 5-1 by the eventual winners, Halesowen Town.

I was up at seven and by twenty five past I was on my way to pick up Alan Oliver. It was just going to be the two of us as Calvin is on parental duties, taking his son to play in goal once again for Rochdale AFC under 18s. I had agreed to pick Alan up at Crewe station and as I turned onto the road of the station, Alan phoned to say he had just arrived.

"I know, mate, I can see you right in front of me," I replied and promptly pulled up alongside him. Timed to perfection, can the rest of the day go so well? Only time will tell.

"Hang on a minute," Alan says before we set off and promptly delves into the plastic carry bag he's holding to proudly produce a Newton Aycliffe scarf, "I got given this last week at the game by Allan Oliver, you don't mind me putting it in the car window, do you?"

"Carry on," I said, not for one minute thinking I had any say in the matter.

I opened the back door of the car and Alan shuffled in and spread the scarf across the rear parcel shelf.

With the scarf in place, we were on the road to Surrey, but we weren't even out of Crewe when Alan chirped up again.

"Do you reckon we'll have chance to stop off at Walsall Woods FC on the way down, mate? It's not far off the M6 and we can wind up Nathan, Saul and the City lads if we do."

Apparently the City lads are always winding Alan up about whether he has ever been to Walsall Woods. Alan then goes on to explain that he's managed to get hold of one of their Manchester City flags and wants to call in at Walsall Woods to get some photographs there with the 'Borrowed' (or 'Stolen') flag ahead of the City lads turning up later in the day en route to their FA Cup match at Aston Villa. It's a flag with the City crest in the middle of the lyrics from the chorus of the James song 'How Was It For You?' Looking at the route timings to Surrey, I knew we had plenty of time, so the plan was hatched and a detour via Walsall Woods was factored into the day's journey.

By quarter to ten, we were at Walsall Woods promptly unfurling the City flag ready to get a few snaps to post on Facebook and Twitter. Staff and volunteers are already at the ground getting ready for the Manchester City contingent who had pre-booked their regular visit there for pre-match refreshments prior to playing away in the Midlands area. We had a couple of coffees in the club tea bar and posted our photos onto social media. As we were enjoying our drinks a call to the club came in to confirm the City coaches were only twenty minutes away.

"Right, let's get out of here," says Alan and the flag was duly thrown into the back of the car and we were quickly back on the road before the flag could be snatched back by its rightful owner.

The journey down South was unusually congestion free, aided by heading down the M6 toll, then the M42 and M40 with Alan updating me along the way with his experiences from the previous week at the Newton Aycliffe v Marske United game. Alan was gushing about the red carpet treatment he had received from his namesake Allan Oliver, the Chairman of Newton Aycliffe, the boardroom hospitality and the Newton Aycliffe scarf.

"Well," I responded, "I've managed to blag us free entry for the game today."

"You get where water can't," Alan replied, "how have you managed that then?"

I explained to Alan that one of the Assistant Referees appointed to the game is a colleague, Nick Dunn, from Kent FA. I'd officiated with Nick at the Iber Cup International Youth Football tournament in Lisbon, Portugal in the summers of both 2014 and 2015, together with working with him on a National FA referee exchange programme with the Danish FA which had been hosted in Liverpool in 2015. I'd contacted Nick and as he hadn't used his guest tickets, promised he would leave them on the gate for us.

By now we were well down the M40 and my stomach was rumbling so I decided to have a pit stop and lunch break at Beaconsfield Services.

"This is the one that has a Wetherspoons pub on the services, isn't it?" I ask Alan.

"You're planning on having a pint, are you?" Alan replied.

"No, was just saying, that's all! I'll be falling asleep at the game if I have a pint now," I laughed.

So, we pull off the motorway towards the service station and just as we do, Alan lets out an excited cry,

"Look! Another football ground!"

Sure enough, just off the M40 and across the road from Beaconsfield Service Station is none other than Holloways Park, the home ground of Beaconsfield CYOB FC who are currently ground sharing with Slough Town FC as their tenants.

"I'm thinking we could wind the City lads up again here," Alan suggests, as we walk into the service station. We sat down for a KFC lunch, during which we are joined by a couple of coachloads of Stoke City fans who were heading towards South London for their team's FA Cup tie at Crystal Palace. A plan was then hatched to nip across to Beaconsfield's ground to give the City flag another outing.

By five past twelve, we had pulled up at the car park at Holloways Park. There were four cars and a white van parked outside the club house and the ground is open.

"Result," shouts Alan, as we drove across the car park, "we won't have to climb over the wall to get in."

It was a result for me too, as I had visions of having to hoist Alan up, with me being over six feet tall and Alan not being much more than five feet tall. He may not be tall but he'd have still been heavy! Out came the Manchester City flag again and we headed down through the tunnel and dressing room area towards the pitch side. As we entered the ground, we spotted two of the club volunteers working in the dugout across the far side of the ground. Not wanting to alarm them, we headed over and asked for permission to take a few photographs inside the ground.

"No problem at all," was the reply, once we had explained our plans.

A nice photo of Alan was then taken with the City flag with a comment saying, 'Your flag has been to more grounds than you', duly posted on to Twitter and Facebook for the attention of Alan's Manchester City mates, Nathan and Saul Foy. We then set off again, chuckling to ourselves, as we headed on to the M25.

From the M25, we headed on to the M3 and by 1.20pm we had arrived in plenty of time at Camberley Town's Krooner Park ground. We took a few obligatory photos outside the ground and put our newly purchased programmes into the car just in time for the Newton Aycliffe team coach to arrive. We headed through the turnstile without having to pay, thanks to Assistant Ref, Nick Dunn and once inside it was time to catch up with Newton's Chairman, the other Allan Oliver, the club secretary Stephen Cunliffe and fellow ground hopper, photographer and Newton Aycliffe fan, Colin McNeillie. We then wandered around the ground for a few photographs before heading into the clubhouse for a chat and catch up with the rest of the Newton Aycliffe contingent and the local followers of Camberley Town.

Whilst chatting in the club house, Alan has one of those looks on his face, the type of look that suggests his mind is working overtime.

"What's his name there?" Al asks pointing to a group stood near to one end of the bar.

I had a look but no names sprang to mind.

"No idea."

"It's Marcus something, he used to play for Wimbledon and Watford."

"Marcus Gayle?"

"Yeh, that's him."

"Are you sure?" I asked, not convinced.

Colin McNeillie came over to join us and Alan asked him if he recognised Marcus Gayle.

"No idea if it's him or not, Alan. Am not sure I'd know even if it was him."

"Hang on a minute," I said and downloaded a picture of Marcus Gayle on Google images. It's a picture from his Watford playing days. All three of us gather around to look at it. Colin and I are now unconvinced and although it has put doubts into Alan's head, he is still repeating, perhaps to convince himself,

"It's him! I'm telling you, it's definitely him!"

"For God's sake, Alan, just go and ask him then!" I urged.

Alan doesn't need asking twice for things like that, so marched straight over to the group of two males and a female at the end of the bar.

"This could be funny," I said to Colin.

Next thing you know, a triumphant smirk spreads across Alan's face and then he shouts across, telling the whole bar,

"I told you! It's him! IT IS MARCUS GAYLE!"

Marcus Gayle is now looking around the room bemused by all the attention he's getting. Colin and I went over to join them. We explained to Marcus that Alan was sure but we had downloaded a Google image of him and it had made us uncertain. Marcus asked to see it. When shown it, he proudly said,

"Yes, that's me at Watford."

To which the lady in the group said,

"Yes, but that's when you had hair."

We quickly concluded that must have been his wife.

Marcus Gayle had a long and distinguished football career. He was primarily a striker, but could also play on the wing and towards the end of his career was sometimes called upon to play centre back. He was London born, but represented Jamaica fourteen times, including playing a key role in Jamaica's appearances in the 1998 World Cup in France.

Gayle started his career at Brentford but in March 1994 moved to Wimbledon in a £250,000 move and had several successful seasons there, including 1996-97 when he scored 13 goals, helping Wimbledon to finish eighth in the Premier League and reach the Semi Final of both domestic cups. He scored the winner in Wimbledon's 1-0 fourth round victory over Manchester United.

In 1999-2000, Wimbledon were relegated after an amazing 14 year stay in the top flight. Gayle stayed loyal but in March 2001 had a £1 million move to Scottish Premier League giants, Rangers. He only played four times though before moving back down South to join Gianluca Vialli's new look side in a £900,000 switch.

Hampered by a back injury, Gayle only played fourteen games in his first season at Watford, but after Vialli's departure, Gayle was switched to centre back by new boss, Ray Lewington and won 'Player Of The Season' in his new role and agreed to defer some of his wages to help with the clubs financial difficulties. Gayle remained at Watford until Lewington was sacked in 2005, departing two days later, when he rejoined Brentford.

After a couple of seasons at Brentford, he joined Aldershot Town and then signed for AFC Wimbledon, becoming only the second player, after Jermaine Darlington, to play for both AFC Wimbledon and the old Wimbledon FC. He helped them to promotion to the Conference South before retiring that summer.

We had a great half hour with Marcus, spent talking everything football, from his career in the game through to the work he currently does in the South London area working alongside Troy Townsend, Andros Townsend's father, for the PFA, acting as a life coach for young footballers, trying to keep them on the straight and narrow and away from the gang culture that is still quite prominent in the South London area. Marcus explained that he was down to watch this game as he lives locally and his son plays for the Camberley Town u18s Youth team. He stated he had a season ticket at Brentford but would come down to Camberley whenever Brentford weren't at home. He advised that Camberley were a big, physical team and were not adverse to 'mixing it' when they needed to.

Before we realised it, it was nearly time for kick off so we said our goodbyes to Marcus and his friends and headed out for the game.

"Shall I go and tell the Newton lads?" Alan asked.

"Tell them what?" I questioned.

"About Camberley being a big, physical side."

"Bit late now," I said, pointing towards the two teams lined up alongside one another in the cage area leading from the dressing rooms to the field of play.

There was quite a good crowd on the ground by now with the majority congregated around the club house and main stand area, so we headed to the opposite corner of the ground from the clubhouse to watch the first half from there. Once in position, we found ourselves standing next to Allan Oliver (Aycliffe's Chairman) and Stephen Cunliffe, behind my assistant referee mate, Nick Dunn. I did try to distract Nick for the first fifteen minutes, but he correctly ignored me and maintained his focus on the field of play.

The game started at quite a frantic pace and within sixty seconds, Camberley's number 6, Dan Jewell, had put a late and heavy challenge on Newton Aycliffe's number 8, Ashley Coffey, bringing the first free kick of the game. A minute later and Camberley's number 9, Perry Coles, put in a similarly late and heavy challenge on Newton's number 3, Neil Pattison, which rightly brought the first yellow card from referee, Ian Fissenden.

"They are a physical lot, aren't they?" shouted out Alan.

"What's that?" asked Aycliffe's Chairman, Allan.

"We got told by Marcus Gayle in the clubhouse that Camberley are a physical team," Alan explained.

"As long as we can keep eleven on the pitch, we should have a chance," was Allan from Aycliffe's response. An enlightened comment given what was to follow in the next hour and a half.

Eleven minutes into the game and following another heavy challenge Camberley's Dan Jewell and Newton Aycliffe's Matty Moffat square up to one another in an aggressive manner.

"Matty! Matty! Walk away, don't get involved," yelled Allan Oliver, Newton Aycliffe Chairman, from beside us.

On this occasion the ref chose to man manage the situation with a stern telling off issued to both players as opposed to resorting to the use of his yellow card again. The tone was certainly set though with the game continuing as a very physical affair. Newton Aycliffe weren't really creating any noteworthy attempts on goal whilst Camberley Town were relying on their long throw specialist, Chris Ellis, to try to creat some mayhem in the Aycliffe box.

After twenty eight minutes Allan Oliver turned to us, and in rather a dejected tone said,

"We haven't got going yet."

It wasn't until the 36th minute that Newton Aycliffe managed to get what was their first real opportunity of the game. They were awarded a free kick just outside the Camberley Town penalty area, to the right side of the field of play. The two centre halves raced forwards, but their efforts were wasted as Dennis Knight needlessly wasted the chance, firing what could only be described as a speculative effort, twenty five feet over the cross bar and into the high netting positioned behind the goal, specifically there to prevent such efforts leaving the ground.

Forty minutes in and it all started to go wrong for the visitors from the North East. They took a short goal kick but lost possession, allowing Camberley Town number nine, Perry Coles, to advance on goal from the right side of the penalty area. As Newton Aycliffe's goalkeeper, James Winter, committed himself, the Camberley striker retained his composure and neatly chipped the ball over the advancing keeper, to put the hosts into a one goal lead.

There were no further clear cut chances before half-time so our motley crew traipsed around the ground, Allan and Stephen heading off for some boardroom hospitality whilst Alan and I joined the long queue to get a half time brew.

By the time the second half started, Alan was still in the queue for the brews. Newton Aycliffe should have come out all guns blazing but they were slow out of the blocks and were duly punished. Two minutes into the second half and Camberley's Number 10, Rob Lazarczuk, was played in one on one with keeper, Winter. Again the home striker kept his calm and slotted home to give Camberley a two-nil lead.

Matters went from bad to worse for Aycliffe. In the 55th minute, they conceded a free kick on the half way line near to the technical areas. Whilst disputing the decision, they switched off, allowing Camberley to take a quick one. The ball was fired forwards towards centre forward, Perry Coles who raced through and slammed the ball into the back of the net. Three-nil.

From the sidelines the body language of the Newton Aycliffe team spoke volumes as heads clearly dropped and shoulders slumped, classic signs of a team resigned to their fate. In an attempt to shake things up, Newton Aycliffe brought on sub, Jordan Laidler, but the game continued to be the scrappy and physical encounter it had been from the start.

With Newton Aycliffe heading out the FA Vase, they may have thought things could not get any worse, but unfortunately they did. In the 76th minute, a Camberley substitute, Marcus Cousins cynically tripped Newton Aycliffe's Ashley Coffey. The Aycliffe player reacted angrily, kicking out at Cousins which resulted in a mass confrontation between players from both teams. The result was inevitable with Cousins booked for the original foul and Coffey sent off for his retaliatory kick. The correct decision by referee Fissenden.

On reflection, I probably shouldn't have said what I did, but a couple of minutes later, I pointed out to Al that Newton Aycliffe hadn't had a shot on target all game. From his facial reaction, I could tell it probably wasn't what Allan, the Aycliffe Chairman, wanted to hear at that point.

With around ten minutes to go, Camberley introduced their third and final sub with two goal hero, James Hubbard came on with Perry Coles coming off to a great ovation from the home supporters. A couple of minutes later, the home side were awarded a corner kick which was lofted high to the far post. Hubbard, having only just entered the fray, rose unmarked to head home the fourth goal of the game with his first touch of the ball.

The home team were now running amok against a crestfallen Aycliffe side. Camberley quickly regained possession from the kick off and had soon gained another corner. Rob Lazarczuk took it and it curled straight into the net, on the far post, without a touch. It had been that sort of day for Newton Aycliffe and was now five-nil.

The game as a contest was already over but it should have finished ten a side. Chris Ellis intentionally pulled back Aycliffe's Stuart Banks and having already received a yellow card, I was expecting him to receive another and his marching orders. Surprisingly, on this occasion, ref Fissenden opted for leniency and Ellis escaped with a ticking off.

To add insult to injury, in the third minute of stoppage time Aycliffe's Thomas Marshall received the final caution (yellow card) of the game for a late challenge on Camberley's Dale Webb. There should even have been a further booking when Jordan Laidler allowed his frustration get the better of him when caught offside and kicked the ball away high over the home team's cross bar. Such an offence should be a mandatory yellow card but Fissenden again opted for a stern talking to. In post-match discussions I did mention the rather inconsistent approach to the application of law by the referee. I noticed he had also allowed Camberley Town players to play in two different colours of long sleeved under armour, red and white, which should not really be happening at this level of football, especially in such a late stage of a prestigious FA competition.

After the final whistle blew, we said our goodbyes to a very dejected Allan Oliver, Stephen Cunliffe and Colin McNeillie from Newton Aycliffe and wished them all the best for the remainder of their season. We quickly nipped in to the clubhouse to say farewell to Marcus Gayle and we were soon our way back on the M3 motorway for the long journey home, contemplating where the Monday morning Quarter Final draw may take us and Camberley Town in February.

We had another good run on the roads and apart from a brief stop at Warwick Services on the M40 to refuel the car and refuel me and Alan with coffee, we arrived back at Crewe railway station for Alan to be dropped off at 8.00pm. I then headed back on to the M6 North for the final leg of the journey and received a call from Alan to say it was perfect timing as he managed to jump on to the 8.11pm train for Manchester.

"Travel arrangements have been good for the day at least," I replied.

"Shame we lost Aycliffe though. They're a nice bunch," Alan said sombrely.

Arrangements were then made to speak on Monday morning after the draw for the next round and I then phoned ahead to the Acropolis chippy in Ormskirk to order a chicken curry with fried rice meal which I happily tucked into when I arrive home just after nine. A very long, eventful but thoroughly enjoyable day was complete.

FINAL SCORE : Camberley Town 5 Newton Aycliffe 0

Goalscorers : Perry Coles (2), Rob Lazarczuk (2) & James Hubbard.

Man of the Match : Perry Coles

Attendance : 460.

FA VASE GOALS :- 33 in 7 games.

Sunday 31st January 2016

Thanks Gordon! Sounds like Alan and Gordon had a cracking day down in Camberley yesterday. It made me laugh thinking of them plotting a flag raising mission at Walsall Woods and Beaconsfield to wind up Saul and Nathan Foy. Two fifty odd year old blokes trying to get the better of two whippersnappers (Saul and Nathan are in their twenties). Us men never grow up.

My 45th birthday yesterday was a really enjoyable too. I took Brad over to Hyde United's Ewen Fields with my Dad to watch the Rochdale u18s game against Accrington Stanley u18s. Dad and I went over to Morrisons before kick off on a bitterly cold morning to have an English breakfast and then watched a highly entertaining game which unfortunately Accrington Stanley won 3-2. Unfortunately there don't appear to be any superstars amongst the second year scholars at Rochdale and other than Johny Diba, the goalkeeper who has already signed professional forms, I would be surprised if they sign anyone else. The lads seem to have sensed that and there is a dejected manner to their play currently. It's great experience for Brad to be playing two years up though and it should stand him in good stead for the next couple of seasons.

After the game, Dad went to have a chat with Paul Lodge, who is in charge of the Academy at Accrington. My Dad had Paul in teams at Everton when 'Lodgey' was just a kid and it still shocks my Dad to see lads he pictures as young men as grey haired fifty somethings. Lodge went on to play for Everton first team 24 times and one of my Dad's favourite football tales is 'Lodgey' playing against Spurs at Goodison and making an attempted slide tackle on Glenn Hoddle, by the dugouts, on a rain sodden pitch. As Lodge slid in, Hoddle dragged the ball away and Lodge kept sliding on his backside off the pitch as Hoddle struck a 60 yard cross field pass.

"Get us an Echo whilst you're out," quipped Colin Harvey from the Everton dugout, referring to the local Liverpool newspaper.

Anyway, after his chat we headed back to the car, put the heating on full blast and attempted to warm up. Once Brad arrived, we headed over to Spotland, Rochdale's ground, to watch them take on League One leaders, Burton Albion. As it was Academy day at Rochdale there were hundreds of kids of all age groups wandering around the ground in their Rochdale tracksuits with their Mums and Dads.

The game itself was an entertaining one. Callum Camps, himself a product of Rochdale's Academy, appropriately put Rochdale ahead in the 8th minute with a 25 yard strike into the keeper's top right corner. Brad said Camps had just gone to the dugouts to change shinpads and had one in his hand and the other tucked in his briefs when he took the shot. Ian Henderson doubled Rochdale's advantage in the 24th minute when he was brought down in the penalty area and converted the resultant spot kick himself.

It was a bitterly cold afternoon and the game was played out amongst intermittent snow flurries. It seemed immediately evident that I had moved into my late forties as I was full of muscular aches and pains from the cold, especially in my neck. I still love watching football with my Dad though, as he still has a coach's eye for the game and spots finer details that I would never spot, especially in relation to centre backs. It's funny how when I'm at a game with Gordon, Alan and my Dad, Gordon focuses on the officials, my Dad on the centre backs, me on the goalkeepers and Alan on the general play!

Rochdale kept their 2-0 lead until late in the second half when Lucas Akins lobbed Josh Lillis in the Rochdale goal, in the 78th minute. It was a nervous final quarter of an hour, including injury time, after that for Rochdale, but they emerged as deserved victors. Burton Albion remain top with Rochdale now in a comfortable mid-table position with an outside chance of reaching the play offs if they finish the season with a run of victories. With average crowds of two to three thousand though, it is a fine achievement for Rochdale to now be considered a mid-table League One side.

After the football, my evening was spent with Alison, Brad and Joel with a good meal (ribeye steak) and a few beers. It did take me half the evening to warm up though. Today, as I update my notes in the car, I am in Rochdale again, as Brad has a match on the all weather for Rochdale under 16s against Wigan Athletic under 16s. I still have a crick in my next from yesterday.

I still help my younger son with his paper round but just on a Sunday now. It gives me the chance to grab 'The Non-League Paper' and then an hour to read it in the car prior to Brad's Sunday kick off.

Yesterday, four of the other FA VASE 5th Round games took place and also a 4th Round game, as a few sides are still playing catch up due to the wet winter. Up in the North East, Morpeth Town against North Shield's 4th Round game once again fell victim to the weather as the pitch was waterlogged. I'm guessing Alan will be pleased he's dodged a bullet though as Cornwall's Bodmin Town managed to play their 4th Round tie against Ipswich Wanderers but lost 3-1. Apparently it was a 750 mile round trip from Ipswich!

In the 5th Round, Sunderland RCA lost 3-2 at home to Bristol Manor Farm who have reached the Quarter Finals for the first time in their history. That is another mammoth journey from Bristol to Sunderland. Mammoth journeys must have been the order of the day yesterday, as Dunston UTS, one of Shaunee Smith's favoured teams, as they are from Gateshead, had to travel all the way down to Kent to play Ashford United. Unfortunately, the two teams could not be separated after two hours of football. The game finished 1-1 after extra time, so Ashford United will now have to travel all the way back up to Gateshead for the replay. In the final two games, Steve Claridge's Salisbury defeated Nuneaton Griff 3-0 and Kidlington won away at Cleethorpes. The draw is tomorrow and no idea where Alan and Gordon (and possibly me) will be heading but one thing is for sure, it won't be local!

Monday 1st February 2016

Alan is excited. The FA Vase Quarter Final draw was made today and Camberley Town were drawn away at either Hartley Wintney FC or Hereford. Having investigated it, Alan discovered that Hartley Wintney is a village between Basingstoke and Farnborough. Always one to see omens in things, Alan is wondering whether we will follow a village side to Wembley like we did in the FA Trophy last season. One thing is for certain, they will have to be a damn fine village side to beat Hereford who are the big favourites to win the Vase.

When I say 'we' will follow them to Wembley, it isn't so much a 'we' as a 'they'. The 'Vase' is very much Alan and Gordon's adventure as fate has decreed my role to be a minor one. The next round is on Saturday 20th February and I'm working that day. We are snowed under with work at Barron Financial Solutions at the moment with mortgages coming in left, right and centre so there is no way I will be asking for the day off or to swop. I'm hoping to get to at least one leg of the Semi Final and the Final, just to finish off the three Cup journey, but I'd put my mortgage on Alan and Gordon heading to Hereford. If Hereford win in the Quarter Final, they will be playing there again in one leg of the Semi Finals so I will hopefully join Alan and Gordon at that one. Watch Hartley Wintney secure a sensational win over Hereford now I've said that.

The full FA VASE Quarter Final draw is as follows :-

Ipswich Wanderers or Bowers & Pitsea v Kidlington

Hartley Wintney or Hereford v Camberley Town

Salisbury v Dunston UTS or Ashford United

North Shields or Morpeth Town or Berkhamsted v Bristol Manor Farm.

Hartley Wintney play their re-arranged game against Hereford this coming Saturday, as apparently this was another game that fell victim to the weather this weekend as the pitch was waterlogged. Heard that one before once or twice this winter!

Thursday 4th February 2016

Since we started our FA Cup campaign, Alan has always wanted to meet the Wealdstone Raider. For those who don't know, the 'Wealdstone Raider' has cult status amongst English football fans following a 'You Tube' clip showed Gordon Hill aka 'The Wealdstone Raider' with a pint in his left hand and a fag in his right, at a game in March 2013 between Whitehawk and Wealstone, drunkenly singing 'You've Got No Fans' at the Whitehawk supporters and then getting into an argument with one of them and repeatedly uttering the immortal words 'Do You Want Some?'

The fact that Gordon is a small, bespectacled late forty something made the whole thirty two second clip particularly amusing and it very quickly became a phenomenon. Alan thinks it is hilarious and in the early rounds of the FA Cup he often spoke about fate conspiring to send us to Wealdstone. It never happened. Undeterred, Alan said he was sure the paths of 'The Casual Hopper' and 'The Wealdstone Raider' would cross one day. Well now they have!

Alan actually crossed paths with Gordon Hill back in April 2015 when Wealdstone's St Georges Stadium became his 382nd ground, but because the FA Trophy finished last March, I only became aware of the meeting when he posted it on Facebook today. I guess because so much happened between March and August last year, Al just forgot to mention it.

I asked Alan how the video clip came about and he said the City lads are often talking about 'The Wealdstone Raider' so one of them, a lad called 'Walshie' said to Alan that if he went to Wealdstone, he wanted to go with him. So, last April Alan and 'Walshie' went to Wealdstone against Ebbsfleet United (Ebbsfleet United won 1-0 – Alan reckons most of the time when he goes to a new ground he curses the home team and they lose!) Anyway, 'The Wealdstone Raider' allows people to make video clips with him, providing they make a donation to the 'British Heart Foundation'. Al and 'Walshie' found him at the bar and there's about a thirty second clip of Alan with 'The Wealdstone Raider with him saying,

"Walshie, I'm with your mate, Alan. Do you want some? I'll give it yer!"

And then Alan cracks up.

It's an amusing meeting of two of the biggest characters of the Non-League scene. Not quite De Niro and Pacino in 'Heat' but still two larger than life characters who, in their own eccentric ways, light up the terraces.

Saturday 6th February 2016

I received a text from Alan just before five this afternoon which simply read, "Hereford, here we come – Hartley Wintney 1 Hereford 4."

I've subsequently read the various media reports on the game and it seems Hereford won relatively easily, taking a 3-0 lead before Hartley Wintney got one back. Mustapha Bundu, Hereford's 18 year old striker from Sierra Leone who is receiving rave reviews in Non-League circles this season, scored twice, whilst Mike Symons and Joe Tumelty grabbed the others. Both sides ended up with ten men after an altercation fifteen minutes from time saw Hereford's Ryan Green receive a straight red and Ross Cook, who had earlier scored a penalty for Hartley Wintney, received a second yellow.

Gordon and Alan have both confirmed that they will be heading down to Hereford on the 20th. Not sure who will be doing the writing duties yet but in the game itself I'm expecting a close encounter. My money is on a narrow Hereford victory. I'm still expecting them to come a cropper against a Northern League side if they come across one in the Semi Final or Final though. Hereford are a massive club at Vase level, but as the last seven years have shown, the Northern League is the strongest Step Five league of the lot. Having said that, Camberley disposed of Newton Aycliffe with ease, so who knows, maybe the Vase will be heading further South this season.

Sunday 7th February 2016

Gordon Johnson has been down in Southampton this weekend with Mrs J for a short break. It wasn't a football free weekend though as they went to St Mary's (Gordon's first trip there) to see Southampton beat West Ham United 1-0.

I did my usual ferrying my sons, Brad and Joel to football yesterday, although it was a quiet weekend as neither had an official game. Brad had to go to Rochdale for an u16s versus u18s game on the all weather and Joel had a 5-a-side game for a friend's birthday.

Given it was a quiet weekend football wise, I took up an offer to go out last night into Ormskirk with the lads I used to play football with at Metropolitan Football Club in the Ormskirk Sunday League. I got the train over about six and then Alison and Joel picked me about eleven. It was a night out to celebrate the birth of a son, Charlie (on 18th January), for manager Mark Pounder and his partner, Louise. Some of them stayed out until 3.30am so will be nursing bad heads this morning.

I don't see the lads as often as I'd like which is understandable as a lot of them have young children. A couple of summers ago, I played in a Dad's end of season six a side tournament in Croston, for Brad's old local side, Croston Juniors. As Dads of the under 14 players, we weren't as fit as some of the younger teams Dad's, so could only muster four players. I even had to play out of goal as one of our four, Keith was injured. So, to make up the numbers I asked a couple of the footy lads, Robbie Knowles and Steve Garcia, to come down. Steve is a year younger than me and Robbie about three or four years younger. They both still play and are both pretty decent so we ended up getting to the final. No doubt that will be the last football medal I ever win, but hopefully my lads will go on to win better football medals than a 'Croston Juniors Parents Six A Side Summer Tournament Runners Up' medal, with a team that included two 'ringers'. Still, I reckon it's the only medal I've ever won as an outfield player so it has pride of place in my office. As it was a sunny, summer's afternoon Alison brought the boys down to watch. She watched me running around for a while in my tight top with my belly and moobs bouncing around and said,

"Steve and Robbie are much fitter than you."

I hope she was commenting on actual fitness rather than looks!

Steve said something to me last night when we were out which I've thought about a fair bit today. He only married his wife Angela when he was 40 and they have a little boy, Lucas, who is now two. We were talking about children, relationships and contentment, probably the type of conversation you only have, as a lad, when you get a bit older and he said,

"I've got in Ang now, what you've always had in Alison and that's a best friend."

He's a bit of a joker, Steve, one of the lads who has always been the life and soul of the party, whilst on the whole I'm a bit more reserved, so it was good to know other people, even those you wouldn't expect to notice, look at your relationship and think they would like something similar.

Today, whilst I've been nursing a mild hangover, Alan took the train up to Newcastle for the last 16 game of the FA Sunday Cup between Burradon & New Fordley and Hardwick Social. The visitors won 1-0 at Bedlington Terriers ground. Alan notched up his 406th new ground in the bargain. Next week, weather permitting, he's off to the Quarter Final, to see OJM host Hardwick Social at Sporting Khalsa FC in Willenhall, West Midlands. He's apparently already been there, so it won't be ground 407.

Monday 15th February 2016

I suspect Alan wasn't in the cheeriest of moods last night when he spent his Valentine's evening with Jo. Heading down on the train to Wolverhampton from Manchester yesterday for the FA Sunday Cup Quarter Final, he received notification from the secretary of the social club that the game had been put back a week. The FA had not updated their website so Alan was fuming as he'd wasted £50 on his train ticket. So next weekend it's Hereford for Alan on the Saturday and Sporting Khalsa on the Sunday.

The draw for the Semi Final was made today and the winners of the OJM v Hardwick Social game will be away at New Salamis, a Cypriot team based in London. 'The Casual Hopper' certainly gets about!

Gordon has had a busy weekend too. On Saturday, he refereed a game in the Wigan Amateur League between Bickerstaffe and Shevington, with the latter winning 6-1. Then, yesterday, he was officiating at a University Futsal tournament at Edge Hill University, Ormskirk between Edge Hill, Leeds, Liverpool, Lancaster and Manchester Universities. Today, Liverpool County FA's Walton Hall Park Headquarters was full of excited staff as they had a visit from Liverpool's manager, Jurgen Klopp. Gordon's Facebook page is littered with photos at the best of times, but today there's a load of photos of Gordon and Jurgen smiling at the cameras. Loathe to admit it as an Evertonian, but Klopp comes across as a good guy. Hopefully he'll move on to pastures new soon enough and they can appoint someone it's easy not to like again.

Gordon is off to Amsterdam tomorrow for a few days with Jackie (they do like their holidays) via a ferry from North Shields. He's back in plenty of time for the trip to

Hereford though. I suspect Gordon will write up the details of the game rather than Alan but neither has claimed ownership of the pad and pen yet.

Even if I hadn't have been working, I would not have gone to Hereford on Saturday. Brad is playing for Rochdale under 18s against Manchester City's under 18s in a friendly at the brand spanking new Academy at the Etihad. Would have loved to watch him in that one, but will have to leave it to my wife, Alison, to take him. Can't see it being a quiet morning for him.

CHAPTER SEVENTEEN

Saturday 20th February 2016

The FA VASE – 6th Round Proper

Hereford FC v Camberley Town

Written by Gordon The Ref

As I've been away in Amsterdam this week, only returning on Thursday, yesterday saw the usual round of email, texts and phone calls to Alan, plotting our Saturday football journey. Once again, I agreed to pick him up at Crewe railway station.

I was on the road to Crewe at 7.25 am, but almost as soon as I left, I received a phone call from Alan to say there had been some changes to the rail services from Manchester and he'd be at Crewe by five past eight. I put my foot down a bit but still only managed to get to Crewe for half past eight. Alan climbed into the car with the now obligatory cup of coffee from Costa and we were off on the road. Good time was made down the M6 and M5 motorways before leaving the M5 near Worcester to head across country towards Hereford.

At about 10.25am we drove past a tank in a layby outside an Army & Navy type store.

"What's that all about?" shouted Alan.

"We're making good time, better than I expected, so let's take a look," I replied.

So, a quick U turn was made and back to the lay by to further investigate. It was in fact an old decommissioned Russian tank so out came the camera and selfie stick for a few pictures to record this part of the journey.

"Let's have a look inside," Alan said.

I had images of his little chunky frame clambering up on to the tank and into the driver's entrance, but he meant a look inside the shop and he duly trooped off into the Army store to have a look around. After a twenty minute mooch around the store and trying on various items of clothing and coats, Alan bought himself a German Second World War army tracksuit top. Happy with his purchase, Alan and I headed back to the car and continued our journey to Hereford.

At about eleven o'clock, on the outskirts of Hereford, the car passed by a football ground on the left hand side of the road.

"Look! What ground is that, Gordon?"

Without even bothering to ask, I took a left turn and then another left into the car park of Pegasus Juniors FC.

"These play in the Midlands League, I think," Alan said, "and look, there's a game on."

We walked into the ground just in time for the half time whistle of a game between Pegasus Juniors Youth Side and AFC Wulverians. The club house was open with a very tempting aroma wafting out from within, so we ventured inside and purchased a couple of bacon sandwiches and coffee before going back out to watch the second half of the youth team game.

As the Youth team game reached its conclusion, we headed back to the car and continued on to Hereford's Edgar Street ground, arriving at the ground for 12.30pm. This wasn't a new ground for either of us. Alan had been here for Hereford United against Crawley on Bonfire's night, 2011, although he said there were no real fireworks at the game. He remembers there was an unease within the home crowd and it turned out it was for a good reason, Hereford United were relegated out the Football League at the end of that season.

I had been to Edgar Street a few months earlier than Alan, on 23rd April 2011, when I was appointed fourth official for a derby game between Hereford United and Shrewsbury Town. It was an Easter Saturday and was an eventful day for a number of reasons. The Shrewsbury Town manager at the time was none other than Graham Turner, the ex-Hereford United manager. He was met with quite a hostile reception which didn't get any easier as the game progressed as Shrewsbury went on to win two-nil.

Another reason the game was memorable was because an hour prior to kick off there was a knock on the referee's dressing room door and in walked Jack Taylor, the retired English referee who was the last Englishman to take charge of a World Cup Final prior to Howard Webb taking charge of the 2010 Final in South Africa. Jack was a lovely bloke who was now an ambassador for the Football League and, hailing from Wolverhampton, had decided to head over to see the 'derby' game at Hereford. Being a retired referee, Jack always made a point of calling in to see the match officials to wish them luck for the game ahead of them. He spent a good ten minutes chatting to the four of us.

The World Cup that Jack Taylor took charge of was the 1974 World Cup Final in West Germany between the host nation and Holland. There were two first half penalties in the game, a yellow card for the legendary Johan Cryuff in the tunnel at half time, but probably less memorable but still very interesting was the fact that Jack Taylor came within about thirty seconds of starting the game without corner flags! If you get chance to play back any old recordings, watch as Jack delays the kick off and two groundsmen sprint around the corners putting flags in place, before Jack starts the game.

So, back outside Edgar Street in 2016, we headed to a steward and asked about getting tickets as a big attendance was predicted for the game. We were directed to the ticket office in the corner of the ground and as we had seen Camberley Town in the last round, we decided to go in the away section with their supporters. The tickets were £8 each. We also bought three programmes at £2.50 each. As Calvin has had to miss a few games this time around, we have made sure we have got him a programme from each game that he's missed. He hasn't had any of them yet, as they are still at my house, but he'll have a nice collection next time I see him. I then headed back to the car as I like to put my programmes in the car before kick off, when I can, so they arrive home in pristine condition. Typically, Alan had got chatting to one of the club stewards, so I left him chatting whilst I went to the car. On my way back, I bought a couple of half time draw tickets, for me and Al, only to discover he had done the same, when we met back up. We had double the tickets but still none of the luck, as we still didn't win.

Match tickets, programmes and raffle tickets purchased, we then headed off for some pre-match refreshments in Addison's Bar which is located within the ground. The bar is named after the former Hereford United manager, Colin Addison, who was in charge of the club at the time of their legendary FA Cup victory over Newcastle United when Ronnie Radford equalised with a wonderful thirty yard strike to take the game to extra time and then sub, Ricky George nabbed the winner.

At about half past two, we headed out of the ground and around to the away section where we took our seats in the upper tier. Initially, we were sat near to a mesh divide which separated us from the Hereford fans in the same tier but were asked to move by stewards, who moved the divide, taking us further away from the Hereford supporters. As more away fans came into the stand though, the stewards had a change of heart and moved the divide back to where it had been in the first place and we returned to where we had originally been sitting.

Camberley kicked the game off, but both sides started tentatively, taking time to gauge each other. Once the game settled down, Camberley Town were the brighter side, but their delivery from crosses, free kicks and their now trade mark long thrown ins were lacking in quality and were being gathered by keeper, Horsell. As Camberley continued to exert pressure, Hereford's Nathan Sumners picked up the first caution of the game from referee, John Busby, for a cynical pull back on Camberley's Bunyan. From the resultant free kick, Camberley took the lead. Lazarczuk delivered a high ball into the goal area and Bunyan himself soared above the home defence to head home. One-nil to Camberley and deservedly so at that stage of the game.

With Camberley continuing to take the game to Hereford in a combative and hardworking manner, Hereford were unable to create more than the occasional opening. The game reached half time with a one-nil lead to Camberley Town. The scoreline was an accurate reflection of the half with the underdogs causing a lot of problems for the FA VASE favourites.

It was obvious to all that changes were needed for the home side and during the interval Hereford's manager, Peter Beadle replaced Pablo Heysham with long standing Hereford play maker, Rob Purdie. As he came on at the start of the second half, I pointed out to Alan that Purdie had actually played for the now defunct Hereford United during their time in the football league and had actually played in the game I was fourth official of at Edgar Street back in April 2011.

Purdie coming on did assist in turning the momentum of the game in Hereford's favour but it was not until the hour mark, with the introduction of Hereford's top goalscorer, John Mills, that the game appeared to be turning more and more in favour of the home side. Mills introduction certainly picked up Hereford's attacking momentum and he immediately began asking questions of the Camberley defence. Within a minute of his introduction, a cross into the Camberley penalty area from Mills was handled and from the resultant penalty kick, Mustapha Bundu scored to bring the home side level. 1-1.

The expectation in the ground from the crowd of 3,329 fans, that were mainly supporting the home side, was for Hereford to run away with the game now and coast to an easy victory. They were, therefore, caught off guard in the 70th minute when there was a calamitous mix up in the home defence, allowing Matthew Bunyan a great chance to restore Camberley's lead. His resultant shot was blocked by Hereford keeper, Martin Horsell, but he simultaneously spilled the ball and it rolled just over the goal line. The correctly positioned assistant referee was on the goal line and awarded the goal to Camberley Town. 2-1 to Camberley. Game on again. I complimented the assistant ref to Alan as he was in a great position to see the incident and come to the right decision.

Dan Turkington's Camberley Town now had twenty minutes to hold on for a sensational away victory that would be the talk of the Non-League football scene. Only four of those twenty minutes had elapsed, however, when Hereford broke forward menacingly. Two of the subs combined as Rob Purdie crossed to John Mills who headed down into the path of Mike Symons, who fired home to bring the home side level for a second time. 2-2.

Hereford continued in the ascendancy for the remainder of the ninety minutes but there were no further goals or clear cut chances so a further thirty minutes of extra time were needed. Hereford dominated the two extra fifteen minute periods but Camberley were defending determinedly as the clock ticked down. Camberley Town's hearts were broken though, in the 119th minute, when John Mills grabbed the winner. Hereford broke down their left and a tiring Camberley defence were unable to keep pace. The ball was driven low into the box and Mills arrived right on cue to smash the ball into the back of the net and send the home supporters into ecstasy. It was a tough blow for Camberley Town and their supporters. Their players had fought valiantly for two hours against a huge and vociferous crowd for this level of football. Alan and I really felt for them. It's funny how football goes as a neutral. In the last round, we were disappointed to see Camberley Town win and today we were sorry to see them lose.

After the final whistle, we headed back to the car, passing hundreds of delighted Hereford fans. Their team, either as Hereford United or as the newly formed Hereford FC had never been to Wembley and now it was only a two legged

Semi Final away. We continued to chat about Wembley on the way home and wondered whether it could be a final between the two big guns, the phoenix clubs, Hereford and Salisbury.

I dropped Alan off at Crewe railway station at 7.55pm with the now customary parting comment from Alan,

"Speak to you Monday, pal, after we know the draw."

FINAL SCORE : Hereford FC 3 Camberley Town 2

FA VASE GOALS :- 38 goals in 8 games.

Sunday 21st February 2016

It sounds like I missed a lot of good football yesterday. I have a desk piled high with mortgage files currently, so needed to crack on with them, but if I could have been at both Hereford's Edgar Street with Gordon and Alan, as well as at Manchester City's Academy with Alison, to see Brad play against Manchester City under 18s for Rochdale's under 18s, then life would have been perfect.

I had regular updates from Alan and Gordon at Hereford but prior to that Alison had been texting to let me know how the lads at Rochdale were doing against City. It was a massive ask of the Rochdale lads to take on City lads who are not only some of the best young players in Britain, but now some of the best players from across the world. Rochdale lost 5-0 but apparently they gave a very good account of themselves and Brad said he had one of the best games he'd ever had in his life, as his goal was peppered with high class strikes.

A former work colleague, Gareth Jones, a big Evertonian who I took as a guest to the 2009 FA Cup Final between Chelsea and Everton, has now left the glamorous world of mortgages to become a football agent. He looks after a lot of the young Manchester City players, including the son of former Everton and Arsenal player Kevin Campbell, Tyrese Campbell. 'Gaz' was at the game yesterday with Kevin and text me to say Brad played excellently. Other than the Youth Cup game against Notts County, Brad hasn't played with the same confidence for the under 18s as he has for the under 16s, so it was great to hear he did well. Hopefully next season when the oldest lads are only a year to 18 months older, rather than up to two and a half years older, then he will come in to his own.

On the Vase front, Hereford made the front of the Non-League paper this morning as their last gasp winner has taken them within a step of Wembley. All the talk seems to be of a phoenix club FA VASE final with Salisbury and Hereford but I'm sticking to my guns and thinking a Northern League side will come along and spoil that party. That responsibility now lies with Morpeth Town as they are the only Northern League side left in the competition! Morpeth knocked last year's FA Vase winners, North Shields out in the 4th Round 2-0, in a game that was played at North Shields ground when it was due to be played at Morpeth, due to the waterlogging issues at Morpeth. Subsequently, they journeyed down to Hertfordshire and beat Berkhamsted Town 2-1. Morpeth still have to play their Quarter Final at home to Bristol Manor Farm as the game was postponed due, once again, to a waterlogged pitch. Now there's a surprise.

Joking aside, the North of England, especially the North East has really suffered with wet weather this winter and it must have had a massive economic impact on non-League football. Instead of teams getting regular income coming in every fortnight, they have had to cope with not playing for weeks on end. The games will be re-arranged for later in the season but they will have to be clustered together and crowds won't be the same on a Tuesday or Wednesday night, as they would have been on a Saturday afternoon nor will as much be spent in the bar.

Morpeth Town, for example, have only played 18 of their 42 League games and it's the end of February. I know they obviously have the further distraction of Cup games because they have reached the FA Vase Quarter Final but their end of season campaign is going to be frantic. They have only lost two of those eighteen games and would perhaps have been title challengers but once they start playing four games in eight days, players will start struggling to get away from work early enough to play and will pick up knocks and the season could just fizzle out. I expect the Vase will be given top priority and the League will become about squad rotation.

Other than Hereford's win over Camberley Town, the only other guaranteed semi-finalists are Salisbury, hence the reason the Non-League paper has focused so much on the phoenix teams. Salisbury beat Ashford United 3-0 with their captain Kane O'Keefe scoring two with Taurean Roberts scoring the other. As readers of my first football book will know, I go to watch Portsmouth from time to time with Alison's Uncle and cousin, so have a fair bit of time for Steve Claridge. He was always a much loved personality at Pompey during his time there as player and manager although it proved too difficult a task for him managerially. Pleased to see him doing well at Salisbury. They had their record crowd (for the reformed club – Salisbury City were the former club) yesterday of 1,791 so they attract a good following. If they drew Hereford in the Semi Final, tickets would be at a premium.

The other tie that didn't reach a conclusion was Bowers & Pitsea against Kidlington which finished 3-3 after extra time. Kidlington went 2-0 up in the first ten minutes, then found themselves 3-2 down with a quarter of the game left before making it 3-3 in the 73rd minute, a scoreline that didn't change for the remaining 47 minutes of play. Both the Morpeth Town game against Bristol Manor Farm and the replayed Kidlington against Bowers & Pitsea game will take place next Saturday.

Today, Alan has been to the re-arranged FA Sunday Cup game between OJM and Hardwick Social that he started heading to last week only to find out it had been put back a week. It was at Sporting Khalsa FC and whilst he was there Al spotted Luke Benbow, formerly Stourbridge's centre forward, now at Rushall Olympic who we had watched several times during our FA Cup travels. Benbow is a lively, dangerous forward when he sniffs an opportunity but conserves energy for when it matters and doesn't tend to keep going throughout the ninety minutes. This gives the impression, rightly or wrongly, that he looks angry and frustrated for most of a game. He definitely has an element of class about him on the football pitch though and is still banging in the goals for Rushall Olympic. Alan had a good chat with him and a photo taken of the two of them which he posted on to Facebook.

Despite being the Quarter Final of the national FA Sunday Cup, Alan said there were only sixty in attendance. A disappointing figure, I thought, as I've played in local Sunday derbies when I played in the Wirral Sunday League when a couple of hundred have wandered down to watch and those games obviously had nowhere near the same prestige as a Quarter Final of the Sunday cup. OJM won 1-0 with Hardwick Social missing a first half penalty. Alan said Darren Byfield turned out for OJM. Byfield must be in his late thirties now, but had a long professional career, starting at Aston Villa, where he played a handful of games before moving on to the likes of Walsall, Rotherham, Sunderland and Gillingham amongst others. Away from football he also found tabloid fame as he was briefly married to the singer Jamelia. I think it's great that people like Byfield still enjoy their football enough to turn out for their local Sunday League side.

Monday 22nd February 2016

The FA Vase Semi Final draw was made today. It has restored Alan's faith in the FA as the two phoenix clubs, Hereford and Salisbury have been drawn against each other ("No warm balls this time", he quipped). If the two clubs had avoided each other and each made the Final, it would have ensured one of the biggest FA VASE crowds in its history. I'm sure Alan never anticipated that he would have to battle for tickets in the FA VASE, but it is a two legged Semi Final and I am sure tickets for both games will be hard to come by.

I have said to Alan that I will go to one of the two Semi Finals but will check what games Brad has on at Rochdale. My Dad is keen to go to Hereford too, so ideally, if Brad's fixtures allow, me and my Dad will go with Alan and Gordon to the 1st Leg at Edgar Street, Hereford on 12th March. In fact, I know I'm working on the 19th March, so it'll have to be the Hereford game for me.

We lived down in Gloucester from 1999 to 2002 and often when driving back to see family for the weekend in the North West on a Friday, Alison and I would have to head up the 'A' roads to avoid the M5 and M6 traffic, so would pass Hereford's ground on the way. I've never been in though, so fingers crossed I'll be able to go.

As it stands, the other Semi Final is :-

Kidlington or Bowers & Pitsea v Mortpeth Town or Bristol Manor Farm.

The Semi Finalists should be sorted out by next Saturday, as the two remaining Quarter Final games are due to be played then.

In the FA Sunday Cup, the Semi Final draw sees the Midlands team Alan is following, OJM being drawn against New Salamis (a London based Cypriot team) at a venue still to be announced whilst the other Semi Final is Barnes AFC (from Chiswick) against current holders, Campfield who are from Liverpool.

Sunday 28th February 2016

Alan and his Manchester City pals are all on Cloud Nine this evening, as City won the first major domestic trophy of the season beating Liverpool 3-1 on penalties after the game had finished 1-1. City's hero was normal second choice keeper, Willy Caballero who made three great penalty saves in the shoot out.

In FA Vase news, the two remaining Quarter Final's did go ahead yesterday. In the game in the North East, Morpeth Town beat Bristol Manor Farm 2-0. Morpeth's first goalscorer was Chris Swailes who is almost definitely the only outfield player, still playing at a competitive level of English football, who is older than me. He is 45 years old, same as me, but was born in October 1970 and I was born in January 1971. I ache for a few days if I run more than a mile or go to the gym for an hour, so how the hell he still turns out for Morpeth Town is beyond me.

Swailes may be one of the fittest 45 year old's in Britain, but he has had more than his fair share of health problems. He had to have a six inch screw inserted into his heel ten years ago and, even more incredibly, he has had the same heart condition as my Dad, atrial fibrillation which is when your heart has an abnormal heart rhythm, normally going through spells of beating excessively fast. Swailes has had four heart operations. Not for nothing is he known as Morpeth's 'Bionic Man'.

Swailes also has an interesting back story with regards to the FA VASE. He had an excellent professional football career, most notably at Ipswich Town, Bury and Rotherham, playing over one hundred times each for the latter two at centre half. Both prior to and post-professional football though, he won the FA Vase. The first victory aged 21, was more of a squad involvement than playing a part in the win on the day, as he was an unused substitute in Bridlington's win in 1992. Then, aged

41, he played for Dunston UTS, when they won the FA VASE in 2012. To be in with a chance of a unique treble, in 2016, is a real life miracle. I am sure no-one has ever returned to Wembley as a player 24 years after their first victory to win a trophy again.

Everyone at Bowers & Pitsea will, I am certain, be determined to stop Swailes and his team mates making FA VASE history. In their Quarter Final replay, Bowers & Pitsea travelled to Oxford to defeat Kidlington 4-0. Stevens, Wilson, Salmon and Adams ensuring a comfortable victory for the visitors, who have made sure some coach companies in Northumberland and Essex will be kept busy on two Saturdays in March. My money is on a Morpeth-Hereford final with Morpeth winning. Not sure how good Salisbury are going to be though. They are eight points clear in the Sydenhams Wessex League Premier Division with games in hand and won again yesterday 2-1 at Verwood Town. Just think it's impossible to rule out the Northern League teams in the Vase though.

Monday 29th February 2016

Alan has text to say the tickets for the Hereford first leg of the Semi Final go on sale online on Wednesday at 10am so he'll be straight on to it. I will definitely be going so Alan is going to get three tickets for me, him and either Gordon or my Dad as Gordon isn't sure whether he can make it. Al is also trying to sort something out for him and Gordon for the second leg at Salisbury. He's been in touch with the club and they've said they will allocate him two tickets but only after they've been made available to Salisbury fans on Saturday. Alan says he's checked and each individual can buy four tickets so he's worried they may sell out and his FA Cup, FA Trophy, FA Vase and FA Sunday Cup 100% record may go. Obviously, he's unwilling to allow this to happen so is intending on getting the train down to Salisbury on Saturday with the sole purpose of buying two tickets for the Second Leg. He's a bit gutted about it as his nephew, Joe Boyling, is playing for Greater Manchester against Lancashire on Saturday at Charnock Richard. A ground I know Alan has been desperate to go to for the three seasons I've known him.

Talking about Lancashire u16s, Brad is pretty much a nailed on second choice goalkeeper for Lancashire behind Billy Crellin from Fleetwood Academy. I have no problem with that at all and Andy Clitheroe, their coach, understands my perspective that when fixtures between Rochdale and Lancashire clash, it makes sense for Brad to be getting game time at Rochdale rather than sitting on a bench for Lancashire. When the fixtures don't clash, I'm more than happy to go along to Lancashire with Brad as a reserve keeper. Brad is playing at the weekend for Rochdale so won't be playing at Charnock. Pity as it would have been good to meet up with Alan. Having said that, I'm pretty sure Rochdale under16s are playing at

Oldham u16s soon. Joe Boyling is now the keeper at Oldham so it will be fun being rivals for the day.

11.00pm

It appears common sense has prevailed. A couple of Alan's mates (Garry and Nathan) have been in touch with Salisbury via Twitter saying it seems unfair after the journey Al has done and the money he has raised for charity (over £15,000) that he has to travel down to Salisbury just to get two tickets. Subsequently someone at the club has been in touch with Alan and said two tickets will be put to one side for him so he doesn't need to journey down this Saturday with the sole purpose of buying tickets. Good work Salisbury FC. They look after the fans in Non-League football.

Sunday 6th March 2016

Mothering Sunday in Britain today. My own thoughts are with the great mother's in my own family especially my wife, Alison and Mum, Jacquie but also interesting reading everyone else's statements on social media about their Mums. Couldn't help but notice Alan's daughter, Jordan, had posted how much she adored her Mum and how strong she has been kicking cancer's arse this year. Long may that continue. She also posted a version of James' 'She's A Star' which was very appropriate. They are a great family and I am very grateful fate brought us all together when the FA drew out West Didsbury & Chorlton FC to face Abbey Hey back in the FA Cup Extra Preliminary Round, August 2013. It's been a hell of a journey, both on the pitch and off it, ever since.

Whilst discussing cancer, just a quick mention to a social media friend of mine, Michael Devereau. I've never met 'Mick' but our paths crossed on Twitter several years ago as he was an Evertonian and he bought my first fictional book, 'Forever Is Over'. Thankfully for me, he loved it and we have been in regular contact since. He is one of a host of people who regularly help promote my books on social media, mainly people in the UK but there's even one guy, Matthew Jarrett (Twitter name @FANGOFOX77) who is always lending a hand from Australia.

Mick Devereau is originally from the Isle of Man but now lives in Northern Ireland. He decided this year that he wanted to do something to help 'Balls to Cancer' and their work for testicular cancer. He asked his nine year old son what would be the worst thing he could do and his son, Jack, suggested getting a Liverpool tattoo. So that's what Mick has done. He said if he could raise over £1,000 for 'Balls To Cancer' he would get a Liverpool tattoo on his leg. The money has been raised and he is now sporting a reasonably large Liver bird on his calf, with LFC underneath and 'Balls to Cancer' underneath that. He's raised over £2,400 now and a huge well done to him for a brilliant cause. I honestly don't think I could ever bring myself to permanently ink myself with the Liverpool badge, no matter how good the cause. Michael is a better man than me.

Incidentally, Alan still hasn't managed to get to Charnock Richard. Lancashire u16s beat Greater Manchester u16s 1-0 yesterday but because of the weather, it was played on the all weather at Skelmersdale rather than at Charnock so he's intending on heading back there to watch a Charnock game later this month.

Friday 11th March 2016

It is going to be Alan, my Dad and me heading down to Hereford tomorrow for the FA VASE Semi Final 1st Leg. Gordon had to rule himself out as Liverpool County FA have a number of referees coming over from Northern Ireland this weekend and he is hosting the event. My Dad was more than happy to replace him, as he fancied coming down to Hereford.

As ever, with Brad's hectic football life at Rochdale, this has taken a bit of logistical planning. Rochdale u18s don't have a game tomorrow, but they still have to go in training. Alison is working so I am going to drive over to Rochdale's ground Spotland to drop Brad off and Alan is going to meet me there (I suggested picking him up at Rochdale train station but he said he'll get himself up to Spotland). Then, I am going to head back to Wigan to pick my Dad up at a designated spot just by the M6 where he will leave his car, then we will head down to Hereford. Once Brad finishes his training, I have given him a tenner to get the train home and arranged for his goalkeeper coach, Ryan to drop him off at the station. I've also given my other son, Joel, a few quid and will leave some sandwiches for him. Thankfully, my boys are pretty independent characters.

CHAPTER EIGHTEEN

Saturday 12th March 2016

The FA VASE – Semi Final 1st Leg

Hereford FC v Salisbury

Today has been another cracking FA day. All the logistical planning worked well and Alan arrived at Spotland within minutes of me dropping Brad off and we headed over to Wigan to pick my Dad up. Dad was waiting for us when we got to Wigan and after the usual warm greetings, we headed towards Hereford. Given we had plenty of time, we decided to go via the scenic route on the A41 and A49 through the likes of Whitchurch, Shrewsbury, Church Stretton, Ludlow and Leominster. It was a bright spring morning and it's a beautiful part of the country to drive through. You can get stuck behind slow moving traffic as most of the time it is only a single lane carriageway, but we weren't in a rush so there was no need to rush.

By late morning, we were all getting hungry so were looking for a place to grab some food. My Dad suggested we stop at Hawkstone Park. My Dad did a lot of work over the years in the Shropshire area and ten years ago, when our boys were only five and three, my Dad arranged the whole family (me, Alison, my sister, her husband and their two children as well as our two) to go on a Santa Safari at Hawkstone Park. We went to Hawkstone Park Hotel and were then picked up by a Land Rover before going up into the hills and meeting up with Santa in a cave at the top. The kids loved it and it brought back some fond memories stopping off there again.

My Dad was originally wanting to take us to Hawkstone Park Golf Club which he thought he would be able to find from memory but we took a few wrong turns before he realised he couldn't quite remember where it was so we just stopped at a café in the hills. Whilst we were having a bit of food we discussed the FA Vase game and also the FA Cup Quarter Finals. Crystal Palace had beaten Reading in the Friday night game, 2-0, so there were now only seven teams left in the competition, with Everton playing Chelsea later in the afternoon, before Arsenal host Watford and Manchester United host West Ham tomorrow. If Everton could win, it could give under pressure boss, Roberto Martinez a lifeline.

During the week, Alan and I had discussed the fact that he wanted to get home as quickly as he could after the Hereford-Salisbury game had finished. He had a gig to go to in Manchester and also knew he would have to head back down to Nuneaton Town the following day for the FA Sunday Cup Semi Final between OJM and New Salamis. Nuneaton Town had been chosen as the designated neutral venue. Al understood that my Dad and I would want to watch the Everton game so he suggested that we drop him off at Hereford train station and then we could find a local pub to watch the game.

After our spot of food, we headed down to Hereford and were parked up just outside the ground just after one o'clock. The Edgar Street ground is just on the outskirts of the town centre and there is a big council car park around the back of it, which is fine, but unfortunately means you have to pay a few quid for parking. Alan showed us where to park so we could get to the exit easily once we arrived back at the car.

Even before we parked up, we could tell the whole town was buzzing about Hereford having a very real opportunity of going to Wembley for the first time in the history of the old and new clubs. There were various stalls set up around the ground, ice cream vans, people wearing novelty wigs and hundreds wearing replica Hereford FC tops. There were still two hours before kick off and the carnival had begun.

We walked around the ground and typically, Alan could not resist getting his photo taken with the Hereford team mascot. Striding purposefully over (I don't think I've ever seen Alan run) when he spotted Edgar, the six foot bull wearing a Hereford top, to add to his growing collection of photos with mascots. This was obviously the human mascot (in a fancy dress outfit) but Hereford also have a real bull as a mascot too. He's called Ronaldo and has become a real hit with fans since he was paraded around the ground before Hereford's first home game of the season in August. Rumour has it that if they make it to Wembley they are going to try to take Ronaldo with them but what the F.A will make of that remains to be seen.

Our tickets were for Merton Stand, an all seater stand on the East Side of the ground, directly opposite the Len Weston stand that Gordon and Alan had sat in for the game against Camberley Town. We didn't have designated seats and with it being a sell out, didn't want to leave it too late before going in, but as it was still not half past one, we decided to go into the town and grab a coffee.

I always think a town looks better on a sunny day and with the sun shining down on it, Hereford created a good impression, clean and modern, with lots of fashionable retailers obviously keen to open stores there and a good selection of coffee shops and restaurants. We had a quick coffee, sitting outside to make the most of the first proper sunshine we'd seen for six months, before heading back over to Edgar Street.

Over the last three seasons, especially in the early rounds of the FA Cup and during the FA Trophy campaign, I have commented that going to certain grounds was like going back in time to the football stadiums of my youth, well, Edgar Street is a perfect example of that. It's like receiving an invitation to go to see what Huddersfield Town's ground or Derby County's might have looked like if they had stayed at Leeds Road or the Baseball ground. It has that mid-twentieth century feel to it, a bit like Goodison still does. It still has big old floodlights in the corners and three of the four sides are at least partially terraced (behind each goal is fully terraced and the Len Weston stand has a tier of terracing below the stand itself). I love stadium like this and felt immediately privileged to be there on such a prestigious occasion for the new club. The ground is only permitted to hold just under 5,000 and today it would be as fully as it is legally allowed to be. In its Hereford United days, Edgar Street's record crowd was 18,114 when they played Sheffield Wednesday in the FA Cup Third Round back in 1959.

Although we always try as best as we can to remain neutral, I felt at kick off that it would fitting for the town and just rewards for those who battled to resurrect the football club, if Hereford could finally make it to Wembley. I must admit, however, that my loyalties swayed the other way due to an incident that happened during the first half.

Games at this tier of English football don't come much bigger than this and with a huge crowd of 4,683 cheering them on, the Hereford and Salisbury players began a three hour battle to win the right to play at Wembley. Perhaps nerves and a poor playing surface played a part but for the most part of the first forty five minutes, Alan, my Dad and I were muttering to each other,

"It's a terrible game this," or similar words with the same message.

There was certainly no lack of effort and it was interesting to see Hereford's big striker, Mustapha Bundu, in action. The striker is from Sierra Leone and is on an educational visa so if Hereford get promoted from the Midland League, which they are very likely to do, as Champions, then Bundu won't be allowed to play. If Bundu plays at any level higher than he does currently, he will be breaching his visa conditions. As he is only 18, very fast and has a real physical presence, the talk is that he will end up going to play somewhere in Europe. He is certainly one to look out for in the future, but for now, Hereford are delighted to have him.

Just before the half time whistle, the game came to life. This was the incident that didn't sit well with me and found me leaning towards a Salisbury victory. An innocuous cross was played in to the box from Hereford's right wing. It was slightly over hit and seemed to be heading towards the safety of Salisbury keeper, Charlie Searle's chest, when Hereford striker, Pablo Haysham sprinted forward and then hurled himself, Superman style, at the ball with his left arm outstretched, pushing the ball in to the net.

The vantage point that we had taken up in the Merton Stand was just in line with the edge of the box that the Salisbury keeper was guarding and we couldn't have had a better view of the incident. I fully expected Haysham to be booked for his impudence and was astounded when the referee, Stephen Martin pointed to the halfway line to indicate a goal had been given. I looked at the Assistant referee, who must have had as much of had almost as good a view of it as I had, expecting him to be flagging frantically but he wasn't. As the Hereford players and fans celebrated, Steve Claridge, the Salisbury manager, raced down the touchline quicker than I had ever seen him sprint in his heyday to protest to the Assistant Ref and he was soon joined by his players.

"Am I missing something here?" I asked my Dad and Alan, "Did Haysham not just push the ball into the goal with his hand?"

"Yeh, it was handball," Alan agreed.

"Handball," my Dad confirmed.

"Well, it was handball, but they've given the goal now, they can't disallow it," was the general consensus of the Hereford fans around us.

Stop right there! There is nothing I hate more about the way modern football has gone than the fact that cheating isn't punished enough. Players, particularly at the higher level, dive around at the slightest of touches, pretend they have been punched in the face when they've been touched on the chest and find any way they can to con referees. Just because cheating may benefit your team, doesn't mean you should condone it. I know sometimes there is a fine line. Did I cheer at Wembley when Steve Sherwood had the ball headed out of his hands by Andy Gray in the 1984 FA Cup Final? Yes, I did. Debatable decisions are just that, but this wasn't a debatable one, this was a blatant handball.

After an elongated debate, jeered by the home supporters, the ref ushered everyone away and after having a word just with his assistant, ruled the goal out. Everyone around us booed wholeheartedly. I didn't get it. What were they booing for? One of their players had just tried to cheat his way to Wembley and after making the wrong decision, the officials had eventually made the right one. I just felt relieved. The Hereford fans collectively seemed like a nice bunch. If you were stuck in a pub with a couple of hundred of them, I presume you would have a friendly chat rather than fear for your life, but this incident made me want them to lose. I know if it happened elsewhere there probably would have been the same reaction, but I just expected Non-League fans to be better than that and perhaps just want their team to get to Wembley based on honest endeavour. I'm guessing 90% of the supporters around the ground didn't get a good view on it but the ones around us definitely did and these were the ones that were winding me up. The whole English nation has never forgiven Diego Maradona for his far more discreet handball thirty years ago, so there's no need to condone something similar now. Anyway, I'll stop moaning on. You get the point. The right decision was made and no-one should feel aggrieved. Apparently Pablo Haysham apologised to Steve Claridge and his players after the game. Claridge admitted he wouldn't have accepted the apology had the goal stood. I suspect there weren't too many fans writing to Stephen Martin saying he had made the right decision and they were sorry for booing him. Perhaps if Martin and his Assistant had got it right first time, the incident wouldn't have even got a mention or even better, if Pablo Haysham hadn't stuck his left arm out.

Half time arrived soon after with the score remaining at nil-nil. When discussing the half we all agreed that the players would probably tire a little in the second forty five and hopefully the game would become more open. Thankfully, we were right.

For all that we may have moaned a little that it wasn't a good game in the first half, Salisbury had done their job well. They worked hard in midfield, looked very solid at the back and on the rare occasion they did break forward, they looked dangerous. Nil-nil would be a fine result for them and the emphasis was on Hereford to come at them.

Three minutes into the second half, Hereford again broke forward along their right wing and the ball was cleared for a throw in near the corner flag. Jimmy Oates hurled the ball in towards Salisbury's near post and it was scrambled clear to the edge of the box, right to the position Oates was retreating to. He knocked the ball down with his thigh then pushed the ball in front of him before curling a deep right footed ball to the far post. Mustapha Bundu had intelligently stayed at the back post from the initial move and leapt higher than his marker and directed a strong header past Charlie Searle's right arm into the net. One-nil.

This was the first of many chances that fell Hereford's way in the second half. Another glorious chance when another lofted ball from the right fell to the feet of Bundu on the far post, in line with the penalty spot. Bundu was facing away from goal when he turned on the proverbial six pence and advanced menacingly towards the six yard box before laying the ball across the box toward Ross Staley. To his credit, Staley beat the defender and keeper to the ball, and prodded a left foot shot towards goal, but saw it strike the bar and bounce back towards him. In the matter of two seconds, he was handed another wonderful chance to double Hereford's lead, he headed the ball towards Searle's left hand post but held his head in his hands after seeing the ball strike the post and bounce wide.

Three minutes after Searle's double miss, Bundu had another golden opportunity. A corner came in from the right which was headed on to Bundu who tried to loft his own header over the keeper but he got a little too much on it and it struck the top of the bar. Just as we were asking whether Hereford would rue their missed chances, Salisbury had a great chance to equalise. A free kick was floated into the Hereford back from their right and Stephen Walker made a back post charge, meeting the ball with power, he tried to direct the ball back towards goalkeeper Martin Horsell's left post, but Horsell reacted quickly making an acrobatic body adjustment and managing to tip the ball over for a corner. One-one would have been harsh on Hereford who had dictated play in the second half.

After Horsell's late save, there were no more clear cut chances and the game finished one-nil, with all still to play for next week in the second leg. We headed back to the car, pleased with an entertaining second half and were soon dropping Alan off at Hereford train station.

My Dad and I ended up listening to the first half hour of the Everton-Chelsea game on the radio as we had decided to head towards home and just stop at a pub en route. The first couple of pubs were restaurant type pubs without televisions and we got all the way up to Stourbridge, a place we had fond memories of, from visiting the War Memorial Athletic Ground in our FA Cup adventures, before finding a great pub and bullying their bar staff into putting the Everton game on. The pub served food so we ordered some tea but it was evident to one and all that we were Evertonians as we roared with delighted when Lukaku picked the ball up on the left wing and weaved his way past four players before neatly finishing in the far corner. A few minutes later, we shouted the place down again when Barkley put a clever ball through to Lukaku who finished with ease and put Everton through to the Semi Finals. We headed home with smiles on our faces and although I knew I would be heading to Wembley for the FA VASE final in May, I asked my Dad to see what he could do to get me tickets for the FA Cup Semi Final. I'm getting greedy now, but even if I don't make every Final myself, the ideal scenario would be to see a great

FA Vase final, Everton to go to Wembley twice (Semi Final and Final) and then Rochdale to sneak into the League One Play Offs and make it to Wembley too. That would just be perfect!

I dropped my Dad off at Wigan and made arrangements to pick him back up on Tuesday as we are off to the races at Cheltenham for the day (my Christmas present to him). I've not been to Cheltenham races for a good few years so I'm really looking forward to it. Not sure we'll find any winners but any day spent with my Dad is a good day.

FINAL SCORE : Hereford 1 Salisbury 0

FA VASE GOALS : 39 in 9 games.

Sunday 13th March 2016

Whilst we were at Hereford yesterday, the other FA Vase Semi Final was taking place between Bowers & Pitsea and my tip for the trophy, Morpeth Town (based purely on the fact they are high up in the EBAC Northern League). The home advantage had been taken away from Bowers & Pitsea somewhat when their pitch was deemed unplayable earlier in the week and the game was moved to the neigbouring pitch of Concord Rangers. At half time, it looked like Morpeth Town were making giant strides towards Wembley as Sean Taylor and then Michael Chilton had given them a two goal lead.

In the second half, however, Bowers & Pitsea fought back with Lewis Manor scoring after a goalmouth scramble in the 61st minute and the tie was beautifully set up for the second leg when Alfie Hilton scored a last minute equaliser. Morpeth Town would probably have settled for a draw before the game but will have been disappointed to see a two goal lead slip away.

Elsewhere in non-League, Cheltenham and Forest Green remain miles clear of the remainder in the Vanarama League with Cheltenham on 83 points, Forest Green on 81 points and Grimby leading the chasing pack on 68 points. There is only one automatic promotion to League Two though with second to fifth going into the play offs. Yesterday, Cheltenham won 4-0 at home to Woking whilst Forest Green won 1-0 at Gateshead.

Solihull Moors lead the way in the Vanarama National League North with Fylde second and North Ferriby defying all expectations currently, as they are in third despite the rumoured sharp cut in players wages. In Vanarama National League South, three Uniteds lead the way with Ebbsfleet first, Maidstone second and Sutton third. In both North and South, the leaders are automatically promoted to the National League with the second to fifth place going into a play off. The bottom four in the National League are automatically relegated.

The Premier League is also more exciting than usual this season with Leicester City still surpassing everyone's expectations. Leicester City and Tottenham Hotspur seem to be in a two horse race for the title now with Leicester City on 60 points with a game in hand over Spurs who have 58 points and Arsenal are third with 52 points. Incredibly, it's Leicester's to lose now. They play Newcastle United tomorrow night and if they win that, they are really in the driving seat.

In the Sunday games in the FA Cup, Watford went to the Emirates and caused a major upset beating Arsenal, 2-1, whilst Manchester United and West Ham United drew 1-1 at Old Trafford. Only five teams left in the FA Cup and one of them is Everton. Fingers crossed we may win something for the first time since 1995.

One trophy that definitely won't be going to Merseyside is the FA Sunday Cup. The Merseyside based holders, Campfield were knocked out today in the Semi Final by London club, Barnes AFC. Alan went to the other Semi Final at Nuneaton Town between OJM and New Salamis which the London based, Cypriot side, New Salamis won 3-0. They hold the final based on where the two teams are from, so given it is two London teams in the Final, looks like Alan will be heading to the capital to watch it. He will be moaning like mad about that (he likes moaning does Alan!) as last year's final was at Ewood Park, Blackburn. I think, like most men, he just likes a good moan. He loves the adventure really and if it was nearby then that's not as much fun.

Alan said before the game, New Salamis were classed as underdogs but they were the better team throughout and deserved their victory. The 3-0 scoreline was about right. Once again, I was surprised to hear that the crowd for the game was really low. Only 71 turned up to witness the New Salamis victory. Hopefully, if it is a decent London venue for the final then there should be a good crowd for that.

Given how low the attendances have been in the FA Sunday Cup, Alan must, once he finishes it, be the only person to have completed every round of the FA Cup, FA Trophy, FA Vase and FA Sunday Cup. Gordon is goading him to do the FA Youth Cup next season and providing Jo continues to do well in her battle with breast cancer, I think he will go for it. For a man who can't drive it is one hell of an achievement.

Monday 14th March 2016

Leicester City beat Newcastle United 1-0 to take them five points clear in the Premier League with a 25th minute goal from Ozaki. The impossible might just become possible.

Tuesday 15th March 2016

Great day at Cheltenham races with my Dad. Called in to see my old school mate (and my Limited Company Accountant), Andrew Moss before the races in Bishop's Cleeve and he bought us a full English breakfast. We then took our car to his house and walked up to the course from there. The downside was that we had to walk back afterwards too. My Dad was noticeably knackered by the time we got back to Bishop's Cleeve and had a cup of tea with Andrew's wife, Sarah before heading home. It's not surprising though, it's a hilly three mile walk and we probably did a couple of miles walking in the day. It was hard work for me at forty five but even harder for my Dad at seventy two. If we go again, I will pay for a taxi.

I had a couple of winners at the races and ended up a few quid up but nowhere near enough to cover the cost of the day, but it was terrific, the atmosphere was brilliant and it was superb catching up with a few old friends like Andrew Elkington (the horse racing fanatic who I saw in Nottingham before Brad's FA Youth Cup game), Mark Sunderland (an old school mate) and his two friends, Martin and Darren. All the improvements made to Cheltenham racecourse are breathtaking too. It has always been my favourite racecourse but it is better than ever now.

Friday 18th March 2016

As was probably anticipated, the venue for the FA Sunday Cup Final has been announced and it's at Crystal Palace's Selhurst Park. The ground is on the Southside of London so it is going to be another long trek for Alan. He is letting out a lot of profanities about it on Facebook, but, as I've said before he loves it really. Why climb a hill when you can climb a mountain?

Tomorrow is the FA VASE Semi Final Second Leg at Salisbury. I will be working so once again, I will pass the pen over to Alan and Gordon. Apparently Gordon isn't well so it may just be Alan going so if that's the case, it will another section written by 'The Casual Hopper'.

CHAPTER NINETEEN

Saturday 19th March 2016

The FA VASE – Semi Final 2nd Leg

Salisbury v Hereford FC

** Written by 'The Casual Hopper' **

It was difficult to know where to start this but in the end I decided I'd start with the moment, last Saturday, when Calvin dropped me off at Hereford train station and I said my goodbyes to him and Richard. I had to be back in Manchester to see a band, Puppet Rebellion, at Manchester Academy.

I had no sooner got out of the car and I felt as if I had been transported, 'Ashes to Ashes' style, into the 1980s. Yep, it was blue flashing lights, tag Vans and police at Hereford station and there they were Salisbury's finest, thirty odd young lads, I'd say each one under twenty three years old. They looked like they had just fallen out of the Stone Island Adidas shop window, all trying their best to put their best game face on. Some were holding crates of Budweiser, others were singing and some were doing both. The police were soon in amongst them, marching them into the station. They'd soon be back with their doting parents in Salisbury. They couldn't throw their voice never mind a punch, but at least they bothered to turn out.

Now then, flash forward a week and here's me, just rolled into Salisbury station, decked out in my regular camo jacket, black jeans and Clarks' originals, heading for the toilet. I notice police, about six of them, waiting on the platform near the exit. I'm going the other way, but notice two of them are now following me. Whoops, I must meet their criteria.

I come out of the toilet and one says,

"Are you here for the football?"

"Me, errr, yeah," I say in broad Mancunian.

"Who you supporting, Salisbury or Hereford?"

"Err, no-one, I'm a neutral."

That baffled him. He gets the story and I'm allowed on my way, there's not a Hereford fan in sight which I found strange as my connecting train to Salisbury was Bristol, easy to connect from Hereford. Salisbury station entrance is lined with police, vans and cameras rolling, the lot. I head for a taxi as it's about three miles to the 'Ray Mac' from Salisbury station. 'Ray Mac' is Salisbury's stadium by the way, it's short for 'Raymond McEnhill' Stadium, named after the former Chairman of the club. The taxi driver starts telling me how there was lots of trouble last week and was blaming the Hereford fans. Don't believe what you hear mate, from what I saw, some of the young Salisbury kids were causing a bit of bother too.

Anyway, I'm here on my own today, Calvin's working and Gordon's come down with flu, but not man flu, proper flu. Gordon told me yesterday that he was too ill to make it, so what I imagined was a drive down with 'Gordon the Ref', visiting Stonehenge and the hippy ley lines and all that, turns out to be an absolutely jam packed 8.05 train, Manchester to Bristol, cross country express.

I've told you before I'm not a good traveller. I have to sit facing forwards otherwise I stand, so I was still stood at Birmingham. They changed the crew at Birmingham and when the guard came and I flashed my rail pass whilst standing, he said, 'there's loads of room in first class, mate, you can upgrade into there'.

"Great," I thought, "don't mind if I do."

It's alright in First Class. No sooner had I plugged my phone charger in and the trolley guy was there with tea and coffee. I didn't have to buy food either as there was shortbread biscuits, a bag of peanuts and raisins, a fruit cake, oh and a glass of water and a can of coke. I offer to pay for the coffee, but the trolley guy says I don't have to.

"No, it's fine, it's on your upgrade."

"Err, nice one".

'I could get used to this,' I thought and then, because it was free, I grabbed another one before I got off.

The real scenery was on the First Great Western train, Bristol to Salisbury. First it's Bath Spa and then Bradford Spa, then Warminster. You can see the white horse etched into the hill at Devizes, then its rows of armoured cars and tanks on the edge of Salisbury plain. The arrival at Salisbury you know about, so it was off up to 'Ray Mac', situated next to old Saurm airfield and numerous light aircraft are up and down.

I arrive bang on 1pm to collect my tickets, kindly donated by a friend at Salisbury. This is where I can say the official gate is 3,449 because if Gordon was counted in, it went in the bin – no resales and no day sales.

As for the game itself, it was a cracker, played to a full house bar one. Salisbury, chasing the tie after losing the first leg, opened up brightly and were the better team early on. They deserved their goal on 17 minutes which brought the tie level. Steve Walker opened the Salisbury account, from a tight angle.

Hereford woke up after the Salisbury goal and in fairness, once they equalised in the 41st minute, scored by the excellent Mike Symons, the big centre forward who wears number eleven, they controlled the game.

In the second half, Hereford were at another level. They were in their change strip of red and black stripes and white shorts. Very AC Milan. They should have gone ahead in the game and further ahead in the tie when they were awarded a penalty midway through the second half but Salisbury's star performer, goalkeeper Charlie Searle, saved. He had made a few decent stops prior to the pen as well, to keep the home side in it.

The impressive Mustapha Bundu was the star man for Hereford. He was always at the heart of their menace. He could definitely play higher up the pyramid later on in his career once his visa issues are sorted.

In the 76th minute, the away fans Wembley songs kicked in properly when Joe Tumelty scored to make it 2-1 on the day, 3-1 on aggregate and out of Salisbury's reach. I noted it was the same aggregate score that Salisbury City had lost to Barrow in the FA Trophy Semi Final back in 2010.

There were no further goals and although it was a disappointment for Salisbury, it was a terrific effort for them to get this far and to draw the favourites in the Semi Final was hard. The streets of Hereford will empty for the Final now though.

The final word has to go to the policeman who approached me on Salisbury station whilst I was waiting for the 17:40 to Bristol.

"Where's the rest of your lot?"

Ha Ha! My lot? My lot are back home in Manchester awaiting Derby day. How little do they know? So, we are almost complete. Just one to go – over to you, Calvin.

FINAL SCORE : SALISBURY 1 HEREFORD FC 2 (Agg:1-3)

FA VASE GOALS : 40 in 10 games.

CHAPTER TWENTY

Sunday 20th March 2016

From speaking to Alan yesterday, it seemed that once Hereford equalised yesterday, it always looked like they would go on and win. To take the club to Wembley for the first time in the town's history is an enormous achievement.

The game that was played up in the North East, between Morpeth Town and Bowers & Pitsea, to decide their opponents, was by no means a straightforward affair and was only decided at the death. Having drawn 2-2 in Essex, Bowers & Pitsea travelled to Northumberland knowing they faced a tough task against one of EBAC Northern League's finest. The task became even harder three minutes in when Sean Taylor put Morpeth ahead with an eighteen yard strike. Morpeth apparently dominated the first half but Bowers & Pitsea looked dangerous from set plays and in the thirty ninth minute they equalised through Lewis Manor's goal.

The reports indicate that the equaliser shook Morpeth and Bowers & Pitsea had a good spell prior to half time but in the second half Morpeth had a foothold on the game and had the better chances. They almost paid for not taking these chances, however, when Tom Hine hit the outside of the post for Bowers & Pitsea.

After eighty three minutes, Bowers & Pitsea were reduced to ten men when their midfielder, Ross Adams was sent off for a second yellow card. Morpeth Town tried to make their numerical advantage count whilst Bowers & Pitsea dug in to try to take the game to extra time.

I watched some of the highlights of both legs of this Semi Final today and in the 93rd minute, the ball was at the feet of the veteran defender, Chris Swailes, in the centre circle. He sent a long diagonal ball to the left wing, which was pulled back to the bald headed figure of Morpeth's Keith Grayson. The Irish 33 year old is a veteran of the non-League football scene in the North East and has already won an FA Vase, scoring the winner in Spennymoor Town's 2-1 victory in 2013. He whipped a low right footed ball into the near post and Luke Carr nipped in front of his marker to prod the ball past the keeper and into the back of the net. Mass celebrations followed and Morpeth Town were heading to Wembley.

A last minute winner must be a wonderful way to secure victory but you have to feel for Bowers & Pitsea. Their manager, Rob Small, was understandably gutted and admitted to the Non-League paper that him and most of his team shed a tear in the dressing room afterwards. He did compliment Morpeth Town though and described them as a "fantastic, attacking team".

Thus, the FA Vase final is between Hereford and Morpeth Town and it should be a cracker. Hereford will no doubt be favourites but as I keep saying you can't rule out the Northern League sides. They've won the competition six years out of the last seven, so Morpeth will go to Wembley determined to make it seven from eight.

Thursday 31st March 2016

The FA Vase Final isn't until Sunday 22nd May, so there is a two month gap between Semi Final and Final. I will just keep putting a few updates into the book between now and then, updating what is going on in our world and also in the world of football (particularly non-League). Obviously both paths regularly cross.

This season, for the first time, the FA are experimenting with having the FA Vase and FA Trophy on the same day. There is a hope some Vase fans will stick around for the Trophy final and some Trophy fans will arrive early and catch some of the Vase game. I hope they do and I hope a lot of other non-League supporters go along too. There are four sections of the stadium for the various fans and there are also neutral sections so we have bought three tickets for the neutral section for myself, Alan and Gordon. Hereford have already tweeted that they have sold an incredible 12,240 tickets for their section already.

The FA Trophy finalists were decided on Saturday 20th too. Grimsby beat Bognor Regis 2-1 (3-1 on aggregate) and FC Halifax Town drew 2-2 with Nantwich Town but FC Halifax went through 6-4 on aggregate. Thus, Grimsby-Halifax is the final. Both finalists are big clubs and former members of the '92' League Clubs (well, Halifax in a former guise were) so it should ensure a nearly full Wembley on non-League Finals day. We will definitely stay and watch that game too.

I've not updated you on Brad's progress at Rochdale for a while. He continues to do well and my old Vauxhall Astra continues to spend a lot of its life on the road or in a car park in Rochdale when it should be enjoying a more relaxed lifestyle as it heads in to later life. He has Rochdale related training or games five days a week – three weekdays and both weekend days and although Alison sometimes takes him, I do the lion's share. There's something wrong with the turbo on my car too so it isn't running as well as it should but when it goes to the garage it gets patched up rather than fixed. It's just a case of trying to running it until it cries enough. I'll be going to Wembley in May on the train though as I think the trip to Hereford was the last long journey I'll risk in it.

Watching Brad play for the under 16s still remains very different to watching him play for the under 18s. For the under 16s, he oozes confidence and pretty much plays well every game. I watch every under 16s game thinking 'he's got a great chance of making it'. The under 18s games are very different though. The games at Notts County in the FA Youth Cup and Manchester City in a friendly are the only two games he has really stepped up to the next level. The rest of the time, he seems to play a little within himself, perhaps inhibited by the older lads. I watch those games thinking, 'He's got no chance of making it'. I know it is 'fickle Dad' syndrome but outside of the bubble of the matches, I realise he's only a baby in goalkeeping terms and will hopefully grow more assured with experience.

Spectator wise, in the last few days I've been to watch Rochdale u18s twice at Victory Park, Chorley and Ewen Fields, Hyde against Preston North End and Wrexham respectively (lost 4-0 and won 3-1). Gordon and Alan have been busy too. On Easter Monday, Gordon did two games in a day going to Wigan v Rochdale and then Skem United v Nantwich. On Tuesday, he went to Wembley to watch England against Holland (the Netherlands won 2-1). There was sad news in the footballing world this week as Dutch legend Johan Cruyff passed away aged 68, so perhaps it was fitting that England lost that one.

Alan has notched up his 407th and 408th grounds, finally making it to Charnock Richard for their game against Euxton Villa and then heading down to Daventry Town on Saturday to see their game with Kidsgrove. Alan has the FA Sunday Cup final coming up in April too so he's looking forward to that one.

Just a final thing before I go. Both our boys were playing football tonight. I was working in Southport so I went to Joel's local game (he won 4-2) and Alison took Brad to Rochdale u16s v Bury u16s. I rang Alison and she reported that Brad had won 5-1. Just had a text from Brad to say they won 6-3! Seems like his Mum has had a few lapses of concentration.

Sunday 3rd April 2016

Today has been a busy footballing day. This morning, Brad was playing for Rochdale u16s against Oldham u16s at Oldham's training ground. Brad only played a half, as Rochdale u15s have recently signed a keeper who has been released by Manchester United, James and this means they now have three goalkeepers at under 15 level. Two of them were playing for the under 15s so the under 16s were asked to play James for a half. Brad was a bit miffed about getting 45 minutes, as he is fortunate enough to be the only keeper at under 16 level. Still, a bit of competition won't do him any harm.

In the Oldham Athletic goal was Joe Boyling, Alan's nephew, who Brad knows from his time at Blackburn Rovers. As mentioned much earlier in this book, I have always been very impressed with Joe. He is an outstanding trainer, kicks well, commands his area, takes crosses cleanly and throws the ball excellently. If he was 6 feet 2 inches tall, he would be at a Premier League Academy but he is currently 5 feet 9 inches tall and genetics are his only weakness. Funnily enough, I watched the game with Joe's Dad, Lee (Alan's brother in law) who is well over six feet tall and with Alan. I ended up with bragging rights this time as Rochdale were the better team and won 2-0 but it was an enjoyable ninety minutes as Lee, like Alan, knows the game inside out. Joel, my younger son, also came to watch but when Brad came off at the end of the first half, he lost interest and spent the second half in the car listening to music.

After the under 16s game, I took Brad back to Horwich railway station, a stone's throw from Bolton Wanderers ground, and whilst Brad was heading home, Joel and I met up with Joel's footy manager, Bill Cecil and his son, Ben. We left my car at the station and the four of us went to Old Trafford to watch Manchester United against Everton. Bill has four seats in one of the corporate sections at Old Trafford, so had kindly offered two of the seats to Joel and me, as Joel (unfortunately) supports United and I'm an Evertonian. The game itself wasn't a classic, Martial scoring the only goal for United, but it was a great day out. Lee Martin came to our table to show the lads his FA Cup Winners medal and Frank Stapleton was also doing the rounds. I was about to tell Frank how he made me cry back in March 1983, when I was twelve (only the second footballer to make me cry). Everton were at Old Trafford for an FA Cup Quarter Final and I was anxiously listening to it on Radio Merseyside on my Dad's portable Bush radio in the kitchen. Everton had defended fantastically throughout the ninety minutes and as the game headed into what seemed to be a never ending amount of injury time, it was still nil-nil. With seconds left, Ray Wilkins pumped an uncharacteristic long ball forward into the box from the centre circle. Of all players, diminutive substitute Lou Macari, standing at all of 5 feet 6 inches tall (if that), managed to slip the attention of Everton's midfield and therefore Mark Higgins, Everton's centre half, had to drop off Stapleton to pick Macari up. Macari headed the ball backwards, to a now unmarked Stapleton. I'm not sure if it was an exquisite piece of skill or pure luck from Stapleton, but, on the volley, he flashed his right boot at the ball and it flashed past a despairing Jim Arnold, in the Everton goal and into the keeper's top left hand corner. I bawled my eyes out. I can still remember my Mum trying to console me by telling me it was only a game and me thinking that she wasn't an Evertonian so she couldn't possibly understand how much it hurt. Thankfully, today, big Frank got talking to someone else just as I approached so I didn't have to relive the nightmare once more.

Interestingly, if Manchester United manage to beat West Ham in their FA Cup Quarter Final replay, Everton will face United at Wembley in the Semi Final. I hope we get West Ham. We still owe them for the 1980 FA Cup Semi Final defeat, when I was nine, when Frank Lampard scored a diving header at Elland Road then danced around the corner flag (the first footballer to make me cry). Souness was the third in 1984 and I don't remember any tears after that, as things, for a while, got a whole lot better.

Sunday 10th April 2016

There are a lot of Facebook photographs at the moment of Alan Oliver and his mates up bloody big hills in the middle of nowhere as they train for the Glencoe Challenge in July. Alan is normally at the back.

"Two stone heavier and twenty years older, that's my excuse and I'm sticking to it," says Alan.

Yesterday, I went to AFC Blackpool's ground to see Rochdale under 18s take on Blackpool's. Brad was on the bench as Johny Diba was available and he played very well, helping Rochdale earn a creditable one-all draw. Other than Diba, none of the other second year scholars have been offered a professional contract and it's now looking almost certain that they won't be. They are languishing in the bottom half of the North West Youth Alliance league and it has been a disappointing season for them. The top two are Wigan and Bury who are battling it out to be Champions.

In the afternoon, I watched the Grand National. I've been following the horses, especially National Hunt (jumps) racing since I was sixteen, so made a real effort to find the winner. Alison, on the other hand, just picked 'Rule The World' on her way out to work because it's the name of a Take That song. All my choices came nowhere and Alison's won at 50-1. Typically, I put her £1 each way on and had to hand over the winnings!

'The Casual Hopper' and 'Gordon The Ref' were also kept busy. Alan went with his daughter, Jordan to Tadcaster Albion against Handsworth Parramore (Tadcaster won 5-2). Gordon went to watch the team he supports, Wigan Athletic take a step nearer a return to the Championship with a 1-0 home win over Coventry

City. Gordon is off to Cape Verde for the week on Monday. Wonder if he'll catch a game over there?

CHAPTER TWENTY ONE

Sunday 17th April 2016

The FA Sunday Cup Final

New Salamis v Barnes AFC

Venue – Selhurst Park

One thing I've learnt about Alan 'The Casual Hopper' Oliver over the last three seasons is that he doesn't stay in much. Not content with heading down to London today for the FA Sunday Cup Final at Selhurst Park, yesterday he headed up to Billingham Town in the North East. He went to watch Greater Manchester play Cleveland, in an Under 16s Semi Final. Joe Boyling, his nephew, was playing in goal for Greater Manchester and they will all have come home very happy as Joe kept a clean sheet in a 3-0 win. That was Alan's 410th ground, presumably Tadcaster was his 409th.

Today, Alan was interviewed in the Selhurst Park stand pre-kick off by KOPA League and the interview was posted on to their Facebook page and shared by Alan. If you picture him, he's got his green camo top on, coffee in hand and he's closing his eyes through most of the interview. The reason his eyes are closed is because he's concentrating hard, tapping into his memory banks, to recall, in minute detail, his whole FA Sunday Cup adventure. The interview went something like this :-

Interviewer :-

I'm here at Selhurst Park, Crystal Palace FC for the FA Sunday Cup Final and here with me is Alan Aliver (*got his surname wrong but never mind), who's got a fantastic story to tell. Tell us about it, Alan.

The Casual Hopper :-

Yeh, Mike. Well, basically, I'm a groundhopper to start with. I've done 410 grounds up to now. Did Crystal Palace years ago. Completed the '92'. But I've done every round of this FA Sunday Cup. Started in October at Allerton FC and the idea is you follow the winning team all the way through to the final, as I'm here today.

Allerton, in October, played a team called 'The Pineapple'. I didn't even know this Cup existed but it's been brilliant. Allerton FC won, they got a team from Leeds called West Bowling, who West Bowling beat. They played in the next round at Hardwick Social which is in Stockton on Tees near Darlington. Hardwick Social won and they drew another Northern team from near Morpeth, Burradon & New Fordley, who they played at Bedlington Terriers after all the rain we've had. It was postponed about three times.

So, they played it at Bedlington Terriers, Hardwick Social won and they earned the right to play OJM at Sporting Khalsa which is in Walsall. If you can understand my accent, I'm from Manchester, so I've been up and down and all over the place.

OJM, very good side, beat Hardwick Social 1-0 and they met New Salamis in the Semi at Nuneaton Town. I've been to Nuneaton Town before, being a groundhopper, but I had to complete this. New Salamis, fantastic performance on the day, totally outplayed them, it could have been a lot more than 3-0 but OJM's goalie played really well as well. And this is like journey's end for me. Seven rounds to the final.

Now, here's a funny one. 'Cos when I looked at these fixtures, the final is usually played at Blackburn, so I was led to believe. And here I am with two London clubs at Crystal Palace. So it just makes the journey for me.

Interviewer

Brilliant. Thanks a lot, Alan. That's a great story and enjoy the game.

Typical Alan. He was asked one question and the interviewer could have gone and made himself a cup of tea and come back and Alan would have still been telling his story. Seven rounds, one take, no prompts.

As for the game, Barnes AFC took an early lead in the seventh minute. Joe Wright in the New Salamis goal tipped over a dipping, long range effort from Alex McGregor but when the resultant Steven Loveridge corner was only partially cleared, Mark Gallagher's well placed effort was accurate enough to beat the two New Salamis defenders on the line and give Barnes AFC a 1-0 lead.

It took until the 69th minute for New Salamis to equalise when Ryan Hervel crossed from the wing and substitute Harrison Georgiou neatly finished. 1-1.

With the game delicately poised, in the 75th minute Jordan Willis from Barnes AFC received a second yellow card for a bad tackle on Deniz Mehmet. New Salamis were then the more offensive team for the following fifteen minutes of normal time and thirty minutes of extra time but a winning goal could not be found and the game headed to penalties.

New Salamis keeper, Joe Wright, saved Barnes AFC's second penalty, from Ben Dyett, so when every subsequent penalty was scored, it was 4-3 to New Salamis with just the fifth and final nominated penalty taker from each side left. Nico Muir stepped up knowing if he scored the Cup was New Salamis but his penalty was saved by Balvinder Khaira in the Barnes AFC goal. The responsibility was now with Barnes AFC's fifth penalty taker, Rob Sheridan, to score and take the penalties to sudden death. Sheridan didn't get a great connection though allowing Joe Wright to make a save that won the Cup for New Salamis, 4-3 on penalties.

After visits to Liverpool (twice), Stockton on Tees, Bedlington (Northumbria), Willenhall (Wolverhampton/Walsall), Nuneaton and Crystal Palace, Alan's FA Sunday Cup journey was over and New Salamis were the new FA Sunday Cup winners. One game left and three seasons and then the journey through four tournaments would be complete.

Wednesday 20th April 2016

The Wade family are in Nottingham Center Parcs at the moment along with several other families we are friendly with in the Chorley area, including our closest friends in Chorley, Jo and Shaun McManus and their daughters, Ellie and Lucy. Tonight, all the blokes went down to the bar to watch the Merseyside derby. I was at the 5-0 drubbing back in November 1982 and tonight's 4-0 drubbing was no less humiliating. At least the Liverpool team of '82 had Rush and Dalglish playing, this Liverpool team weren't all that fantastic, it was just Everton were incredibly poor.

Like Glenn Keeley in 1982, our cause wasn't helped by a sending off. Funes Mori, who still hasn't convinced me that he is the answer to our centre back problems if John Stones leaves at the end of the season, was deservedly sent off for a terrible tackle. He then had the audacity to shake his badge as if he loved the club. If you loved the club, you would stay on the pitch for the full ninety minutes you fool!

At the weekend, we have Manchester United in the FA Cup Semi Final. They defeated West Ham in their Quarter Final replay 2-1. My Dad tried his damnedest to get tickets for me, but with us not being season ticket holders these days and most of my Dad's old contacts at Everton having retired, it proved to be impossible. After tonight, I don't hold out much hope of us having to try again for FA Cup Final tickets. If we lose on Saturday, Martinez has to go at the end of the season.

Saturday 23rd April 2016

I am not one to scream for a manager's head. These days I don't really feel I have the right to anyway, as although I still watch a lot of football, only a small proportion of it is Everton games. Still, after this evening, I do really think the game is up for Roberto Martinez. Everton lost their FA Cup Semi Final against Manchester United 2-1. It wasn't a bad performance and for a spell we were even the better side, but we just lack that bit of resilience to get us through the bad spells and take advantage of the good ones.

Having mentioned Stapleton's injury time winner in this book, this time we fell victim to another one, Anthony Martial's composed 93rd minute taking United to the Final. John Stones, who I felt played very well, had switched off for a second and only woke up as Martial was closing in on goal. Another season without a trophy, that's twenty one now. Brad has never seen Everton win a thing in his lifetime. With the team we have now, he never will. Major rebuilding is necessary, starting from the top.

The only good news from the day was that Evertonian 'Speedo Mick' walked the two hundred miles to Wembley (in his speedos, naturally) and raised £46,000 for charity.

Sunday 24th April 2016

In tough times for Everton, Rochdale under 16s are really cheering me up, football wise, at the moment. Last Sunday, before we went to Center Parcs, they beat Tranmere Rovers under 16s 4-0. After the game, I overheard a couple of the Tranmere Rovers parents chatting and they said they were given a footballing lesson. The Rochdale side had five under 15s and three under 14s playing, so it bodes wonderfully for the future.

Today, Rochdale u16s had a friendly at Leeds United's training ground, Thorp Arch. It's a terrific set up and great for the lads to play on a top class pitch. Leeds took an early lead and at that stage, I was worried Rochdale would get comprehensively beaten but they fought back superbly. Brad made an excellent penalty save at 1-1, keeping up his record of being great at spot kicks and eventually Rochdale ran out 3-2 winners. Great stuff.

In FA VASE news, the Non-League paper reports that the FA have given permission for the Hereford mascot, Ronaldo the bull, to be paraded around the Wembley stadium prior to the Vase kick off. Apparently the club were supported by the Herefordshire FA in their bid. John Hale, Hereford's Chairman said,

"It will only serve to make this special day even more memorable."

I guess that's true, unless you're the Wembley employee given the task of cleaning up the bull****.

Monday 2nd May 2016

Apart from a few mad Leicester City fans that put a few quid on it, no-one would have guessed it, Leicester City are Premier League Champions. Leicester drew at Old Trafford yesterday, 1-1, which meant that Spurs had to go to Chelsea and win to prevent the title heading to Leicester City for the first time in their history. At half time, Tottenham were 2-0 up and it looked like it would go to Leicester's next game, at home to Everton, however, Chelsea fought back in the second half and when Eden Hazard equalised in the 83rd minute, a party like no other ever experienced before in Leicester kicked off and I am sure it will now go on to the early hours of the morning.

I am really pleased for Leicester City and their fans. Their Italian manager, Claudio Ranieri is a real gentleman and a lot of their players have been around the lower Leagues. Jamie Vardy, their striker, has played Non-League football for Stocksbridge Park Steels, FC Halifax Town and Fleetwood (when they were still in the Conference) before signing for Leicester City for £1 million, in May 2012, in the process becoming the first £1 million non-League player. Tonight, it's looking like a bargain.

I know a few Leicester City fans including Rob Prior (from my Yorkshire Building Society days), Alan Green (from my BM Solutions days), Rob Davies (my first boss at World of Warranty) and Chris Ayres, one of my closest friends who I worked with at Yorkshire Building Society and again at World of Warranty. They are all great lads so I know how much they will be buzzing tonight. The stuff dreams are made of.

Wednesday 4th May 2016

Today has been one of the saddest, most shocking days of my life. I tend to work, on average, four days a week in Southport for Barron Financial Solutions, but today, I was working from home, putting a few things together for this football book and my next fictional book, which will come out a few months after this. I sometimes need the help of Facebook to piece together what Alan and Gordon have been up to in this footballing season, so nipped on to Facebook with the intention of checking their historical statuses.

Whilst on Facebook, I noticed a post from the manager of my old Sunday football team, Mark Pounder, which simply said, 'Great Friends are Hard to Find, Difficult to Leave and Impossible to Forget'…with a comment above it which just said 'Going to miss you buddy x'. It was apparent that it was a message relating to a friend that had died and although I went to the same school as Mark, Ormskirk Grammar School, he is three years younger than me, so other than football friends, we don't share many friends. Nevertheless, I was sorry to hear he had lost someone close to him, so sent a message across asking him who had died. I was stunned by the response.

'Steve Garcia'.

Steve is one of the lads from football. Not just one of the lads, he was central to everything that happened at Metropolitan. When you turned up on a Sunday morning, Steve would always be in the centre of the group of lads, laughing, joking and putting a smile on everyone's face. There are probably only three or four of them that I've regularly kept in touch with since I stopped playing and Steve is one. I went to Aintree races with him a few years ago and he slept the night on the floor of the twin room I was sharing with 'Elks' in Liverpool, as we'd been drinking all day and all night and he didn't want to go home. I'd have woken up moaning, saying my back was aching but Steve just laughed it off and said as floors go, it was pretty comfortable. That was the only day, out of hundreds of race meetings I've been to, that I hardly saw a horse because I was having such a laugh with Steve Garica, Elks and another football mate, John Wilson, that I couldn't drag myself away from the bar to watch the races.

When I needed a computer, I contacted Steve to sort it out as he had a computer business. When I needed some lads to play in the parent's footy tournament at Croston, Steve was the first person I asked and he was so enthusiastic about it, it was like I'd asked him to play at Anfield. I chatted regularly to him on Facebook. He wasn't my closest friend nor was I his closest friend, but realistically I only have twenty or so close friends who I have known for a long time, who would describe me as their 'mate'. Steve was one. Being told he was dead seemed preposterous and although I knew this was not the type of thing 'Pounder' would ever joke about, I found myself typing back,

'NO'.

I still don't know the full details, nor do I ever want to know the full details, but Steve went to play five a side football last night and at some point, during the game, he tragically collapsed. He was 44 years old. I feel desperately sorry for everyone there, but more so for Steve's family and especially his wife, Angela and his son, Lucas who is only two and not yet old enough to fully appreciate what a wonderful man his father is. A lot of tears will be shed by a lot of people over Steve's death and rightfully so. He was one of the best, most positive, most energetic, most amusing people I have ever had the great fortune to meet and to have him taken away from his family just seems dreadfully wrong.

NOTE - My mind hasn't been on football this evening, but Manchester City played Real Madrid in the second leg of their Champions League Semi Final at the Bernabeu. The first leg was a goalless draw and from all accounts, Real Madrid bossed the Second Leg and won from a deflected Gareth Bale cross shot that struck Fernandinho. Real will now meet Atletico Madrid in the Final at the San Siro. Right now, it hardly seems to matter.

Saturday 7th May 2016

I understand that ultimately this is a football book with a central theme of the FA Vase and a lot of people reading it won't have been in the fortunate position to have met Steve Garcia or classed him as a friend, so I don't want to spend thousands and thousands of words telling stories about Steve. I do think, however, that as he was a close friend that I met through playing football and a man who died playing the sport he loved so much, that it would be wrong not to write about the last few days.

The reaction to Steve's death has understandably been one of shock but it has also been really touching how people have been posting on Steve's Facebook wall with their memories of him. The words that come up most regularly are 'gentleman' and 'lovely lad' and people consistently pointed out that he always had a smile on his face and (other than when he was on the football pitch) how he was always so positive. He was fiercely competitive on the pitch though and it has brought a smile and a tear reading stories about how frustrated he would get when team mates would lose possession, whether it was a game at the weekend, five a side or just a kick around at the park.

I have been thinking back this week to when I played for Metropolitan. I have played for several teams that never properly warmed me up as a goalkeeper. Too many people just wanted to kick the ball into the back of the net before the game started and I, as a goalkeeper, would just be in their way. It wasn't like that at Metro. Every game I played, Steve would say,

"Come on Calv, I'll warm you up," and he did. He didn't want to break the back of the net with his shots, often we would just go near the corner flags to warm up because the pitches were so muddy (especially at our home ground at Abbey Lane, Burscough, which was like a paddy field from October to March) but he'd just chip the balls in for ten minutes and we'd have a chat. It was a simple gesture but one that I appreciated as so many others wouldn't bother.

I think the most touching messages of all this week came from Steve's Dad, Gerry and his best mate, Andy Whalley. Gerry spoke of how it was a pleasure being Steve's father, how he loved to compete, how there were no words to describe how much he loved him and he wished he had told him every time he saw him. He pledged to give Steve's son, Lucas, as much love as he had given Steve, so he will be a joy to everyone he meets, like Steve had been.

It seems to me that Steve was a fine man in no small part because he was from a fine family. I have no doubt he will have known how much everyone around him loved him. Positivity stems from appreciation and as so many people have said, Steve was one of the most positive people they've known.

Andy Whalley wrote about how Steve and Angela had bought a new house in Burscough. The sale had gone through on Friday and on Saturday, Andy had gone over to help him unload stuff from the van. Steve had talked about the plans he had for the house and what he was going to do with it. They had also talked about Andy having a Euro party on 11th June, for the European Championship game between England and Russia and how Steve was so looking forward to it and talked about how he wanted to 'get on it from midday'

'Steady on son, maybe one!' Andy had joked.

He said right now he's just numb.

The one thing that this week has really taught me is to treasure the people around you because none of us are here forever. Too many people, including me sometimes, get worked up by trivial nonsense when in the big scheme of things it doesn't really matter. It's a miracle to be here in the first place and every healthy day is one that has to be treasured. I won't fundamentally change as a person through Steve's death, but I will make sure I take a moment to reflect before allowing something stupid to bother me.

Today, Brad had a football match at Radcliffe Borough for Rochdale under 18s against Wigan under 18s. Wigan needed to win to clinch the title whilst for Rochdale u18s it was the final game of the season and the last time the lads would play together. You could tell from the warm up which team wanted it more and there was no doubt in my mind that Wigan would get the three points they needed. The lads at Rochdale under 18s don't seem to have the same hunger and enthusiasm as the under 16s, so I'm hoping next season, with fresh faces in the squad, it will give those that remain a lift.

Before kick off, I ran into Pete Baxendale. Pete was mentioned very early in this book as the man who rang for the ambulance at Eccleston Cricket Club when Brad was hit with the cricket ball. I had no idea why he was at Radcliffe, but it turned out he has an older son, Arnie Baxendale, who is an under 18 at Wigan Athletic and he has just signed his first professional contract at the club. I had a good chat with Pete and he told me Arnie could play full back or centre back, but was playing centre back today. He wasn't the biggest centre back, but was a muscular, well built lad who I would imagine will be more likely to make it as a full back professionally. Having said that, Mascherano and Lucas have been asked to play centre back at times. These days you don't have to be a giant to play there (although apparently you do have to be a giant to be a keeper, as Joe Boyling has found to his expense at Blackburn).

The game finished 3-0 to Wigan and they were crowned Champions. They didn't celebrate excessively, which I guess was for a number of reasons, amongst which I presumed to be that some of them were staying on and some would be getting released so for some, it wasn't a day for wild celebrations.

For Brad, his season is over now and it's time to concentrate a little less on football and a little more on schoolwork with his GCSEs quickly approaching. Come the end of June he will be moving to digs in Rochdale and will begin a new stage in his life. Twelve months ago, he was training at Fleetwood as second choice keeper for the under 16s and thinking a season in grass roots football lay ahead. His development this season has been 'phenomenal' (to borrow a phrase from Roberto Martinez) and although he is still a raw talent, if he keeps on progressing the sky is the limit. Whether it works out or not, we'll be there encouraging him for every step of his journey.

Sunday 8th May 2016

Yesterday, whilst I was watching Wigan being crowned Champions of the North West Youth Alliance under 18's league, Alan was at the Etihad Campus watching his nephew, Joe Boyling, play in the under16's Northern County Cup Final between Greater Manchester Schools and Northumberland Schools. Manchester won 2-0. Great win for them and brilliant for Joe to have kept a clean sheet.

Today it was Gordon's turn to be witness to celebrations and again he was on the right side of them, as he went with wife Jackie, daughter Heather and son Kieran to see Wigan Athletic crowned League One Champions. They lost the game 4-1 to Barnsley but it didn't seem to bother anyone too much as Wigan still won the League by two points and it ensured Barnsley's place in the play offs too, so added to the carnival atmosphere. Brad's club, Rochdale finished five points behind Barnsley in 10th place. As far as I'm aware, this is the highest finish in their history. Hopefully, next season they'll make the Top Six.

Two weeks today it will be the FA Vase Final. Gordon is taking Jackie down for the weekend to stay in the Premier Inn at Wembley on Friday and Saturday night, going to the FA Cup Final on the Saturday (between Manchester United and Crystal Palace) and the Vase/Trophy Finals on the Sunday. Alan is going down to London with Jo, also staying at the Premier Inn at Wembley, for three nights, Friday, Saturday and Sunday, but as a City fan he isn't going to watch the United game.

I'm heading down to London on the Saturday afternoon. On the Friday night, I've booked a table at a MS fundraising event at the Ramada Hotel in Southport. An old school friend, James Coates has MS and the event was initially to raise money for him to have pioneering surgery in Mexico, which involves in layman's terms taking stem cells out, blasting your body with chemotherapy and then putting the stem cells back in. Thankfully, however, James has now been accepted for the surgery in London and is going through the process as we speak. He won't be at the event as he's not well enough to travel up but his wife, Alison and his family will be there and they want to raise as much for MS as they can. It should be a great night and I'm anticipating going down to London with a hangover.

On the Saturday afternoon, I am meeting up with another school friend, Nick Woodward, who was probably my best mate at school from the age of eleven to sixteen. He was always a very intelligent lad and is now a consultant in a hospital in London. His wife Sarah is also currently going through the same process as Alan's wife, Jo, as she has been diagnosed with breast cancer. Providing Sarah is feeling well that weekend, I am meeting Nick at Euston and we are going to watch the FA Cup Final in a pub somewhere, then have a few pints and some food around London. I'm already looking forward to that weekend but my liver is probably dreading it.

Sunday 15th May 2016

One week to go until the FA VASE final and most of the English Non-Leagues promotions and relegations have been sorted out, with just the Cup Finals left. In the National League, CHELTENHAM TOWN stretched away from their main title rivals, Forest Green Rovers and won the League by twelve points, to ensure a return to League Two. This sent Forest Green into the play offs with Braintree Town, Grimsby Town and Dover Athletic. Forest Green beat Dover Athletic 2-1 on aggregate and Grimsby Town beat Braintree by the same aggregate score, 2-1, despite losing the first leg at home 1-0.

Today, saw the first of two Wembley visits for GRIMSBY TOWN in May. This one was the main priority though, as winning would ensure a return to League status. Omar Bogle scored two goals for Grimsby in quick succession just before half time and despite Jon Parkin being introduced for Forest Green at half time and the some relentless pressure from Forest Green in the second half, especially after they pulled a goal back from a quality goal from Keanu Marsh-Brown on the hour mark, Grimsby held on and nicked a third in injury time when Nathan Arnold sealed their victory.

I felt a little sorry for Forest Green as they had accumulated nine points more than Grimsby Town in the regular season. From the outside, it seems a strangely run club though as they sacked their manager Ady Pennock just before the play offs and last week appointed former Notts County manager Mark Cooper to take his place from next season. You would have thought they would have waited until after the play offs but I guess an outsider like me doesn't know what is going on at the club on a day to day basis.

So that was Step One promotion sorted, CHELTENHAM TOWN and GRIMSBY TOWN were promoted to League Two. At the bottom, the four unfortunate teams to be relegated were Welling United, Kidderminster Harriers, Altrincham and FC Halifax Town, the FA Trophy Finalists. FC Halifax went into their last game of the season needing a win against Macclesfield Town to stay up. Despite taking the lead 1-0, they ended up drawing 1-1 and with other results going against them, particularly Guiseley's remarkable 4-3 win over Torquay at Nethermoor, Halifax will drop down to National League North next season.

In Step Two, National League North was won by Solihull Moors, who won by nine clear points to earn their place in the National League next season. Our old friends at North Ferriby United finished second, with AFC Fylde, Harrogate Town and Boston United joining them in the play offs. This pitted Boston United against North Ferriby United in the play offs and as Alan and I had come to witness last season, there was no love lost between the two. Boston United looked like they may well have done enough to reach the Play Off Final when they beat 'Ferriby' 2-0 in the 1st Leg, but we know from experience, North Ferriby United stormed back in the second leg, winning 3-0 with goals from three of their FA Trophy heroes, Liam King, Tom Denton and Danny Clarke.

In the other National League North play off, AFC Fylde overcame Harrogate Town 2-1 over the two legs so travelled to North Ferriby for the Final (the Final takes place at the home of the team who finished higher in the League). AFC Fylde took the lead midway through the first half with Sam Finley scoring from a knock down from Fylde captain, Tom Hannigan. Wayne Brooksby equalised on the stroke of half time though and with no further scoring in the second half the game went to extra time.

I was following the game on the internet and felt that if the game went to penalties, Ferriby would triumph. They won both their FA Trophy Semi Final and Final last season on pens and with a keeper like Adam Nicklin and a deadly penalty taker like Liam King, they would be supremely confident. As it happened, penalties weren't necessary. Five minutes into extra time, impressive centre back, Danny Hone had a header saved by the Fylde keeper Unwin, but the rebound fell kindly to Hone and he made no mistake second time around, striking the ball over the keeper and into the back of the net. North Ferriby United saw the game out and the 'Villagers' were promoted to the National League for the first time in their history. Whether they manage to retain their squad and their manager, Billy Heath, who must be attracting a lot of interest, remains to be seen, but for now, their supporters can wallow in a success that is probably even greater than last year's FA Trophy win.

So, that means SOLIHULL MOORS and NORTH FERRIBY UNITED will be in the National League next season with Lowestoft Town, Hednesford Town and Corby Town all relegated.

In National League South, it looked for much of the season that Ebbsfleet United would go up to the National League as Champions but when they faltered SUTTON UNITED kept their winning streak going and eventually pipped Ebbsfleet United by six points. Ebbsfleet were joined in the play offs by Maidstone United, Truro City and Whitehawk. Maidstone beat Truro City 3-0 on aggregate but the Ebbsefleet United against Whitehawk play off was much tighter finishing 3-3 on aggregate and eventually being decided 3-2 on penalties. I'm not sure I agree with penalties settling a Play Off after a long season, I think it would be fairer if the team finishing higher in the League were awarded the tie. You could finish second, twenty points higher than a team in fifth but lose out because your penalty takers had a bad day or the opposition keeper had a great few minutes. I know others will argue everyone knows the rules at the start of the season but it seems harsh.

As it happens, Ebbsefleet United beat the lower placed League team, Whitehawk in the Play Off Semi-Finals on penalties but their penalty luck ran out in the final. Yesterday, they drew with Maidstone United 2-2 after extra time after taking the lead twice, once in normal time and once in extra time. Agonisingly for Ebbsfleet United supporters, they were moments away from promotion when Maidstone substitute Dumebi Dumaka scored a 121st minute equaliser. Worse was to come, Danny Kedwell, the impressive striker who we saw last season at North Ferriby United, had scored two penalties in the actual game, but his attempt to score a hat trick of penalties with another in the shoot out, was saved by Maidstone keeper, Lee Worgan and Maidstone United won 4-3 on penalties.

It was therefore SUTTON UNITED and MAIDSTONE UNITED that were promoted to the National League. Havant & Waterlooville, Hayes & Yeading and Basingstoke Town were relegated.

Further down the Non-League pyramid, several teams we have come across in the last three seasons were involved in promotions and relegations. New Mills fared the worst. We saw them at Mickleover Sports in the FA Trophy but they must have lost a lot of players as they only managed three draws all season (and no wins) as they were relegated from the Evo Stik Northern Premier League Division One North. On a brighter note for them, their Church Lane ground is used for the Sky One comedy programme 'Rovers' starring Sue Johnston and Craig Cash.

Warrington Town, who we also visited in the FA Trophy actually won New Mills League by fifteen points. Their demonstrative manager, Shaun Reid, controversially departed before the end of the season though when he discovered he would not be having his contract renewed by the club. Some of his touchline antics received a few negative comments from myself in 'Brutal Giants' but he had obviously assembled a fine side and I was sorry to see him depart.

As predicted, the amount of games Morpeth Town had to play from the end of February onwards caught up with them and they could only finish fourth, nineteen points behind EBAC Northern League Champions, Shildon. That will soon be forgotten if they win the FA VASE next weekend though.

Hereford won the Midland League Premier Division by seven points from Alvechurch so will go to Step Four next season, competing in the FA Trophy rather than the FA Vase. A Wembley Final will be a lot harder to get to next season in that one, so they will be hoping they seize the opportunity to finish the season on a high next week. Their promotion also ensures Mustapha Bundu will need to be playing for a different side next season and will have to leave the club after his Wembley appearance. Wonder if fate will conspire to see him score the winner?

Colne, another club with an eccentric manager in Steve Cunningham, finished as Champions of the North West Counties Premier Division. Danny Boyle scored the winner in their last game, a 1-0 win over to 1874 Northwich to secure the title with a two point gap to Runcorn Linnets.

Hartley Wintney also won the Cherry Red Combined Counties Premier Division with Camberley Town finishing third in the same League.

So, that's everything rounded up and all that are left now are the FA finals next weekend. It will be Alan's 45th consecutive FA game spanning the FA Cup, FA

Trophy, FA Vase and FA Sunday Cup. Next stop the FA Youth Cup next season but we'll leave that one to Alan and read the stories on social media. He's the only real groundhopper amongst us anyway. Me and Gordon are just football fanatics.

Saturday 21st May 2016 – 4pm

I'm on the train down to Euston and I'm feeling rough. Hangover from hell but sometimes you look back on a night and think it was worth it. Last night was one of those nights. The Charity evening for Multiple Sclerosis arranged by James Coates wife, Alison, was superb. Great food, great company, lots and lots of drinks, a Katy Perry tribute act, a Robbie Williams tribute act and we even managed to get Joel to my Mum and Dad's so we stopped over at the hotel. I don't remember what time we got to bed but I do remember drinking in the Hotel bar long after the actual event was over with some old school friends.

I can see from Facebook messages that Alan and Gordon have both safely arrived in London and are separately doing their 'touristy' bits with their wives. Alan is doing a bit of training for his 'Glencoe Challenge' by walking from Westminster Bridge to Tower Bridge and back with Jo, which he says is 5.2 miles whilst Gordon and Jackie have been to The Mall, Marble Arch and Buckingham Palace and are now having a couple of drinks before the FA Cup Final which kicks off at 5.30pm this year, apparently to ensure a bigger TV audience. It should be 3pm in my opinion. Some traditions need to be respected.

Anyway, the late kick off has given me more time to get over my hangover but I am now on a busy train carriage next to four girls, probably in their early twenties, who are doing their utmost to wind me up good and proper. One of them is travelling down with rollers in, whilst another one is getting her hair done by her mate on the train. All four of them are wittering away incessantly, drowning everyone else out on the train with their dramas and false laughter. The hairdresser of the bunch has had her boyfriend on loudspeaker on her phone for the whole bloody journey from

Preston to London and he has some sort of throat infection so sounds like a Dalek. You're away on a girlie weekend, talk to your mates. Oh and boyfriend, go out and see some of your mates whilst your girlfriend is heading to London, don't be sat in, speaking monosyllabically to her in your croaky voice whilst she does her mates hair.

It's going to be hair of the dog for me. As soon as I get off this train at Euston, I'm going to be head for a pint. That's if I don't get arrested beforehand for grabbing a phone off a fellow passenger and throwing it out the window along with 'poorly throat' boy. As you can probably tell, I'm not good with a hangover.

11.30 pm

Now tucked up in bed in a Travelodge in Greenwich High Road. I booked in here for £58 which is pretty reasonable for London on Cup Final weekend. Not as nice as the Ramada Plaza where I stayed last night, but I'll be leaving soon after I wake up in the morning, so it'll do the job.

Nick met me off the train and as soon as I got away from those four girls my mood lifted. The girl who was on the phone to her boyfriend for the whole journey, said, on arrival at Euston,

"I'm going now, babe. We're going to get a taxi to the hotel. We'll be fifteen minutes. I'll ring you as soon as we're in the room."

Honestly! I wanted to go out and buy them two badges saying 'I'm In The Saddest Relationship Of All Time'. I'm very much of the opinion that you have to give each other space in a relationship and allow each other time with friends. Maybe the hangover didn't help but there were a lot of sober looking train travellers who were huffing, puffing and rolling their eyes at the foursome/fivesomes total disregard for their fellow travellers.

Nick has lived in London for a long time now, at a guess about twenty years, so he knows his way around very well and soon found us a good looking pub. It was perfect timing as the FA Cup Final was about to kick off. There were a few giggles and guffaws in the pub prior to kick off as the 24 year old former X-Factor contestant, Karen Harding, missed her cue and the National Anthem was almost finished by the time she joined in. A terrible moment for her but I guess I wouldn't have looked up her name or taken any interest in who she was unless something extraordinary had happened.

This was the start of a pretty incident packed FA Cup Final. I'm not Alan Pardew's biggest fan, I think he becomes a bit of a thug when he gets riled and don't mind Manchester United so, on balance, I would have slightly preferred a United win. I knew the occasional press comment about Pardew for England would only gather pace if Palace won the FA Cup and as I'm expecting another English failure in the Euros, I'm hoping Pardew isn't touted as the new Messiah.

It was a tight game that took a long time to fully come to life and to be honest we were only half watching it at times as trips to the bar were necessary and it was good catching up as I hadn't seen Nick for a good while. Marcus Rashford went on a run down the left wing in the first minute which prompted me to tell Nick about my Dad spotting his talent less than twelve months ago when he was on the pitch next to Brad at Blackburn Rovers Academy. As with everyone else I have told this story to, I told Nick to watch out for Angel Gomes too.

Chris Smalling was booked for a foul on Connor Wickham when Mark Clattenburg really should have played an advantage to Palace, who 'scored' from the resultant move although a lot of the United players had stopped running by the time the ball went in the goal. Still, it was a decision that stoked up all the Palace fans in the pub and they shouted abuse at the televisions. There was a healthy contingent of both sets of supporters in the pub which added to a lively atmosphere.

Later, Juan Mata had a great opportunity to score but Wayne Hennessey pulled off a good low save to his right. Soon after, Fellaini hit the corner of post and bar with an effort he smashed towards goal with his right foot after a sublime flick on by Rashford. Manchester United were dominating at this point and another chance went begging when Martial's header hit the post.

With twelve minutes left, Crystal Palace took a surprise lead. Fellaini partially cleared a ball that had been played into the United box but when the ball was played back in to Puncheon on the Palace left he was allowed the freedom to run deep into the United box before smashing a shot past De Gea on his near post to put Palace 1-0 ahead.

You could possibly blame De Gea for allowing Puncheon to exploit a gap on his near post or perhaps Juan Mata who was the closest man but failed to close Puncheon down quickly enough, but credit where it was due, Puncheon was given a half chance and he took full advantage. Pardew did an embarrassing Dad dance on the halfway line which took over from the National Anthem as the most cringeful moment of the 2016 FA Cup Final.

If Mata was partially to blame for the Palace goal he quickly atoned for his error. Three minutes after the Palace goal Rooney tried to dance around several

Palace players to get a shot on goal, but when he was forced wide to the right by the Palace defence, he chipped a ball across to the back post. Fellaini tried to bring it down on the world's most used footballing chest, but the ball ran dropped behind him where Juan Mata was perfectly placed to drive a low shot on target which was deflected past Hennessey into the Palace goal. 1-1.

Yannick Bolasie almost won it for Palace when he drilled a low 25 yard shot towards the bottom left hand corner of the United goal but it was expertly saved by De Gea's outstretched fingertips. Soon after Bolasie was wrestled to the ground by Smalling just as the Palace attacker turned him and was about to use his speed to run into space in the United half. Smalling spotted Clattenburg running towards him, fiddling in his pocket for his notebook and knew his fate was sealed. A second yellow was brandished by Clattenburg followed by a red and for the first time since Kevin Moran's red card in 1985, United would have to fight out an FA Cup Final with only ten men.

Like 1985, this game headed to extra time too and also like 1985, Manchester United grabbed a winner. It perhaps wasn't quite as fine a goal (how I hate writing that) as Whiteside's curler past Southall in 1985, but it wasn't far off. When Valencia's cross from the left was cleared it looped up to the onrushing Jesse Lingard who smashed the ball right footed, on the volley, into the top right hand corner of Hennessey's goal. 2-1 and the FA Cup was United's.

Nick and I left the pub soon after the final whistle and went to a few pubs and bars around 'The Shard' but we heard later that Van Gaal was stepping down and Jose 'The Special One' Mourinho would be taking over at United. With Pep Guardiola leaving Bayern Munich to take over at Manchester City, the Manchester derby's are going to be interesting next season. Incidentally, Everton are another club who will have a new manager next season with the board losing patience with Roberto Martinez after declining form over the last two seasons. Not sure who I want to take over, but whoever it turns out to be has as big a rebuilding job as Mourinho will have at Manchester United but without the same budget.

So, that's the FA Cup sorted and I've actually gone easy on the beer tonight (unlike last night) as I know I have a big day ahead tomorrow. After three seasons of FA journeys, ours comes to an end tomorrow. I've faded out the picture this season, largely because of work commitments, bad weather causing postponements when I was all set to go and especially Brad's football at Rochdale but Alan has kept strong and this is his swansong with Gordon and me. Let's hope Hereford against Morpeth Town turns out to be a classic.

CHAPTER TWENTY TWO

Sunday 22nd May 2016

The FA VASE Final – Non League Finals Day

HEREFORD FC v MORPETH TOWN FC

Venue – Wembley Stadium

I don't drink very often these days. I'd say I only have more than a couple of pints about once every six weeks or so, so having had a skinful on Friday and quite a few more yesterday with Nick, my body felt a bit achey this morning and for the second day on the trot I had a hangover, but thankfully this time it was only a mild one. I was going to have to get the Docklands Light Railway and the tube to Wembley and I was just hoping those four girls from yesterday were nowhere in sight.

As I wasn't feeling at my freshest I decided to walk down Greenwich High Street towards the town centre. My Dad will be ashamed to read this, but my sole purpose was to seek out a McDonald's to have a McSausage & Egg McMuffin breakfast. I found one and was pleasantly surprised to see the Cutty Sark a couple of hundred yards beyond it. My geographical knowledge of London isn't the greatest and I hadn't realised where it was situated. After my McDonalds (I had to get my priorities right), I went up to inspect it. It's a fine old ship, designed for the nineteenth century tea trade, but it brought back more recent memories for me, running past it three times in the early stages of the London Marathon, when you delude yourself into believing that you are going to feel great throughout, before every muscle in your body aches and every step seems like a journey of a thousand miles. Still something persuades you to try it again. I applied this year to do it for 'The Christie' but my application (like so many others) was rejected.

After a few tourist related stops at places like Canary Wharf and Westminster, I was soon at the Premier Inn, Wembley. I rang Alan when I was at reception and he told me to grab a coffee at the bar and he would be down in a few minutes. He said Jo was knackered from the five mile walk yesterday so he was just making sure she was sorted for the day before leaving. I wasn't surprised she was knackered, she's just been through extensive rounds of chemotherapy and radiotherapy and five miles seems like a hell of a lot in the circumstances. It shows how tough she is though.

Whilst I was waiting for Alan, Gordon and Jackie walked through the front entrance. Like me, they had been out in search of a McDonalds to ease a hangover. After the FA Cup Final, they had hit the bars of Wembley and had been drinking into the early hours with fans of Manchester United, Crystal Palace, Morpeth Town, Hereford, Halifax and Grimsby. Keeping up North East stereotypes Gordon said the Morpeth lot stayed out longest and partied hardest.

During the course of our conversation, Gordon also revealed that despite us buying four tickets for the Finals Day (the extra one was for Jackie), he had subsequently won two Club Wembley tickets in the Liverpool County FA draw. He was going to make use of the facilities prior to kick off, have some food and hot drinks and check the seats out. From what he could work out, they were in a prime spot, in the lower level, right on the halfway line. Not wanting them to go to waste, he suggested that him and Jackie watch the FA Vase final from there and then once that game finished, he would swop with Alan and I, and we could use the Club Wembley tickets for the FA Trophy game. Gordon and Jackie were having to drive home and they said unless the Trophy game started brilliantly and looked like being a cracker, they probably wouldn't stay for the whole ninety minutes of that one.

Soon Alan was down and we made our way across to the stadium. After a bit of a wander up to the Bobby Moore statue, we headed in. There were rumoured to be around 19,000 Hereford fans heading down for the Final, whilst Morpeth were also bringing about 4,000. It was certainly going to be a bumper crowd for an FA Vase Final (boosted further with the early arrivals from Halifax and Grimsby) as last year's final between Glossop North End and North Shields had attracted a crowd of 9,674. There had been 535 teams who had entered the competition and we were down to the last two.

After saying temporary farewells to Jackie and Gordon, we headed to the next tier up and checked our seats out. They were decent seats, just in front of the corporate boxes on the 18 yard line of the goal Hereford were warming up in and straight across from the masses of Hereford fans. Gordon text Alan though to say that their seats were out of this world. They were right on the halfway line, twenty two rows up, in the padded seats reserved for dignitaries just in front of where the players would go to receive their medals and just above where the players come out. A few rows back from the coaching staff for both sides. Despite the hospitality and fantastic seats he still said he would swop with us after the first game. It was really good of him that. Upgrading is brilliant, downgrading isn't so great.

As we still had forty five minutes to kill before kick off, Alan and I decided we'd go and put a bet on. We went down, grabbed a couple of betting slips and checked out the odds.

"What are you thinking?" Alan asked.

"I'm thinking the odds for Morpeth are ridiculous! 9-2? Do they not know that Northern League teams have won this six times out the last seven?"

"The bookies are thinking Hereford are nailed on. Also if there's almost twenty thousand Hereford fans here, they're going to take a lot more money on Hereford than they will on Morpeth," Alan reasoned.

"You've seen Hereford three times Alan, do you think they're nailed on to win this?"

"No, mate, could go either way."

"Exactly. I reckon Morpeth might just edge it, but I can't see them keeping Hereford out the whole game. 2-1 for Morpeth maybe. Hang on, what's the odds on both teams to score and Morpeth to win?"

Alan scanned his sheet.

"11-2."

"Right," I said with confidence, "my fiver's going on Morpeth to win with both teams to score at 11-2."

"Mine too," Alan replied.

I used to like a decent punt. I was never a big time Charlie when it came to gambling but when I had a bit of money, I would put a tenner or twenty on a horse sometimes. Tighter times over the last few years has called for tighter restraints and my William Hill betting account has a maximum deposit of £10 for a day now and I'd never put more than a fiver on a single horse (which I rarely bother with these days) or a single football match. I tend to have a bet one or two Saturdays a month. Sometimes you feel like the bookies have priced something up wrong. This felt like one of those days. Part of my brain was telling me to lob a tenner on but I knew I'd be cursing my profligacy if it went to waste and it had been an expensive weekend. Incidentally, 'profligacy' is a word I wouldn't know the meaning of if it wasn't for football. Often, if a team has a load of chances, spurn them and go on to lose, the football journalists will write about them cursing their profligacy. Maybe that's why I've been going to football matches for the last forty something years, for an education.

Bets were placed. Battered fivers were handed over and Alan started calculating how much we'd win.

"£32.50 each," I said as I could see him doing mental arithmetic in his head.

"Be decent that," Al said as we took our seats again. No gambler ever places a bit with any other immediate thought than ones that tell them that they are going to win. That's why they placed the bet in the first place. Reality tends to bite a little further down the line.

Prior to kick off we chat. I ask about Jo's health and Alan says she's doing wonderfully well and all the signs are positive. She sometimes feels so well she does too much, like yesterday, and then realises she is getting ahead of herself, but overall, they feel like since the breast cancer diagnosis things could not have gone better.

We also get on to discussing 'The Christie' and Alan confides that after the 'Glencoe Challenge' in July, he is going to draw his fundraising to a close as says every time he does fundraising, he asks the same circle of friends for support and he can't go on indefinitely asking them for money, as they have been fantastically supportive to raise £15,000 plus already. He says he will keep his justgiving site open and I say I will keep totting up the royalties from my first two football books and will keep donating my 50p a sale, throwing the money in every few months. We then get to talking about the Vase book.

I must admit, because my participation has been limited, I have had my doubts about doing a book for this journey. It has been Alan and especially Gordon who have pushed for us to do it between us. The FA Trophy was about one team's journey to the Final (North Ferriby United) but this year everything has chopped and changed. The lads felt that there was still enough of a story to tell and I hope they are proved right.

"Al, how would you feel if I didn't donate the money to 'The Christie' for this book?" I ask.

"It's fine, mate. You've kept the money consistently coming in for the first two books at times when we had no events planned. You've done enough, mate. I've appreciated all your help. You don't need to do any more. I wanted to raise £1,000 for the Christie doing the FA Cup 14 Rounds. After Glencoe, I reckon we'll have handed over £17,000. It's been superb."

I explain my thinking. I tell Alan about how it's been a tough few weeks. How Steve tragically died earlier this month. I was thinking I could maybe give the 50p a sale to Steve's widow, Angela, this time around and she could donate it to the charity of her choice.

"I think that's a brilliant idea," Alan agrees.

With plans in place, the teams arrive on the Wembley turf and we settle down to watch the match. It's a bright sunny day with a shapr breeze. Hereford are predominantly in white, Morpeth are in what I would describe as a wasp coloured kit, predominantly black, but with orange and black vertical stripes running down the chest and back. We noticed Mustapha Bundu isn't starting for Hereford, the big Sierra Leone striker has been a constant headache for defenders in the games Al has witnessed so it seems a strange decision.

"Perhaps he's had a knock or perhaps Peter Beadle (Hereford's manager) has one eye on next season," Alan concludes, knowing Bundu won't be at the club next season due to visa complications.

Once the game kicks off, Hereford start confidently. Passing the ball around confidently and restricting Morpeth Town to an initial chasing game. After the ball ricocheted around a little, Joe Tumelty picked the ball up on the Hereford left, just inside the Morpeth Town half. Four Morpeth players advance towards him from North, South, East and West but none put a challenge in, allowing Tumelty to cut inside a lay a ball off to Rob Purdie. Purdie is about forty yards out with a clear sight on goal, he takes one touch to push the ball forwards with his right foot and then from thirty five yards unleashes a low, fierce drive that narrowly avoids the fingertips of the diving Karl Dryden in the Morpeth Town goal and finds the bottom right hand corner of the keeper's goal. Two minutes in and Hereford are 1-0 up. Their contingent go wild.

"What a goal but that's our bet screwed," Alan said in a voice which was a mix of admiration and despair.

"Not necessarily, we needed Hereford to score. What a screamer though!" I pointed out. I've been to both the old and new Wembley's many times and don't think I've seen a better goal than that. It was wonderfully struck.

After the goal, it was more of the same. Hereford controlling the game, Morpeth chasing shadows.

"Morpeth haven't started," Alan observed, "if the game carries on like this it could be four or five," perhaps making comparisons with Camberley Town's 5-0 hammering of Newton Aycliffe on a day when another Northern League side just couldn't get going.

Hereford's dominance was rewarded with another great chance. Sirdic Grant played a neat one two and found himself through on goal with only the keeper to beat. Karl Dryden was off his line like lightning and Grant was forced to shoot early. As Dryden dived bravely at Grant's feet, he tried to lift the ball over the keeper but didn't get enough lift on his effort and Dryden was able to parry clear. It was an important save. Morpeth couldn't allow Hereford to run away with the game in the early stages.

Dryden was called into action again soon after. Hereford crossed from the left after some neat inter play involving Joel Edwards, the ball was flicked on by Symons to Pablo Haysham on the back post who powered a header low to Karl Dryden's left. The ball bounced awkwardly in front of the keeper, but Dryden managed to get enough on the ball to force it out for a Hereford corner.

From the resultant corner, the ball was cleared to goalscorer Purdie, who crossed from the left, Joe Tumelty made a near post run and caught the ball sweetly on the half volley forcing Dryden to make another good save low to his left and send the ball out for another corner. It was one way traffic and the stocky, fair haired figure of Dryden was keeping Morpeth in the game. He had been receiving rave reviews for his performances in some of the earlier rounds, particularly against North Shields and South Shields and was now being called upon to show his goalkeeping talents once more.

Morpeth's first real decent passage of play in the opposition half created their first decent chance. Keith Graydon, a calming influence in midfield brought the ball down just in front of the centre circle with a deft touch and laid the ball off to James Novak. The number three sprinted forwards down the left, playing a great one two with Luke Carr. Novak cut the ball back to Sean Talor who was just inside the Hereford box. He attempted a right foot shot to the keeper's top left hand corner, but Martin Horsell managed to knock the ball out for a corner in an unorthodox style. It wasn't the most convincing of saves by the keeper but he had kept the ball out and prevented what, at that stage, would have been an undeserved equaliser for Morpeth Town.

The corner came to nothing and Horsell's next involvement was to pump a big long ball forward with his left foot that landed deep in the Morpeth Town half. 45 year old defender, Chris Swailes won the header and it went towards Luke Carr who, under pressure miscontrolled the ball, allowing Sirdic Grant to nip in, take the ball and charge quickly towards goal. He was running with the ball at his right foot but foxed a Morpeth Town defender with a step over which allowed the ball to run on to his left foot and lashed an effort from the edge of the box that rattled the crossbar and bounced over for a goal kick. It would have been a great goal by Grant but Luke Carr was breathing a huge sigh of relief.

Sirdic Grant was the most impressive player on the pitch at this point. The Ghanian was another, like Mustapha Bundu, who studies at Hartpury College in Gloucester and is in the UK on an educational visa so will not be allowed to progress with Hereford beyond the Step Five stage they have been at this season. He was trying to leave Hereford FC in style and very nearly had a wonderful goal in his farewell performance. Morpeth Town's goal was leading a charmed life.

The chances just kept coming for Hereford. The stocky frame of Mike Symons won the ball down the left, after a neat chipped ball from Aaron Birch and the centre forward's run finished with him cutting a great ball across the six yard box. Pablo Haysham thought he had a simple tap in but he held his head in his hands as his effort was diverted to safety after a desperate lunge from a Morpeth defender. Hereford could and should have been two or three up at this stage and we wondered whether Morpeth could manage to get to half time still in the game.

For all Hereford's dominance, Morpeth were occasionally creating some good chances of their own. Graydon won a tough tackle in midfield. He slid in ferociously and would have been in trouble if he hadn't won the ball cleanly. It was the type of tackle I used to love to see thirty years ago but has seemingly been almost outlawed from the modern game. The ball fell to Sean Taylor on the Morpeth left. He played the ball inside to Ben Sayer. James Novak had darted forward along the left but 30 yards out, Sayer chose to choot. It was an ambitious effort but was well struck and it flew only inches over the bar. It seemed like Hereford keeper, Horsell, may have applied a fingertip to ensure the trajectory was above rather than below the crossbar but referee, Stuart Attwell, gave a goal kick.

"It's a good game, isn't it?" I said to Alan.

"Yeh, quality," he replied, "not sure some of these older lads at Morpeth will appreciate having the legs run off them in this heat though."

It wasn't a scorcher but it was a warm Spring day. How the likes of Graydon and Swailes would last for ninety minutes on a big pitch that was being exploited by a busy, neat passing Hereford team remained to be seen. The next goal would be vital. If Hereford scored it, we could see no way back for Morpeth Town. We kept saying though that it was imperative that Morpeth got to half time no more than one down.

In the 34th minute, Morpeth had their third corner of the game. Ben Sayer took the corner and drove it into the six yard box but it looked too close to keeper, Horsell, rose for the ball, challenged by his own centre back and a Morpeth forward. I'm not sure whether the other two players also jumping for the ball distracted Horsell or whether he just timed his jump a little wrong, but the ball cleared all three of them. Chris Swailes was standing behind them and, surprised to see the ball bouncing towards him, he just stuck his chest out and watched as the ball rebounded off it and towards the goal. There were Hereford two players on the line and they both tried to scramble it clear whilst Swailes chased the ball down hoping to get a firmer touch on it and ensure it crossed the line but no further touches were necessary. The Assistant referee indicated to Attwell that the ball had crossed the line and 45 year old Swailes had become the oldest ever scorer of a goal in a competitive match at the new Wembley. 1-1. About seven Morpeth players ran towards Swailes and contemplated dragging him down on the floor and then thought better of it. Swailes probably packed a fair punch and at his age, if he was dragged to floor, it might take him five minutes to get back up. It wasn't one of the greatest goals Wembley had ever seen but they all count and somehow the game was level.

The goal was a game changer. Hereford had bossed the first half hour but now their player's minds seemed to be filled with doubt and frustration whilst the Morpeth Town players seemed to be thinking, 'You know what, we can win this'. Morpeth's Luke Carr was buzzing around midfield in lively fashion and when he received the ball from Graydon, he looked to turn but was tackled and the ball fell to Sayer, who played a sensible ball to Novak who had been one of Morpeth's most impressive players in the first half. The left back once again ran into space before playing the ball back to Sayer who had made a run to support his team mate. He continued forwards and played an incisive pass through to Carr who had made a penetrating run beyond the Hereford defenders, defying the offside trap in the process. He could have shot but unselfishly squared the ball to Michael Chilton who was screaming for the ball to be laid off. Horsell had come to his near post to cut off a direct effort from Carr, so Chilton had the whole goal to aim at from six yards out. The Morpeth Town forward had time and space to pick his spot but allowed the ball to run across his left foot and tried to prod it into the far corner with the outside of his right foot but only managed to steer the ball wide. It was an awful miss. Chilton is a prolific Northern League goalscorer and it was now his turn to hold his head in his hands, hoping he wouldn't be thinking back to his golden chance at the end of ninety minutes at two o'clock.

Pablo Haysham had one more half chance for Hereford but soon after Attwell blew for half time and a frenetic, incident packed first half finished 1-1. For the first half hour, Hereford were by far the better team but Swailes scrambled goal had lifted Morpeth Town and for the last fifteen minutes they had edged it. If Hereford got back on top in the second half, Chilton could rue missing an easy chance. One thing was for certain, it didn't look like it would finish one each. There had been a steady flow of great chances throughout the first half.

It only took forty three seconds of the second half for the next goal to come. Luke Carr combined well with Sayer, Graydon and Fry before making a run into the box. He received the ball, evaded a tackle and put the ball to Sean Taylor on the left of the box. Taylor was short of options so chipped the ball back to Carr who was on the near post. He clipped a left footed shot that was all about accuracy rather than power across the body of Horsell and into the far corner of the goal. 2-1 to Morpeth Town!

Hereford were stunned and Morpeth, aided by the hard work of Carr and Sayer and the calmness of Graydon in midfield were pushing Hereford back. In the 59th minute, Stephen Forster came forward from right full back to take a throw in deep in Hereford's half. He threw the ball to Jordan Fry, who knocked it back to captain, Keith Graydon. Graydon tried to put a diagonal ball through to Sean Taylor, but it was diverted by a Hereford defender into the path of Michael Chilton. Facing away from goal, Chilton span around before putting an inch perfect ball through to Taylor who was now running through on goal. Horsell was perhaps half a step too far to his right and Taylor found the narrowest of gaps to slide the ball past Horsell on his near (left) post and extend Morpeth's lead. 3-1. This time there was a pile on, on top of the goalscorer, but old stagers, Graydon and Swailes made sure they were last to arrive, so they were on the top.

Hereford were now chasing the game and Mustapha Bundu and John Mills, two strikers, were introduced. They almost had an immediate impact too, Bundu lofting the ball over the Morpeth defence to his fellow striker, Mills who failed to get a good connection on the ball and it ran tamely through to the grateful arms of keeper, Karl Dryden.

Hereford were now all out of sorts and when they had a dangerous free kick, thirty yards out, after a foul by Graydon, Pablo Haysham played a quick one two with Aaron Birch before sending a tame lofted effort well over the Morpeth Town bar. Hereford were still trying to play good football, but they were now lacking a goal threat in the final third.

Steven Anderson came on for Morpeth Town and he had a great chance to score a Wembley goal. Anderson turned on the left wing and when the ball was passed to Ben Sayer, Anderson made a darting run inside which was found by a clever ball from Sayer. He let the ball run past his right foot and when he spotted a defender about to dive into a tackle Anderson pushed the ball beyond him then struck a low, hard shot that was gathered well by Horsell.

Morpeth were now rampant as Hereford were looking dejected as the clock ticked down. A few minutes later, Ben Sayer, who had been terrific, put another great ball through to Sean Taylor who struck a fizzing shot that Horsell did very well to get down to his right to save. It had been a mixed afternoon for Horsell but he had made some fine stops.

Mustapha Bundu had been very quiet since his introduction, expertly marshalled by Chris Swailes and Michael Hall, but when Sirdic Grant's deep cross found Bundu on the right of the Morpeth box, he tried a curling effort that was similar to Ronnie Whelan's Milk Cup effort in 1983, but sadly for Bundu his was inches wide rather than into the top corner. Bundu had another great chance soon after, meeting Rob Purdie's corner with a firm header that was tipped over the bar by Karl Dryden.

That was what I thought initially anyway, but Alan pointed out it had actually been headed over his own bar by another Morpeth Town substitute, Damien Mullen.

As the fourth official was holding up the board to indicate that there would be four minutes of injury time, Mike Symons had a great chance to pull a goal back, but his shot from ten yards out lacked pace and was easily saved by Dryden. Hereford needed that to set up a grandstand finish and once the keeper saved, it seemed certain to finish 3-1.

Keith Graydon had been sitting very deep in the second half, since Morpeth had taken the lead, almost acting as a fifth defender, but once Symons missed his chance, he must have sensed the game was over and suddenly appeared in a far more offensive position. When Hereford tried to play the ball out from the back, he made a crunching tackle and the ball fell to Steven Anderson. Anderson intelligently spotted the run of fresh legged fellow substitute Shaun Bell and weighted a lovely ball into Bell's path. His left footed shot was deflected and it squirmed into the back of the net. 4-1 and the Vase belonged to Morpeth Town!

Karl Dryden ran the length of the pitch to join in the celebrations in the Hereford box and then had to quickly run back again when someone perhaps pointed out there were still three minutes to go. I remembered what Gordon used to say in the earlier rounds,

"First to four wins!"

There were no further chances and the Morpeth Town, players, staff and supporters celebrated exuberantly once the final whistle had blown. They had been under immense pressure for the first thirty minutes but after that had been the better team. It had been an immense performance by all fourteen Morpeth Town players and we were delighted for them.

After watching Keith Graydon and subsequently the rest of the Morpeth Town side lift the cup, we went to collect our £32.50 winnings. It was the seventh time in eight years that a Northern League side had won the FA Vase. The clubs in that League are reluctant to move up to Step Four as the cost of travelling would increase rapidly with the much greater distances involved and working on tight budgets, they are doubtful whether it makes economic sense. Thus, the Northern League is the toughest Step Five league in the country. To dismiss Morpeth Town as big outsiders in this game seemed naïve and so it proved to be.

We subsequently met Gordon and Jackie outside the Club Wembley entrance. They had thoroughly enjoyed the Vase game but, probably a little jaded from their late night, had decided to head home. They handed over the Club Wembley passes and we headed in.

Once we were in there, we spotted a few familiar faces from the Non-League scene. Alan spotted a couple from the Newton Aycliffe committee who he had met in previous rounds. They had come down to support Non-League day and also to see how Morpeth Town fared. They considered their club to be not far behind Morpeth in terms of playing staff and were bitterly disappointed with how the wheels had come off at Camberley Town.

Subsequently, I spotted Paul Fairclough, England 'C' Manager. He formed part of our story during the FA Cup visits to Stevenage. Paul had previously managed Stevenage and his late father, Eric, had worked for my Dad for many years. Dad contacted him and asked if he could put us in touch with people at the club and our fantastic treatment from Stevenage was, in no small part, down to having the connection with Paul. I went over, told him I was Richie Wade's son and we had a good chat with him for five minutes.

We saved the best until last though. As we were heading out to take our seats prior to the FA Trophy game between Halifax Town and Grimsby Town, who should come into the bar at Club Wembley other than several of the Morpeth Town players and staff . What did they carry in with them? None other than the FA Vase trophy! Alan and I had got our hands on the FA Trophy last season when we were invited into the Directors Lounge by the former Chairman of North Ferriby United, Les Hare, to have our photos taken with the trophy and now we had a chance to get our photos taken with the FA Vase.

I am normally a little less forward in such circumstances than Alan, but for once Alan hesitated and I was in there like a flash. As soon as the trophy was with Chris Swailes, I pounced.

"Excuse me, Chris. I'm writing a book about this season's FA Vase and Alan here has been to every round of the FA Cup, FA Trophy, FA Vase and FA Sunday Cup in the last three seasons. A photo of us with you with the Vase would be the perfect cover. Would you mind having your photo taken with us and the trophy?"

Having just become the oldest scorer at Wembley and won the Vase for the third time, we weren't exactly going to catch him in a bad mood.

"Not at all, lads. It'd be a pleasure. Come on, stand either side of me lads and each grab a hold of the trophy."

Neither Alan or myself are going to win any modelling contracts any time soon, but Chris was patient enough to stick with us until we'd taken a photo we were happy with and we wished him all the best and left him to his celebrations. We subsequently text the selected photo on to Gordon, who was driving home.

"Bloody hell!" he moaned, "that's the last time I'm passing my tickets on to you pair."

The adventure was over and what a way to finish. Have you ever lifted a trophy at Wembley? I can now honestly say that I have. Hopefully if Brad ever gets to lift one, it will be outside.

FINAL SCORE : HEREFORD FC 1 MORPETH TOWN 4

TOTAL GOALS : 45 in 11 games.

FA VASE WINNERS 2016 : MORPETH TOWN.

EPILOGUE

Alan and I stayed around to watch the FA Trophy Final but it had none of the drama of the FA Vase final. Grimsby Town had won the game that had mattered most to them, which was the Play Off Final against Forest Green and Halifax were out to salvage some pride after their bitterly disappointing relegation so it was no real surprise that FC Halifax Town lifted the Trophy. They won 1-0 with a 48th minute goal from Scott McManus.

After the game, I walked with Alan down to the Premier Inn, shook him by the hand, thanked him for everything and said we would stay in touch. We have. I took the tube back to Euston but had time to kill before my designated train back to Manchester, so went in a pub near the station to watch the end of an England friendly match against Turkey. Although the FA had classed the Trophy & Vase day as 'Non League Day' they had still seen fit to arrange an England international friendly at the City of Manchester stadium. Alan was disgusted!

The pub was called 'The Doric Arch' and I had just settled down to watch the game when I spotted a familiar face. Although I had never met him before, the flat cap was a clue. It was groundhopper, Matt Harrison, a Swansea City fan who had been in contact with me since reading 'Another Saturday & Sweet FA'. Like most groundhoppers he travels all over the place watching football, but what makes Matt's journeys particularly memorable is that he always wears a flat cap and always gets people to make a two thumbed salute to the camera for photos he posts on his Twitter and Facebook pages. He is an English teacher, I'd guess he was in his late twenties and is moving from his job in Irlam soon to take up a post in Slovakia. After introducing myself and having a good chat, I asked him why Slovakia and he replied that he had no idea! I was glad I'd had the opportunity to meet him before he headed over to Slovakia. After I joined him for a photo with two thumbs up, I headed home.

On the Tuesday after the Vase final, Alison and I attended Steve Garcia's funeral in Burscough. Not surprisingly the church was absolutely jammed packed and I'd guess about thirty former football friends of Steve's turned up as well as hundreds of others. The reception afterwards was at Briars Hall, Lathom and Alison left me there late in the afternoon with all the football lot. I ended up going into Ormskirk with about a dozen of them and getting a taxi home in quite an inebriated state. I had sent letters to Angela and also to Steve's Mum and Dad so I had a little cry when Gerry, Steve's Dad said he'd always remember what I'd written. I just wished it had never needed writing. As I have probably said before, I feel very privileged to have had Steve as a friend.

June brought an English exit from Europe at the hands of Iceland in the European Championship and also a British exit from Europe after the people of the United Kingdom voted not to remain part of the EU (well, the English and Welsh did, the majority of Scots and Northern Irish folk voted to remain).

In July, following his GCSEs, Brad moved into digs in Littleborough. He lives with two other first year 'scholars' at Rochdale and a very brave landlady. I also had a sensational few days of football watching in July. On the 20th July, after watching Brad play for Rochdale u18s against Bolton Wanderers u18s (and win 4-2 in a pre-season friendly), I was told he was being loaned to Manchester United for an u16s tournament on Friday, Saturday and Sunday at Liverpool's Academy.

Dave Barron, my boss, kindly arranged for me to juggle my working days around and on the Friday, I watched Brad play against Aarhus and Liverpool. He played against Stromgodset and Tottenham Hotspur on the Saturday and then on the Sunday against Ipswich Town and Sheffield Wednesday. Each match was forty minutes long.

I think Manchester United finished third overall. Brad looked very tentative at first, but as the weekend progressed, he got better and better. Each game, irrespective of score, had a subsequent penalty shoot out and after losing the first one, they won the last five and Brad made eleven penalty saves, some of which were fantastic.

I only went to watch Brad on the Friday and Sunday, as Alison and I had already been invited into a box at York races on the Saturday to help celebrate Karen, Bill Cecil's partner's, 50th birthday. My Dad and my nephew, Max went to watch Brad on the Saturday and I had text messages with very positive comments from my Dad.

Whilst at York races, I was heading down from the box after a race to put a bet on and standing waiting, on his own by the lift, was a footballing figure I knew very well, Sir Alex Ferguson. His horse had been running in the first race and had won. I had backed some other donkey that had finished last. An old lady working at the races was apologising to him for the delay in the lift arriving and saying she needed to get a manager. I made some cheesy comment about not needing a manager when she was standing next to one of the greatest managers of all time (it was lucky Alan wasn't with me, he'd have kicked me in the shins for that one). Sir Alex laughed and we got in the lift and began chatting. I told him that my son was playing for United's under 16s over the weekend and he was asking what position he played, how long he'd been at United and taking a real interest. I explained it was just a weekend thing, explained he was at Rochdale and after Sir Alex said it was a terrific experience for him, he said his goodbyes and got out the lift. He only went from the 5th Floor to the 3rd Floor and that was it. No selfie opportunities, no trading of mobile numbers, no hair dryer treatment, just a brief ninety second conversation. I enjoyed it though. He seemed like a nice guy. The likes of Lee Sharpe, Jim Leighton, the City half of Manchester and the Liverpool half of Merseyside may beg to differ.

Earlier in July, Alan posted the following message after heading up to Scotland to do the Glencoe Challenge :-

"Just like to say a big thanks to **Nathan Foy**, **Phil McArdle** and **Adam Heap** for an outstanding achievement in completing this gruelling event. Also a massive thanks to **Tudge Tilley** for his help and support along the way he was immense! This is hard for me to write but as most people know i run an honest book. Having completed approximately 6 miles of the journey and just before the Devil's staircase (the most difficult part of the challenge) I fell down two massive potholes waist high in water. The first one damaged my right knee, described as a soft tissue injury, basically jarring my right knee but i still managed to drag my right leg up and down the Devil's staircase to the 2nd checkpoint at Kinlochleven, that's half the course. At this point, i was told by medical staff to not complete and worsen the injury. The paramedic was surprised I'd made it to that point with the injury. I am extremely gutted in my own personal effort but immensely proud to be part of our team who completely smashed it. If anybody who has sponsored me personally wants a refund i will be more than happy to (give it them). Yours gutted Olly X"

Prior to this little setback there had been some significant good news from the Oliver household. I hope Jordan Oliver won't mind me taking the following passage from her Facebook wall :-

"Hearing the news that your mum has the all clear on her twelve month mammogram has definitely made my day, my week, my month and my year! Puts everything else into insignificance. Knowing my mum is all good. Knew you'd smash it from day one and not let the illness take hold of you. Strong and determined from the off! Another four years of mammograms every year and we'll get through those like this one. Absolutely over the moon. Best news in the world. 💜
<3 #TeamOliver #Winningfromdayone #Smashedit"

Just a few things to update you on before I draw things to a close. Shaunee Smith suggested the title 'The Unbreakable Vase' back when we started the FA Vase. At the time, unaware of what the season would throw at us, I thought 'Smashing The Vase' would be a better title. Alan did smash it, Gordon almost did, but for me it was an FA journey too far, so 'The Unbreakable Vase' seems about right. Thanks Shaunee!

The 2016-17 season has seen Rochdale u18s significantly improve results on last season. They are currently through to the Semi Final of the Youth Alliance Cup and the Lancashire Cup, as well as being one of seven sides with a realistic chance of winning the North West Youth Alliance League. They didn't fare too well in the FA Youth Cup though. After beating Ryton & Crawcrook Albion 7-0 at Spotland in the First Round, they were drawn at home again in the 2nd Round against Shrewsbury Town. It was certainly a night of mixed feelings for Alison and I. Brad probably had his best ever performance for Rochdale and was given 'Man Of The Match' (which was announced over the tannoy system) by Keith Hill, Rochdale's first team manager and Tony Ellis but they lost 2-1. He's about half way through the season and has done very well most games but there's still improvement needed if he wants to get a professional contract in eighteen months time.

One of Brad's friend's from the under 18s, another first year scholar, Aaron Morley, has had a rapid rise up the footballing ranks at Rochdale this season. He's sixteen like Brad, but has already played for the first team half a dozen times. I went to watch his League debut against Southend United and he came a whisker away from scoring a goal that was almost a carbon copy of Wayne Rooney's goal against Arsenal at the same age. Aaron Morley is definitely a name to watch out for.

As well as watching Rochdale, another side I have been watching regularly recently is Southport. Dave Barron, my friend and now boss, has become a Director there this season so I've been with him to a few games. He's also sponsored one of the stands and had a marquee for its launch and kindly gave me a table for the event, so I asked the likes of my Dad, Gordon (and his son Kieran) and a few other old friends along. That game finished 5-4 to Braintree Town, but overall Southport seem to be improving after a poor start.

My car was on its last legs for a while so this time I did go to Andrew Gartside to get a new one. It was great seeing Andy again, he sorted me out a cracking Ford Mondeo (59 reg, I'm doing OK financially now but I'm not rich) and we had a good footballing chat, he runs his son's under 15 team and he's a keeper too. Andy was off to see Celtic-City at Celtic Park the following day. He loves Pep but personally I think he made a significant error in judgement dispensing with Joe Hart.

Around the time I played at Burscough, there were two lads from Ormskirk who were starting to make a name for themselves in lower League football, Kevin Formby and Tony Rigby. I had played football with Kev at Ormskirk West End for a short while so knew him better than Tony 'Tigger' Rigby, but me and my mate who played at Burscough, Matt Helme, often used to run into Kev and Tony in a club in Southport called the Kingsway (which burnt down several years ago) so I got to know 'Tigger' as well. Kev was at Rochdale for a couple of seasons amongst other clubs and Tony had several seasons at Bury. There were rumours at one stage that Newcastle were interested in Tony but nothing ever materialised. There was a touch of 'Gazza' about him both on and off the pitch, but like Gazza he had his fair share of injuries too. Anyway, in May, when I put the photo of me, Alan and Chris Swailes on my Facebook page, 'Tigger' was in touch straight away. He said he'd played with Chris at Bury and that he was a great lad. He said he could tell me some cracking stories about him, but when I prompted him to let me know one for the book, he back pedalled rapidly and said they were to be told over a pint not in a paperback. I'm presuming they aren't for family reading! Hopefully, I'll get to hear them one day.

Finally, as I write it is Sunday 11th December 2016, so I am looking back on this Vase trail six or seven months after it finished. I continue to be really busy at work but still enjoying it and when it's not work calling, it is (primarily) Brad's football. Due to those distractions, this book is a few months later than I originally intended. I'm really sorry about that. It would have been great if it could have been a summer read but it's taken a while to piece everything together.

Alan has moved on to doing every round of the FA Youth Cup now. He started at FC United of Manchester v Curzon Ashton in early September, with FCUM winning 3-0. Gordon and I then joined him at Ashton Town against FCUM which the away team won 4-2 in a feisty affair. Since then there's been FCUM-Gateshead (3-0), Nostell Miners Welfare-FCUM (2-3), FCUM-Carlisle (0-2), Chesterfield-Carlisle (1-2 aet) and this Friday is Barnsley-Carlisle. The next round will see the winners play Leicester or Leyton Orient away. The Casual Hopper keeps on hopping.

As for Alan's nephew, Joe Boyling, he has signed a two year scholarship at Oldham Athletic and is playing regularly for their under 18s. Oldham Athletic are in the North East Youth Alliance rather than the North West, so his path isn't likely to cross with Brad's again anytime soon, but I am sure at some point it will happen.

Not much else to add. It has been great meeting Alan and the rest of the Oliver family. They have hearts of gold and have provided 'The Christie' with a significant boost. I didn't know Gordon Johnson half as well as I do now before all of this either and we've met a whole host of other wonderful people along the way. My Dad's regular presence has been much appreciated too. Billy Heath did leave North Ferriby United, by the way, as many of you will know. He's at FC Halifax Town now with several of the other Ferriby lads. North Ferriby are still making a fist of it in the National League though, despite their absence.

I still think of Steve Garcia every day. I've taken to doing a two mile walk every lunch time to the end of Southport pier and then back to work. It tends to be a time of quiet reflection (and it's helped me go to below 15 stone for the first time in a long time). We had a memorial game for Steve, which was my first game in goal for many a long year, a few months back, between his old Sunday team and the Veterans team he has been playing for recently (several lads played for both teams) and it was superbly organised by Shaun Heath and Jerry Lamb. Angela Garcia made a great speech too, as it was a fundraising event for the British Heart Foundation. I think I've just about stopped aching now. I made some great saves but still kick like a five year old. Even when everything changes some things stay the same!

PHOTOGRAPHS

Ebook Cover/ Paperback Front Cover

The cover for the ebook and the front cover for the paperback is of myself and Alan Oliver standing either side of Chris Swailes, Morpeth Town's giant centre back, in Club Wembley, an hour after their FA Vase victory. We had no-one else with us, so presumably a member of the Swailes family took the photo.

Paperback Back Cover

This photo is of Gordon Johnson and Alan Oliver with Marcus Gayle at Camberley Town prior to their 5-0 victory over Newton Aycliffe in the FA Vase.

OTHER BOOKS BY CALVIN WADE

Football Non-Fiction

Another Saturday & Sweet FA

Brutal Giants & The Village King (A Ferriby Fairytale).

Fiction

Forever Is Over

Kiss My Name

Waiting For The Bee Stings

Living On A Rainbow (due out February/March 2017).

Printed in Germany
by Amazon Distribution
GmbH, Leipzig